Beyond the Rivers of Babylon

Beyond the Rivers of Babylon

My journey of optimism and
resilience in a turbulent century

By Joseph Samuels
يوسف ساسون شميل

Written with Julie Gruenbaum Fax

Book design and cover by Daria Lesnik Hoffman
www.dariadesign.com
daria@dariadesign.com

Written with Julie Gruenbaum Fax
juliegfax@gmail.com

Julie Gruenbaum Fax, an award-winning
journalist, is a writer living in Los Angeles.

Dedication

This book is dedicated to all Jews who, like me, suffered across the Middle East, North Africa and Iran. Especially to the many who, unlike me, did not make it to a life beyond.

I also dedicate this book to my loving family, who are the light to my eyes and the beat to my heart.

אני מקדיש ספר זה ליהודים אשר סבלו כמוני ברחבי מזרח התיכון, בצפון אפריקה ובאיראן, ושלא כמוני, לא ניתנה להם הזדמנות לחיים של בחירה וחירות. אני גם מקדיש את הספר הזה למשפחתי האוהבת, שהיא מאור עיני ופעימות לבי.

اهدي كتابي هذالكل اليهود الذين عانو مثلي في جميع أنحاء الشرق الأوسط، شمال إفريقيا وايران. وخاصةً للكثيرين الذين لم يصلوا إلى الحياة التي وصلتها. ايضاً أهدي كتابي هذا لعائلتي المحبه نور عيني ونبظات قلبي.

Ce livre est dédié à tous les Juifs qui, comme moi, ont souffert à travers le Moyen-Orient, l'Afrique du Nord, et l'Iran. Surtout pour ceux qui, contrairement à moi, n'ont pas réussi à vivre une vie au-delà.

Je dédie également ce livre à ma famille, qui est la lumière de mes yeux et le battement de mon cœur.

ACKNOWLEDGEMENTS

I would like to express my deep appreciation to all those who supported me and helped me turn my story into this book:

Julie Gruenbaum Fax, for using her masterful command and fluency of the English language to help me write this book.

Monona Wali, my writing instructor at Santa Monica College Emeritus, for teaching me how to tell my story.

Luca Chitayat, for his tireless editing, revisions, and rewrites, and for adding a youthful dimension to my aging perspective.

Evelyn Salem, for being my second pair of eyes, and for being honest when honesty was not always the easy option.

Glenn Benest, whose skills as a screenwriter helped to make my words jump off the page.

My wife, Ruby, for standing by me for more than 60 years with patience, support, and the kind of love we all look for in this world. With Ruby as our matriarch, our family has prospered and continues to do so.

And to my children Sharon, Lisa, Jeff, and his wife Benedicte, and my five grandchildren Elana, Rebecca, Eden, Claire, and Zach, for making my life a continuously brighter adventure.

From the bottom of my heart, thank you to each and every one of you who helped me along the way.

My book has turned from a dream into a reality.

WHY I WROTE MY BOOK

Until I was 76, I didn't intimately share the events that shaped my life. Not even my wife knew the whole story. The first time I wrote about my escape from Iraq was after I enrolled in a memoir writing class at Santa Monica College Emeritus, in 2007.

As I read my story to the class, I cried right through. Those were bittersweet tears that I had repressed over decades, which on the one hand were for the mourning of a beautiful life in Baghdad, and on the other hand, for the joy of liberation from the very same place.

It was after this moment of catharsis, of reliving and re-examining these pivotal moments of my life, that I decided to write about what and how I faced both the terrific and horrific events of my life, and the ways I reacted to the unpredictable hardships and opportunities along the way.

I want to share everything I have experienced, heard and seen, everything I have learned from others that has helped to take me from the bottom of the pit to the peak of happiness. I want to share this with those who want to listen, especially with the youth, the builders of the future, who stand to make the world a better place for all.

Joe Samuels, January 2020

TABLE OF CONTENTS

PART 1

BAGHDAD

1930-1949

CHAPTER 1

THE WIND IS AGAINST US

A Current of Fear

Crouching in the dark space, I felt the straw poking into my back from the cover of hay above. Around me, about a dozen teenage Jewish girls and boys, including my younger brother, breathed slowly, afraid to make a sound.

We were crammed into this hidden compartment in a low-lying river vessel illuminated only by the faint light of the moon, gliding atop a shallow tributary in Basra, the southern port city of Iraq. As our Muslim smugglers slowly punted us downstream, the sound of deep water hitting the sides of the boat broke the stillness of the cold December night and offered hope that we had made it to the main river, the Shatt Al Arab, and were on our way to safety in Iran. From there, the promise of a journey to freedom and dignity in the newborn State of Israel awaited us.

Soon the gentle motion of our boat stalled. We had come to a halt. Fear began to set in, and I couldn't stand waiting and wondering in the claustrophobic space any longer. I was only nineteen years old, but I had somehow been appointed the leader of this small band, and I felt the responsibility weighing upon me. I wormed my way through a little opening in the haystack to find out what was happening.

"*Ahmad, ish'sayer?*" I asked the worried-looking smugglers in Arabic. "What is going on?"

"*Ya achi Yousuf, almud wyana bas alhawa thidna,*" he answered, "My brother Yousuf, the tide is with us, but the wind is against us."

This couldn't be. Fear gripped me and nearly paralyzed my mind. I knew that if we missed our original crossing time, our chances of getting caught were much greater.

Our facilitators had figured out which border officers they needed to bribe to ensure our safe passage into Iran. If we missed this low tide we would have to wait until tomorrow night. What if different officers were on duty when we crossed?

I had heard that when police were suspicious of these boats, they inserted steel bars into the cargo spaces to be sure no materials were being smuggled out. What if they jammed the steel bars into our space and hit human cargo? What if we couldn't get food or leave to go to the bathroom? And what if some villagers were to spot us outside the boat and tell the Mukhabarat?

As a boy in Baghdad, I had lived in dread of the Mukhabarat, the Iraqi secret police. The Mukhabarat was infamous for torturing suspects to force false confessions to crimes such as Zionism and espionage. My friends and I traded stories we had heard about their methods: beating people with sticks, fists, and feet; pulling fingernails; burning cigarettes into skin; hanging people upside down for long periods. Outright execution.

The crime we were in the middle of committing—where I was suddenly a leader—was a capital offense in Iraq in 1949.

We were Jews trying to smuggle to Israel, via Iran, with no papers. For Jews, just trying to leave Iraq, let alone sneaking to Israel, was punishable by torture or even death. I could not forget the sight of the bodies I had seen hanging from gallows in the public square in Baghdad, some of them the brothers or fathers of my friends, accused of Zionism or Communism. We knew that if the Mukhabarat caught us, we risked being tortured into false confessions, sentenced to hard labor, or possibly hanged.

Growing up in Baghdad, I had never envisioned my future anywhere but in that maze of twisting streets and narrow alleys, where I made mischief with my brothers and found sweet solace in the delicacies prepared by my mother. Despite terrifying instances of anti-Jewish discrimination and even brutal violence, my childhood, as the second youngest of seven brothers and one sister, had been a happy one.

I loved my hometown. The spirited wave of humanity on the banks of the Tigris River had shaped me. I thought about the endless hours I had spent riding over bumpy dirt lanes on the back of my brother Eliyahoo's bike, using our horn to playfully terrorize the innocent shopkeepers and pedestrians who shared those spindly streets with us in Baghdad's Old Jewish Quarter. Our game had earned us more than one black eye.

At this moment on the boat, I felt the same stubborn indignation that had welled up in me when I was around six years old and my oldest brother, Shumail, tied me to a post in our central courtyard to try to beat me into submission. But I also knew that for the first time, the warmth of my grandmother's unquestioning embrace as she called me *Ayuni* (my eyes) would not be waiting for me in my moment of despair.

I conjured the aroma of my mother's *tibeet*—chicken with cardamom, cloves, and saffron that she set to simmer late on Friday afternoon for Shabbat. And I imagined the peace of Shabbat as my brothers and sister, all of us dressed in white, lined up to kiss my father's hand and receive his blessing under the warm glow of the Shabbat candles suspended above the table in a *karai*, a special metal and glass candelabra.

This was my town, my country, my home—the place that had shaped me.

Now, on the cusp of adulthood, I had left all that behind. I knew that my only hope for freedom and dignity lay in getting out of Iraq.

No Future in Iraq

I had slipped out of Baghdad quickly and quietly just days before, along with my sixteen-year-old brother, Nory. I didn't even get to say goodbye to my beloved grandmother. With tears in their eyes, my parents and my brother Elisha, fourteen years my senior, had put us on an overnight train to Basra, where we would stay with my mother's sister, my *Khala* Freeha, until our scheduled rendezvous at the small waterway. Two other Jewish boys traveled with us.

Nory and I spent that train ride not daring to think about whether we would ever see our family again. To think of everything we were leaving behind was too overwhelming. Besides, we had a dangerous road ahead of us, which became apparent the minute we got off at the station in Basra the next morning. A Mukhabarat officer approached us in the station.

"*Shismac?*" the officer asked. "What is your name?"

"Yousuf," I replied.

"And you?" he asked of my brother.

"Nory."

Neither of our names sounded Jewish.

"And your father's name?"

"Sasson," I replied. The alarm had been sounded, and the officer's face turned stern.

"You're Jewish!"

"Yes, sir."

"What are you doing in Basra?" he demanded. "Smuggling

to Iran?"

He looked as if he were ready to catch a mouse.

I knew our lives depended on my answer.

"We are going to visit my *Khala* Freeha and my cousin."

"What's the name of your cousin?"

"Agababa."

"Does Agababa have a store in Ashar district?" Ashar district was the most fashionable district in Basra.

"Yes, sir, he has a men's store there."

A smile erupted on the officer's face. "I know your cousin well! I get my Arrow shirts from him."

I sighed with relief. I felt God's intervention, a miracle.

"When you see Agababa, tell him Abbas says hello."

He let us go. I knew this encounter would cost Agababa a few more shirts but felt that was a fair price for our safety. The two other boys who travelled with us from Baghdad were not so lucky, and we had to go on without them. I never found out what happened to them. How easily that could have been my and Nory's fate as well.

I hoped our luck would hold out for the rest of our journey. We stayed with my aunt and cousins for a few days until our rendez-vous at the waterway. We rarely ventured out of the house for fear of being discovered.

Our escape had been arranged by the *Tenuah* (The Movement), a local Jewish organization guided by the Zionist movement, which for the last few years had been secretly teaching Hebrew to the Jewish youth of Baghdad and training us in self-defense for the day we might have to leave Iraq.

Jews had inhabited Babylonia, renamed Iraq after World War I, for 2,500 years—since 586 BCE. They managed to survive emperors, monarchs, rulers, and conquerors. A thousand years later, in the seventh century, Muslims conquered the region. Within two centuries, the Jews had adopted the Arabic language instead of their native Aramaic and blended with Arabic culture. From that time on, even after the Ottomans took over, as long as we Jews could pay our bribes and stay out of trouble, we were a tolerated minority. Many Jews, such as my family in the last few years before my journey to Basra, even enjoyed wealth and stature.

But thirteen centuries of mostly peaceful coexistence ended when the State of Israel emerged as a political reality in the early twentieth century and the government of Iraq turned on its oldest and largest minority.

In the late 1930s and early 1940s, Arab nationalism and Nazi-inspired anti-Semitism combined to make anti-Jewish legislation and unbridled civilian brutality a regular part of life.

In June 1941, when I was ten years old, anti-Jewish rioting erupted during the Farhud, a brutal and horrifying pogrom by civilians and military and police officers that took the lives of hundreds of Jews. A few years later, I was chased by knife-wielding Muslim youth, and my brother Aboudi was beaten nearly to death by Muslims. I witnessed Jewish leaders arrested and hanged on trumped-up charges.

Once Israel became a state in 1948, it was clear that Jews had no future in Iraq. Young people like me were getting out any way we could. My favorite brother, Eliyahoo, had left to attend the Hebrew University of Jerusalem in 1942. My plan had been to attend university in America to become a nuclear physicist. After I graduated high school in 1948, I got a passport and a visa to enter the U.S. and was accepted to university. But the Iraqi government refused to let me leave the country. In this new era for Jews in Iraq, we were both subjected to debilitating discrimination and barred from leaving.

The only way out was to take advantage of an international network that was smuggling Jews into Israel. My older brother

Elisha had made the arrangements for Nory and me to sneak across the southern border into Iran, where the infrastructure had been established to get Jewish refugees to Israel.

Under the Cover of Darkness

When we met up that night on the tributary in Basra, our *Tenuah* contact appointed me as the leader for the journey, though I don't know why they chose me. Maybe I was the oldest, or they could tell I was accustomed to devising clever ways to get out of trouble—a skill I had honed as a mischief maker with Eliyahoo. Our group was composed of about twelve teenagers, mostly boys and a few girls; the youngest boy was only thirteen. We didn't know each other before we boarded, but we instantly became bonded in our common goal. We had no luggage, food, or water. The only possessions we brought were the multiple layers of clothing we could fit on our body: three shirts, two pairs of pants, and an overcoat. Sewn into my pants was one hundred dinars, hopefully enough to get me through any troubles I might encounter along the way.

Despite the fact that the night of our escape was bitter cold—colder than usual for Basra in December—sweat collected on my forehead. My mind was crippled with fear.

The boat was shaped like a canoe but was much bigger—about twenty feet long by eight feet wide. It was originally designed to carry light cargo such as manure, hay, and dates to the farmers in the southern delta, but the smugglers had devised a false space, about ten feet long by eight feet wide by two-and-a-half feet high, that they covered with hay. There were no seats, beds, toilets, motors, or drinking water. Although the smugglers were putting themselves at great risk, it was not without reward: in one trip, they would earn what they could in a normal year of hauling.

We boarded under the cover of darkness, ducking into

Under the cover of darkness, we huddled in a small space beneath a haystack on the smugglers' small cargo boat. (Drawing by Jerry Gratch)

the opening in the haystack one at a time at varying intervals to avoid raising suspicion in the neighborhood. When we got into our makeshift dungeon, I bored holes through the hay cover so that we could breathe.

The plan was to start down one of the narrow tributaries in Basra, which spread like a web to irrigate the fields and date groves and spilled into the Shatt Al Arab, the main waterway that began where the Tigris and the Euphrates rivers merged to form the southern tip of the border between Iraq and Iran.

The smugglers moved the boat through shallow water by rowing and punting, a method of propelling the boat forward by pushing long poles against the riverbed. Once we got to deeper water, our escape depended on luck and the tide. The Shatt Al Arab flows into the Persian Gulf about one hundred kilometers south of Basra, so the tides of the gulf determine the river's level and current. High tide pushes the river's current upstream and raises the water level, while at low tide the river switches directions and pulls the water from the tributaries back down toward the gulf.

We needed to hit low tide to be carried downstream toward Khorramshahr, the town about fifty kilometers south of us and just across the river in Iran, where Iranian-Jewish members of the *Tenuah* would meet us. Our crossing was coordinated to the tide schedule, and if all went well we would be in Iran before dawn.

But on that first night, our plan had gone awry.

The tide was with us, but the wind was against us.

We were stalled in the middle of the Shatt Al Arab.

"What is going to happen?" I asked my Muslim handler.

"If the strong wind doesn't subside in the next couple of hours, we will hit high tide and won't be able to move," the smuggler told me.

"When will we be able to move again?"

"We will have to wait for the low tide, tomorrow night."

I forced myself to put on a brave face as I went back through the hole to break the news to my peers. As the leader, I suddenly felt the full responsibility to keep the teenagers calm. I decided not to share how dangerous our situation could be. I told them to close their eyes and sleep while we waited for the winds to subside.

Haskel, the thirteen-year-old of our group, started to cry. I felt the same way but held back my tears. I put on a stoic face and assured them that everything was going to be all right.

Just a couple of hours after we had set off on our journey, we pulled off the main river onto a smaller tributary to wait beneath the swaying date palms. The hours passed slowly. I watched, wide awake, as most of the kids slept fitfully over the next few hours.

When the sun's rays finally pierced the long, dark night, it was time for a necessary bathroom break. One by one, we climbed out of the cell. I advised the youths to stand slowly and stretch. They crept in between the date palms one or two at a time as I stood guard to make sure there were no police watching. One boy,

*I wore a typical Muslim keffiyah and robe such as this,
so I would blend in on our dangerous journey.*

Sion, whose older brother had been arrested on Zionism charges in Baghdad just a few weeks earlier, shook so much he couldn't urinate.

I asked the boatmen where we might get some food, and one of them offered to walk to a village. He returned after nearly two hours with some flatbread, cheese, and dates and, like rats, we followed each other out of the hole, ate something, got on our knees to drink water from the polluted stream, and went back in, until we were all fed.

While in my everyday life I dressed in Western clothing such as shirts and pants, for this journey I donned Arab garb over the layers of clothing I had on. I wore a *keffiyah* on my head and a long white robe, just like the Muslim boatmen. That disguise gave me a little more freedom to wander away from the boat. I stretched and sat under a date tree, closed my eyes, and yearned to sleep. Instead, my mind wandered to the Mukhabarat, to my childhood, to my family, and to my uncertain future.

A River of Dreams

Baghdad would soon be far behind me, and with it both the joy and pain of my childhood. Yes, there had been the constant and overriding fear of the secret police, or of brutal anti-Semitism, especially in my later teenage years. But for much of my childhood and adolescence, I did not feel the reach of anti-Semitism on a daily basis. My family made enough money to pay our bribes, and I enjoyed a life of great material comfort, familial love, and mischievous fun with my siblings, cousins, and friends.

Sitting now along those same waters that had flowed south from the Tigris, I let my mind drift back to memories of this river I had known my whole life.

In the spring, the Tigris was fierce—the snowmelt from the Taurus Mountains in Turkey overwhelmed the river, and the water

Starting upon the waterways of Basra, I and a group of teens smuggled from southern Iraq to Iran to Israel.

23

level in Baghdad got dangerously high, often flooding the river plain, where many poor people lived in tents. By the time I was a teenager we lived in a grand home, and with no dam or levees to control the river's rise, sometimes the water even reached our basement, where we stored most of our food.

But in the summer the river receded, and the *jazra* (the river islands) emerged. It was there that we had our summer fun.

When I was just a little boy, Shumail and his friends, maybe four or five of them, would allow me to tag along. They hired a boatman to row them out to the islands for an afternoon and evening of swimming, picnicking, and campfires. Later on, I would have the same adventures with my closest teenage friends, Nadji Ambar and Haskel Katsab (whom we called Ambar and Katsab).

I let my mind wander to a trip to the *jazra* with Ambar and Katsab. We brought a large tin ice bucket full of summer fruit like watermelons and cantaloupes, and the boatman purchased live fish called *shaboot*, freshly caught from the Tigris, and dragged the fish in our wake. We floated gently downstream, caressed by the lines of date palms on both sides of the river. Seagulls accompanied us and caught any scraps we threw their way.

We reached the island just in time to watch the sun slowly melt away between the palm trees. An army of stars began to sparkle in the pristine skies, and the rising moon announced the beginning of the night's festivities.

The boatman took the *shaboot* from the water, banged them on the head, and slit them open from the back while keeping the fish in one piece. After cleaning the fish, he stood them on stakes facing the campfire. When the front of each fish was charred and the flames were low, the boatman put the whole fish over the campfire, sprinkled it with curry powder and other spices, and topped it off with onions and tomatoes. This was the famous *samak masgouf*, and as night descended, the aroma wafted over the island. We all ate with our hands, wrapping the *masgouf* in a flatbread called *laffa* and dressing it with *amba*, made from pickled mango. It was scrumptious.

The darkness of the night was brightened by the reflection of the moon's rays on the water and sand. We gathered around the fire with violins, oud, doumbuk, and tambourine and sent Arabic music rippling across the gentle waves.

On the way back, the boatman had to pull the boat against the current using a long rope. I helped row the boat against the current, directing it as he pulled. When we arrived home I was so tired that I went straight up to the roof, took a sip of cold water from the clay jar, and tucked myself into my cool bed. Evenings like those were the best of the best of Baghdad's summer nights.

Now this river would take me to a new life, if we could once again pull ourselves to our destination. I woke from my reverie under the palm tree, energized by memories and determined to care for my charges. I returned to the boat, hoping that freedom was just hours away.

To the Banks of Freedom

We waited out the day in the boat, staying out of sight until we could try again to cross the river under the cover of darkness. I worked to keep morale up as I prayed that the wind would be in our favor that night, that it would carry us to safety. "God, please let it be night so that we can make our final escape."

I assured everyone that by the next morning we would be in Iran and that in a few days we would be free people in our homeland, Israel.

We crouched together for hours. A river patrol passed by, unaware of the human cargo hidden under the haystack. I was frightened and frustrated. I waited for the steel bars of the border police.

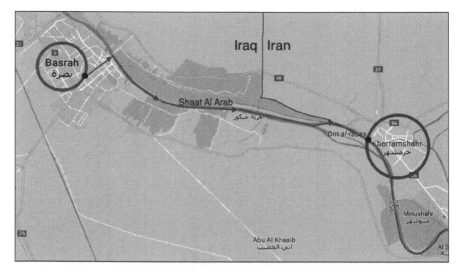

*Our 45-kilometer journey on the Shatt Al Arab River from
Basra to Khorramshahr was delayed by unfavorable winds.*

Finally, darkness settled onto the waterways, and the moon shimmered on the face of the water.

Once again, we crouched and waited as the smugglers slowly punted the boat back onto the Shatt Al Arab. Just as we had the night before, we heard the water slapping against the sides. I was afraid to get my hopes up, but I felt the boat slowly pick up speed. This time we had both the tide and the wind working in our favor, and we were able to move at the appointed time. Some of the teens dozed off. I sat in full alertness, monitoring our speed and our movement, waiting for any sign that we might slow down or that we were being stopped by patrol boats.

We sailed on for several hours, and my hopes continued to soar. Finally, before dawn, the boat slowed nearly to a stop. I poked my head out of our burrow.

We were in Iran.

We had reached the other side of the river.

I saw three frantic men waiting for us on the banks, excitedly waving us in. They had been there since the night before. Our angels from the *Tenuah* had worked overtime.

"We are safe, we are in Iran!" I shouted happily into our stuffy hold.

One by one, my fellow travelers came out. Eleven teenagers, drained and haggard, emerged into freedom. Some were in tears, others had a smile as wide as the river we had just crossed.

I stood on the edge of the river, looking back upstream at the home I had left behind. The river, the swaying palm trees—everything looked familiar, but I felt so different. My homeland had ejected me and my people in the most brutal way. I knew that I had made the right decision in leaving and that my future would be brighter outside of Iraq. But what I was leaving behind was everything I had ever known.

Chapter 2

Boyhood in Baghdad

A Labyrinth of Amusement

Like all of my siblings, I was born at home behind the heavy, reinforced door of my family's house at the far corner of a dead-end lane shadowed by overhanging balconies. The midwife helped bring me into this world with a slap to my tush on a cold and damp December night in 1930. The exact date was not recorded; I only know that I was born during the festival of Chanukah, and it was frigid and rainy.

As a young child, I felt I owned the streets of Taht Al Takia, our neighborhood in Baghdad's Old Jewish Quarter, Hart Al Yahud. The quarter was a jagged maze of narrow passageways with lanes bending unexpectedly into uneven stairways and stubby cul-de-sacs behind brick archways. Two-story masonry homes with protruding balconies and iron grillwork over the windows housed much of the city's Jewish population for centuries. The buildings, some with stores on the ground floor, were connected to each other on three sides, exposed only in the front to a street so narrow that neighbors across the way could reach through open windows to shake hands.

An unconvincing veneer of asphalt covering the dirt roads was broken into shards and pocked with potholes that were filled with mud and donkey dung. In the shadow of Baghdad's many minarets, Hart Al Yahud had no central square and no main thoroughfare. No cars passed through these streets—only the occasional donkey squeezed through to carry a heavy load.

To a young boy, that labyrinth of streets and its cast of characters provided endless opportunities for mischief and fun. When I was young my family did not have a lot of money, but I never felt we were poor. I never had toys, never got presents, and never celebrated my birthday, but my brothers and I always found ways to amuse ourselves. I was a master at the game of marbles, and we played a game called *tirra u bilbil,* where we balanced a small stick on the edge of a pothole and hit it with another stick to launch it into the air. The goal was to smack the stick midair to see who could sent it the farthest. Somehow, my older brother Eliyahoo always beat me.

We had everything we needed in the few blocks around our home in the Old Jewish Quarter—the baker, the butcher, and, most importantly, the sweet shop owned by my relative, Abed Al Shakartchy (*shakar* means sugar). My father always gave me a few *fils* (pennies) to keep in my pocket, and we would go to *Amu* Abed (*amu* means uncle, and all adults were called *amu* or *ama,* auntie, out of respect) to get all kinds of sweets—sesame crisps (*simsemye*), nougat stuffed with almonds, sugar-coated almonds (*mlabas*), *halva,* or a confection called *sha'ar al banat* (girl's hair), a puff of thin strands of sugar similar to cotton candy. We often stopped in on our way home from school. One of my favorite treats was *luzina,* a thick quince paste topped with almonds or pistachios and cut into a diamond shape.

My father and my brother Shumail, who was twenty years older than me and thought he could act as my father, ran a small fabric business in the *souk,* about a fifteen-minute walk from our home. It was a good enough business that kept my family fed,

*I spent my childhood in bustling lanes like this one
in Baghdad's Old Jewish Quarter.*

*Neighbors were able to shake hands across balconies in
the narrow streets of the Old Jewish Quarter.*

clothed, and minimally comfortable.

On summer afternoons, when the temperature could reach 110°F or more, Shumail and my father returned home around two in the afternoon for siesta. We all gathered to rest and sleep in the *neem*, the cellar salon that was the coolest room in the house. It was my job to pull the rope to operate the ceiling fan—an eight-foot paddle with a heavy cloth hanging from it that circulated the air while my father and brother napped.

Other than that, I had few chores and spent most of my time making trouble with Eliyahoo. Eli was six years older than me, and I idolized him. He didn't seem to mind that I followed him around everywhere, and we became a duo in many of our antics, especially on his bike.

Eliyahoo was adventurous and mischievous and had a talent for getting out of the trouble that he was always looking for. I developed my naughty streak under his guidance but didn't quite reach his level of expertise in getting myself out of sticky situations. He was my mentor and, at times, my protector.

In the unbearable summer heat of Baghdad, Eliyahoo taught me the art of flying a kite on the roof. Kite flying in Baghdad was not just a game—it was all-out war. We laced our string with crushed glass and tried to cut off or capture our neighbors' kites. From the roof, we would peep over the wall to make eyes at the neighbor girls. There was no physical contact, of course; no girl would even talk with a boy unless they were engaged or married. But we could look and smile.

One of our favorite targets of mischief was Yahye. Nearly all of our neighbors were Jewish, but each small enclave in the Old Jewish Quarter had a Muslim protector, respectfully called the *Sheik Al Hara*. Yahye was our protector, but we called him *Yahye Al Araj* (Yahye the Lame) because he walked with a distinct limp. He ran a small dry-cleaning plant from his house, on the same dead-end street as our home. To us young boys, Yahye looked big, fat, and ugly. Eli and I used to entertain ourselves by imitating him, provoking him into chasing us down the street as he hurled curses and waved his cane. My parents were not at all happy about the way we antagonized Yahye, and we would receive a sound beating when we got home.

Some of our pranks ended up really harming others. Eli and I liked to trap bees—big, ugly bees, about one or two inches long and dark brown, with a sting that was especially dangerous to anyone who was allergic. We would stick dates to the wall surrounding the top of the staircase on the roof, gather the bees using heavy towels, and put them in jars. Then we would amuse ourselves by releasing them near people and watching them run away in fright. One day we released some bees in the house, and one stung my mother. Her face was so swollen she could barely open her eyes. Luckily for us, she was okay in the end, but again I managed to get rewarded with a good beating.

Despite the adventures I shared with Eliyahoo, if I got on his bad side I had to run for my life. Every Erev Yom Kippur, we would get white roosters for *kapparot*—an atonement ritual where each of us would symbolically transfer our sins to a poor rooster, wave it over our heads while reciting an incantation, and bring the bird to the *shohet* (kosher slaughterer). With eight children, my parents, and my grandmother, that meant we did this eleven times with eleven roosters. We gave some of the slaughtered poultry to the poor, and some we ate. Eliyahoo loved to eat the neck; it was his exclusive privilege.

One year on Erev Yom Kippur I felt I was entitled to enjoy a few necks as well. I found my chance to swipe some that my mother had just cooked while everyone was busy building the *sukkah*, the temporary structure we ate and slept in for the weeklong holiday of Sukkot. We always began to build it right before the fast day of Yom

Kippur, which is just four days before Sukkot.

While my brothers and father mounted the wooden lattice across our home's central courtyard to support the palm fronds for the *sukkah* roof, I snuck away to savor those tasty chicken necks, picking off the bits of meat and sucking the juice from the bones.

When Eliyahoo noticed that some of his eleven necks were missing and found that I was the culprit, he chased me, screaming and threatening to kill me. I had to run all the way to the nearby home of my *Amu* Moshi, my father's brother, to get his family's chicken necks to bring home to Eliyahoo as a peace offering. Thankfully, on the eve of that Day of Atonement, my brother spared me.

I was no less of troublemaker at school.

As a young boy in Rahel Shahmoon, a primary school in the Old Jewish Quarter funded by a wealthy Jewish family, I was defiant and rebellious: if they said no, I said yes; if they said yes, I said no. I was not interested in learning and did the minimum I could get away with—and often that was not enough.

I walked to school every day. Rahel Shahmoon was only a few blocks away on Kouchat Bahar. In the winter, despite the rubber galoshes I wore over my shoes, I always managed to get dirty before I got to school. The rain made so many mud puddles on the unpaved walking lanes that the mess became unavoidable.

I was always terrified of being late, because I knew the stick awaited me if I walked in past starting time. Any student who arrived late had to stand in line for a beating by the principal. He used to hit me on the tips of my fingers, which was particularly painful in cold weather. Cries and excuses didn't help. The teachers also came to class with a big stick to control the students. If anyone made noise or disrupted the class, they got beaten. The teachers thought fear would instill respect and discipline, but it didn't always have the desired effect on me.

At Rahel Shahmoon, we learned all the usual subjects

required by the Iraqi Ministry of Education, plus Hebrew for reading and prayer chants. We learned the *Haggadah* (the Passover story), which I still enjoy singing.

We learned to read and write Nahawi Arabic, a form of standardized literary Arabic that could be universally understood among all Arab-speaking countries regardless of regional dialect. At home, we spoke Judeo-Arabic, which was an ancient dialect spoken by the Jews of Iraq—an Arabic with Hebrew and Judeo-Aramaic influences, written in Hebrew characters.

Around grade three, my parents switched me from Rahel Shahmoon to the Alliance Israelite, a school sponsored by the French-Jewish community to promote Jewish education. My sister, Marcelle, had gone to the girls' division. However, the switch did little to change my insolent behavior, and I remained unmotivated in my work and studies. It was not long before my parents sent me back to Rahel Shahmoon, where I remained until I was ready to move up to junior high school.

The Oldest Diaspora

Iraq, previously known as Babylonia, or Bavel in Hebrew, is home to the oldest Jewish Diaspora, dating back thousands of years to the exile of the Jews from the First Temple in Jerusalem around 586 BCE. The prophet Ezekiel is buried in Al Kifl, in the south of Baghdad, and Ezra the Scribe's grave is in Al 'Uzair near Basra. Three prophets—Jonah, Daniel, and Nehemiah—are buried in the north in and around Kurdistan. Muslims built a beautiful shrine over Jonah's grave near Mosul, a rectangular structure about ten or twelve feet high, with a brass rail all around it, draped in black cloth with Arabic script honoring Nebi Allah Yunis ("God's prophet Jonah"). I visited the grave with my mother as a child. In a horrific terrorist act, this site, holy to both Jews and Muslims, who used to pray there together, was totally destroyed by ISIS in 2014.

Under the Persian Empire, Jews built a successful and educated community that became the center of Jewish scholarship, especially following the destruction of the Second Temple in Jerusalem in 70 CE. The Babylonian *Talmud*, the main rabbinic text of Judaism to this day, records the teachings of the sages who sat in the study halls of Iraq in Sura and Pumpedita in the second to fifth centuries CE.

After the Muslim conquest in 661 CE, despite occasional periods of persecution and discrimination, the Jews prospered under various caliphates and continued building up academies and synagogues. Over time, they adapted to Arabic culture. Within two centuries the Jews, who had previously spoken Aramaic, adopted

The Prophet Ezekiel is buried in a tomb in Al Kifl. (1932)

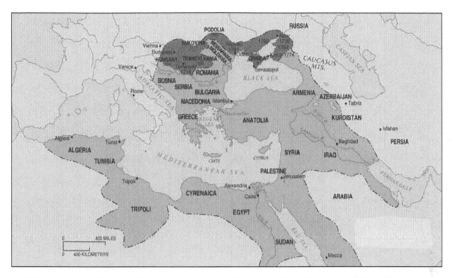

Like most of the Middle East, Baghdad was under the rule of the Ottoman Empire until 1918.

the Arabic language, though in their own Judeo-Arabic dialect, and had become a part of the daily society.

Under Mongol rule in the thirteenth and fourteenth centuries, Jews rose to positions of prominence, including in the court of the sultan. However, Mongol rule also saw the torching of synagogues in Baghdad and general destruction of Jewish property in many of Iraq's cities.

The Ottomans, a generally moderate regime, ruled Iraq from 1534 to 1918. The Jews, along with Christians and other religious minorities, began to live as a recognized but heavily taxed social caste known as *dhimmis*. While *dhimmis* were taxed more than their Muslim counterparts, they were mostly equal under the laws of property, contract, and obligation and experienced only occasional flare-ups of violent anti-Jewish activity. As they had done before, the Jews administered their own communities: they collected local taxes for the Ottoman rulers and managed their own community affairs.

The Jewish population of Iraq greatly increased during this

period. In the mid-1800s, general movement from the rural north into larger urban cities brought the Jewish population of Baghdad to twenty thousand. At the peak of this movement, Jews made up nearly 25 percent of the city's population and held positions in the highest-ranking professions. Jews staffed nearly every bank in Baghdad, were some of the best doctors, engineered city projects, and built businesses that significantly contributed to daily life.

After World War I, under the Sykes-Picot Agreement, the territory around the Tigris River was carved out as the State of Iraq, to be a British mandate. In 1932 Iraq became nominally independent from its British protectors. King Faisal, a member of the Sunni Hashemite family from Mecca and a leader of the revolt against the Ottomans, was appointed leader of Iraq during the British mandate and during Iraq's early independence. King Faisal recognized the importance of the Jewish community; he supported Jewish schools and opened up professional pathways for Jews. Jews even held high-ranking government positions during the 1920s and early 1930s, including Sasson Eskell as the first Iraqi minister of finance.

The Jewish community's success under King Faisal proved to be a final burgeoning before the buildup to the founding of the State of Israel in 1948, after Arab nationalism and Nazi anti-Semitism combined to eject the Iraqi Jews from their home of 2,500 years. I was born during the reign of King Faisal, and my family enjoyed the freedoms and opportunities he put in place.

My Nemesis and My Refuge

In our home, Shumail, not my father, was the unrelenting disciplinarian, and my mischievous nature set me up for constant clashes with him.

My father, Sasson Shumail Hakham Sasson (whom we

My father, Sasson, wore a sidara, a symbol of respect for Iraqi men. (1942)

called Baba), was, of course, the undeniable head of the family. His word was final. He commanded my fear and respect, but we all knew he was actually a placid, good-natured guy, easygoing and happy-go-lucky. Every once in a while, he would give me a good slap on my face or my tush without explanation. I suspect that Nana, my mother, must have reported to him some of my mischief, cursing, or sassy talk.

Shumail, on the other hand, was harsher than anyone else. His punishments were severe and cruel, and under today's laws I have no doubt he would have been arrested for child abuse.

Once, when I was around six or seven, my mother reported to Shumail that she had heard me say, *"kus immak,"* which roughly translates as "f--- your mother." Shumail tied me to the post in our courtyard and beat me with a stick. He ordered me to apologize and to promise never to say the words again. But I refused. The more he beat me, the more I said it. He would not relent, nor would I. Eventually he beat me so much tears came to his own eyes. He put down the stick and began bribing me with candies, but I still

My brother Shumail was 20 years my senior. (1942)

refused. I didn't want to give in to him. I could not let him win. I didn't like his ways, and I didn't like him. I took his beatings to save my pride.

Whenever I got in trouble or received a beating, I always ran to my Youmma ("my older mother" in Arabic, a name was so associated with her, I do not even know what her first name was). Youmma was my father's mother who lived with us and was my comfort in a house where competition for attention was considerable. Without questioning what or why, she would soothe me with hugs and assurances.

Youmma always wore a wide, baggy, long black gown and a white long-sleeved blouse with a series of buttons down the front, traditional dress code for Iraqi women under the Ottoman Empire, which was in power most of her life. A narrow black fez crowned her head, and her long, silver braid with a little white ribbon at its end rested on her back. It's hard to believe that Youmma was likely only in her fifties when I have memories of her—she seemed so old, frail, and wrinkled, and she walked with a limp. Her left foot was

This typical Turkish dress was my grandmother's everyday garb.

twisted, but I never asked her what happened to make it so.

My Youmma had a hard life. An epidemic in the late 1800s wiped out a significant percentage of Baghdad's population and claimed the life of her husband, Shumail, leaving my grandmother a widow with three boys when she was in her twenties.

My grandfather, Shumail, had come from an important rabbinic line. Shumail's father, a religious leader to Baghdad's Jews, was known as Hakham Sasson Adjmeye. *Adjam* is Arabic for Iran; however, we do not know if this means my great-grandfather came from Iran or simply spent time studying in Iran. Whichever was true, I knew my family had lived in Iraq for generations.

My father, who was born in the late 1880s, grew up during the Ottoman period, which followed a millennium of Muslim and Mongol rule. My father and his two brothers learned Turkish in school and, like my grandmother, dressed in the Turkish style. My father told me stories about how people used to avoid having their sons drafted into the Ottoman military by hiding them in false spaces between the cupboards and the walls.

My father was about thirteen years old when his father died in the epidemic during the late 1800s and the family was forced to turn to community charity. My father was left with responsibility for his widowed mother and his two younger brothers, Moshe and Meir. Even though my father came from a family with a long heritage of rabbis and leaders of the Baghdad Jewish community, he was forced to drop out of school and take a position as a bookkeeper at a fabric warehouse to support his family.

My mother, Aziza Sion, also came from a family that went back centuries in Iraq and was also quite poor. Nana was the second of four daughters, and from a young age she helped with the cleaning, washing, and cooking. She never went to school and never learned to read in Arabic, not even Judeo-Arabic, and her father prepared her for a future husband of his choosing. These were the

My mother, Aziza, was 12 years old when she married my father. (1932)

norms of the time.

Though my mother's parents had little for her dowry, the matchmaker easily convinced my father to marry Aziza because she was a stunning and rare beauty. She had radiant white skin and green eyes, in contrast to the dark skin and black eyes of most other women. Her hair had highlights of rich orange-red that contrasted with her flawless complexion. My mother was eleven when she became engaged to my father. She saw him once when he came to check her out before the engagement. She was married at twelve years old. My father was seventeen.

On their *lelt al dachla* (wedding night), the women elders waited outside the bridal room for the bloodstained linen. It would have been solid grounds for divorce if there were no stains, a sign that the bride was not a virgin. I can't imagine the trauma this event brought on such a young girl.

Throughout my childhood I never saw Nana smiling or laughing. She had a difficult life. My mother gave birth twelve

In my parents' ketubah, my father promises "to protect, to feed, and to clothe" his new wife. (March 22, 1906) times; only eight babies survived. My brother Shumail was the first to be born, when my mother was around fifteen; then came Aboudi, Elisha, Marcelle, Eliyahoo, Yaakub, me, and Nory. Marcelle was the lone girl. Daughters were considered much less desirable than sons, so having seven boys and one girl was a mark of stature and pride for my parents.

My father's mother moved in with my parents when they got married, and my mother had a difficult relationship with my Youmma. The kitchen was Nana's domain, and while Youmma was always in there working with her, it was never a true partnership. Still, they worked together, always bustling to feed our hungry family of so many boys. For both of them, cooking was an art and an expression of love. Nana was, to me, the best cook in the world. Cooking was her signature vocation, pride of achievement, and lifelong hobby.

For breakfast, my mother rose early to prepare fried eggs, along with *jibin* and *basal*, dried feta cheese boiled with onions. Dark tea was the daily warm drink, and our samovar was ready with hot water and a teapot on top throughout the day.

I can still taste the juicy mutton stew my Nana made for our main meal at around one o' clock. We often had her kabob, skewered with ground mutton or *mishwi* (chunks of meat), onion, tomatoes, and peppers and barbequed by the charcoal of the *jafoof* (grill). And every meal came with delicious rice, prepared in different ways—with dill or tomatoes or beans, or with spices or dried fruit.

Nana and Youmma baked the most delightful treats for us. In our home, the *tanoor* (clay oven) stood at the back of the kitchen under a wide chimney-like opening that ventilated the smoke up to the sky. Large, blackened pots seemed to always be simmering with fragrant stews on a brick stove that stood over a wood fire. A nearby storage area held onions, drawers of spices, jars of cooking oils, and burlap sacks with hundreds of pounds of rice, flour, beans, chickpeas, and red lentils.

When I was a baby, my mother used to rock me on the *jillala*, a wooden swing near the kitchen, while she gossiped with her lady friends. As a little boy, I would linger around the kitchen and watch my mother cook. I was never required to help but was always given something delicious to eat.

Nana and Youmma may have shared the kitchen, but they had a terrible rivalry. My mother was disrespectful and openly hostile to Youmma, especially when my father was not around. As a child, I was saddened by the clear friction between the two women. I didn't understand why my mother behaved that way, and I felt awful for my Youmma.

When I was six I moved out of the room I had been sharing with my parents, Nory, Yaakub, and Eliyahoo and into Youmma's room, which Aboudi also shared. Shumail, Elisha, and Marcelle were in a big room that had a window onto the lane. At that age I was still wetting the bed, too afraid to go to the bathroom at night. The "toilet" was a smelly hole in a dark room, which led to an underground septic tank. There was no toilet paper—just a jug of water with which to clean yourself. You were supposed to squat over the large hole, but in the dark of the night I never knew if I would fall in or what might jump out. Youmma held my hand to go to the toilet and helped me to conquer my fear of midnight relief.

Youmma gave me attention when my mother was occupied with Yaakub. Yaakub was three years older than me and had cerebral palsy. The story I heard was that Yaakub was born with jaundice, but due to lack of medical advice and his hard luck, they held his *brit milah* (his circumcision ceremony) on his eighth day of life despite the fact that he was sick. After the circumcision he bled continuously, which caused him to go into a coma and likely led to brain damage.

Yaakub didn't walk until the age of three and always did so with a wobble in his gait. His muscles were very weak. He was smart and did well in school, though his speech was halting and not always clear. I used to walk to school with him so that I could protect him from the cruelty of the other children, who would imitate him and make fun of him, showing no sensitivity. When he was in the fourth grade, my parents took him out of school. They were always searching for better doctors and treatments for him, hoping for a miracle, but nothing improved the situation.

When I was around three, my parents traveled to Palestine with Yaakub because they had heard about a new doctor there. But they never told me they were leaving. Parents back then thought that kids would be less distraught if they didn't know their parents were about to disappear.

It was summer, when we slept on the roof to catch a breeze for some relief from the hot, dry air. The whole family had steel beds up there, covered in mosquito netting, and we kept a clay jar full of water, from which we could draw cool drinks.

One night on the roof, my grandmother's usual bedtime fairy tales were particularly enchanting. Youmma painted a picture of a lonely woman who had fallen from wealth and become a widow and who survived on only a few raisins that she ate for breakfast, lunch, and dinner. When the woman would wake up the next morning, new raisins were always somehow waiting for her. "Oh, raisins! You keep me alive. Thank you for keeping me alive! You are my lunch and dinner."

The next morning, I woke up and could not find my parents. I looked for them on the roof. I looked in the bedroom downstairs. I could not find them anywhere! I began to cry. I didn't know what had happened to them.

My grandmother came to comfort me. "Don't worry, *Ayuni*," she told me. "They will be back soon." I waited until the end of the day. When night descended and there was no sign of my parents, I began to panic. After three days, I was hysterical. My grandmother finally told me that my parents had taken Yaakub to Palestine for therapy and that they would be back in a few days. I cried and cried, thinking that I would never see my parents or my brother again. Every day my grandmother told me that maybe they would come back that night, but it was a good few weeks before my parents returned.

Yaakub's condition brought out the superstitious nature that dominated our culture. Youmma and Nana prayed and lit candles and mixed together special herbal medicines for Yaakub and for any of the rest of us when we got sick. Getting sick back then was serious, and people would do anything they thought might appease the higher power.

When Nory was born, I was three years old. As an infant, he suffered from pneumonia, which in those days could be fatal. My parents took him to Meir Elias Hospital, built by philanthropic Jews, and doctors inserted a pipe through his back to drain the fluids from his chest. My mother, who had lost four babies, cried at night. An older woman came and boiled herbs and said all kinds of mysterious words to push away the evil forces. Whether it was the potions and prayers or the doctors' intervention, Nory survived the life-threatening sickness, unlike many others.

One summer, Elisha came down with a terrible fever that resulted in a spell of weakness and delirium. My mother cried and prayed for his recovery, and several doctors were immediately summoned. He was diagnosed with typhoid fever, a disease that was often fatal. They moved his bed into the courtyard, kept cold compresses on his head, and put him on a liquid diet. As his condition improved, he was given soda biscuits and exotic red delicious apples. I was happy for his recovery, but I was jealous of those apples.

To this day, I consider myself blessed to have the strong genes and the luck that helped me and my siblings survive childhood, when the afflictions of the era claimed many others around us.

Courtyards and Clay Jars

In the first room that I shared with my parents, Nory slept with my mother in a bed with beautiful brass head- and footboards. Against one wall was a large, mirrored armoire where Nana kept linens, sheets, towels, and clothes. Eliyahoo had his own bed, and Yaakub and I slept with my father in the large double bed, which was made of plywood and covered with a stiff mattress and a thick Persian woolen rug. To keep us warm during the long winter nights, we had comforters filled with cotton; only the wealthy had feathers.

Once a year, a man came to the house to fluff the cotton in the mattresses and comforters. He was equipped with a wooden instrument, approximately six feet long, with a wire strung taut from end to end, almost like an archery bow. He emptied the old cotton from the mattresses and comforters into a big pile and used a wooden club shaped like a bowling pin to beat the cotton across the wire, which broke up the compressed clumps. While he did this, small pieces of cotton flew around the house, and his banging on the wire made a musical sound, earning him the nickname Ti-Ti Pam-Pah Man. It was lovely to sleep on a soft mattress with a fluffy comforter at the end of Ti-Ti Pam-Pah day. It felt like resting on the clouds.

The temperature rarely reached freezing in Baghdad, but it dropped into the forties at night, and with no central heating system, the house, made of plaster-covered brick and stone and with tile floors, could get frigid. We had a *soppa*, a kerosene heat tower, which gave off hot air. Sometimes we roasted chestnuts on top as we settled in for the evening. We also brought the *jafoof* into the bedroom, even though it was dangerous to inhale partially burnt

Our mattresses and blankets felt like clouds on the days
the Ti-Ti Pam Pah Man came to fluff the cotton.

Sometimes we roasted chestnuts on top of the soppa,
the kerosene tower that heated our home.

charcoal. People lost their lives every winter from the carbon monoxide it produced.

I remember some nights in my parents' room, snuggled into my corner of my father's bed dreaming of the mischief I would do the next day, when I would suddenly be awakened from my deep sleep. The whole room was shaking—was it an earthquake? Then I realized that only the bed was shaking. I could hear my parents' soft voices and heavy breathing. This often occurred in the predawn hours, before my father left for morning prayers, and sometimes late at night, when the kids had finally fallen asleep. Sometimes I pretended to be asleep, waiting to see what would happen. It usually started with whispering, then my mother would come to our bed. The whispering would continue, and the bed would start shaking, culminating in heavy breathing. Then quiet would come.

All of the second-floor bedrooms faced the big, open courtyard, which had a covered walkway and was surrounded by a steel railing. The courtyard was the center of action in our house. Eliyahoo and I considered it our playroom. We would play ball there, in the middle of the house, and he taught me how to climb up to the second floor with a rope, despite the fact that the stairs were right in the courtyard. He showed me how to chase and kill the snakes and scorpions that lived in the woodpiles and charcoal kept in the courtyard storeroom. In winter we used to sail small paper boats down the rivulet that formed in the floor where the rainwater drained.

During the fall holiday of Sukkot, the courtyard would become our *sukkah*, the temporary room where we ate, prayed, slept, and greeted company. We fit wide wooden lattices across the expanse of the courtyard to support the palm branches for the *sukkah* roof and unrolled swaths of canvas to attach to the lattices for walls. We hung pomegranates and apples from the beams and moved our six couches and dining room table into the *sukkah*. Because it was early autumn, the rains hadn't started but the summer heat had died down, so sleeping there was a pleasure.

On the eve of Hoshanah Rabbah, the last day of Sukkot, many men would gather in our home to pray all night. We would fill trays with candles to honor the dead. My cousins Aboudi Moshe and Aboudi Meir, (fathers' names were often used in place of last names in Iraq, so this was how we distinguished the two Aboudis) who were around my age, came for the all-night prayer vigil, and we would play with the candle wax, making sculptures. We always planned to stay up all night but would lose steam by midnight and fall asleep on the many couches inside the *sukkah*.

Around our courtyard were two sitting rooms, called *tarars*, as well as a dining room, which were completely open to the court-yard and had no walls, just pillars. A canvas shade between the pillars rolled down to keep the *soppa*-heated area warmer during the winter. In the summer, an icebox replaced the furnace, and every couple of days a man with a donkey hauled in slabs of ice to keep our summer fruit cold. We had only one electric fan, which Shumail got to use. Dim incandescent bulbs, powered by a small electrical room on the first floor, lit the house. The electricity was 220 volts, which was extremely dangerous. One wrong touch could kill you.

Stairs went from the courtyard up to the second floor and down to the basement, where we had the *neem*, the cool sitting room with the ceiling fan.

Right next to the *neem* was the *surdab*, a cool storage cellar twice the size of the kitchen. That was where we kept huge, beautiful clay jars full of apricot and nectarine jams, barrels of pickled mango from India, and large jars of homemade pickles. The shelves were full of dried fruits and fresh vegetables that needed to be kept in a cool place. In the summer I helped my mother bring tomatoes to the roof to smash them so that they dried into a paste that would last all winter. We would store the paste in the *surdab*.

A huge branch of bananas, which my cousin sent from Basra, dangled from the ceiling. On the floor were heaps of watermelon, cantaloupe, and different fresh fruits. The summer fruit was amazing—sweet yellow nectarines, grapes, peaches, watermelon, and melon. That was our dessert; we didn't usually have cakes after meals, but we did have lots of fruit.

Our distant relative, Khazna, lived with us and worked as a maid, helping with the cleaning and cooking, while her young daughter, Salima, helped with smaller chores, like washing mud from the shoes. Every Tuesday night, Esther, a Kurdistani woman, came early in the evening and slept over. My mother would wake her around two in the morning, and they would boil water to wash our clothes. She and my mother would work all morning over washbasins and scrub boards, then hang the clean laundry on lines to dry by noon. Besides paying Esther modest wages, Nana fed her and sent her home with food and gave her clothes we didn't need anymore.

In addition to the terrifying toilet room upstairs, we had one downstairs and we had a *hammam*, a small Turkish bath on the ground floor of our house. Friday was bath day for everybody. I would sit on a *tachta* (a wooden bench about three inches high) as Nana poured water from a tin cup over my head, the soap stinging my eyes, until I was old enough to do it myself. The bathroom had a special fireplace under the floor to heat the tiles and the room, as well as the hot water tank. There was a clay sink on the floor where we mixed hot and cold water.

On Friday, the fire stayed lit all day. Starting at dawn, we all took turns bathing in preparation for Shabbat. The feeling of the house transformed as everyone got ready for the day of rest.

Friday, When the Sun Descends

My father started Friday like he started every other day: waking at 4:00 a.m. to attend prayers at the synagogue. From there he went to the market to get whatever we needed for Shabbat—live chickens and fresh eggs and yogurts and cheeses and loads of vegetables and herbs and fruit. He often came home with two or more straw baskets, carried by market boys. During the summer months he bought so many melons that they had to be carried in by donkey.

When Baba returned with the chickens, Nana sent Khazna to take them to the *shohet*, our kosher slaughterer. Khazna then brought them home and plucked the feathers. Nana would prepare *tibeet*, a special dish for Shabbat that simmered continuously from Friday afternoon until it was ready for Saturday lunch. Nana filled a family-sized pot with whole chickens stuffed with rice, small pieces of giblets, and *bahartat* (a spice mixture of cardamom, cumin, fenugreek, turmeric, saffron, and cloves). Once it was set on the stove, small, thick blankets were tucked over the pot to keep it warm. A couple of dozen eggs nestled between the blankets, slowly cooking to a warm shade of brown, ready to be eaten for breakfast on Shabbat morning with fried eggplant, finely chopped salad, parsley, *amba*, and flatbread.

On Friday Nana also cooked for the poor and needy, who knew they could rely on her kindness and generosity on Shabbat. She prepared a big pot of meat and *kubba* (dumplings) stuffed with *shwander* (beets), *bamia* (okra), or squash, and white rice, or sometimes chicken with rice.

The aroma of the cooking *tibeet* would help usher in Shabbat. Before the sun set, my father left for synagogue (occasionally succeeding in bringing me along), and then my mother lit her *triyah*, the candelabra that was suspended above our table. Each metal ring cradled a glass bowl with a mixture of water and oil topped with

Family Portrait, 1942
Standing: Elisha, Marcelle and Aboudi,
Sitting: Yaakub, Baba, Nana, Shumail and Joseph (Me) Floor: Nory
(Missing: Eliyahoo)

a wick balanced in a delicate metal tip. As soon as my mother lit those flames, the spirit of Shabbat would descend upon our house, bringing a sense of quiet and harmony.

All of us gathered together for Shabbat dinner. It was not an option to miss dinner, even if some of my older brothers, who were not so religious, went out with their friends later in the evening. Most of the time we had family guests, like Abed Al-Shakartchy from the sweet store and my brothers' friends.

As darkness fell, Baba returned from the synagogue looking regal. On Shabbat, he dressed in all white—his suit, his shirt, even his socks and shoes. Only his *sidara* was black. This brimless, oblong hat with a crisp point at the forehead and back was the national symbol for respected men in Iraq. Like my father, I was also dressed in white shorts and shirt for Shabbat, symbolizing purity, happiness, affluence, and honor.

We sang "Shalom Aleichem," welcoming in angels of peace, and "Eshet Chayil," the last chapter of the book of Proverbs, to praise the hardworking women.

After the *kiddush,* sanctifying the homemade sweet raisin wine, and the *hamotzi,* the blessing as we broke the *khubez* (flatbread), all seven brothers and one sister waited for Baba's Shabbat blessings. One by one, we kissed Baba's hand and kissed Nana.

Shabbat dinner was a festive and scrumptious affair. We always had fish and a nice soup with chicken. Most of the week we had mutton, but on Friday night chicken was our delicacy, prepared with tomatoes, saffron, slivered almonds, and raisins. Shumail was Nana's favorite, so after she served my father, she served Shumail the chicken breast before filling any of the other siblings' plates. Nana and Youmma also made *kubba bamia* or *kubba shwander.* And of course, everything was served with *timman,* rice cooked to perfection—no two grains stuck together.

While the grownups didn't refrain from arguing all week long, on Shabbat there was an unwritten truce. We talked, sang, ate together, and ended the meal with *Birkat Hamazon,* the blessing to thank God for his bounty.

On Saturday morning, after our breakfast of brown eggs from the blankets around the *tibeet* pot, my father dragged me and Nory, and sometimes Yaakub, to the synagogue; my older brothers had already grown past the stage where he could make them go. We stood with him, all of us dressed in white, seemingly for hours, chanting the words and singing the songs. I didn't really like to go to synagogue, but that was just what everyone did on Shabbat morning. I was obedient to my elders and respectful to my culture. But to a child, the words were meaningless, and I made no connection to God. I would sit near my father and he would teach me the prayers, but parents of the era didn't explain spirituality to children, so no one showed me the deeper meaning behind our actions. Still, I enjoyed celebrating the festivals; they were social and joyful times.

After the service we would come home and enjoy the *tibeet,* which had been simmering since Friday afternoon. I can still bring to mind the smell of that *tibeet* and the aroma of my mother's kitchen. Food was how my mother expressed love for us. She didn't hug or kiss her children much. I never saw my father holding hands with my mother, and certainly not kissing her in front of us. But when the aroma of that *tibeet* was wafting through the courtyard, I knew my house was filled with love.

Chapter 3

Changing Times

Moving Up and Out

Everything changed when I was around ten years old, when my family moved from the Old Jewish Quarter to Bab Al Shargi.

Shumail's determination and hard work to improve the family's financial situation had paid off for all of us. Using his street smarts, fueled by his brilliance and business acumen, he had taken my father's business to the next level by schmoozing government officials for exclusive import permits. The small stall in the *souk* was now a huge enterprise that imported cottons from India, silks from Asia, fine woolens from England—whatever people might use to make dresses, robes, shirts, pajamas, or suits.

My father and Shumail operated the expanded business from a two-story fabric warehouse called a *khan*. On the ground floor, bales of cloth were piled so high they reached the second floor. Walking amid those giant rolls of fabric felt like walking through a tunnel.

On the second floor was the office space—a large room with two big desks, one telephone, two couches, a number of chairs, and a big stand-up safe. Ali, an extremely trustworthy Kurdish man who worked and lived in the *khan*, doubled as our security guard. He was so strong that he could carry a bale of cloth weighing more than two hundred pounds on his own.

My father and Shumail helped Elisha establish a successful textile shop in the city. The money from both businesses started rolling in, and now we were ready to move out of the Old Jewish Quarter.

There were several areas in Baghdad outside the Old Jewish Quarter where Jews lived, but the wealthiest and largest concentration was in a collection of neighborhoods on the eastern side of the Tigris River: Bistan Al Khaas (Lettuce Garden), Bataween (a large Jewish neighborhood of single-family homes), Al Alwiya (beautiful private homes near the American embassy), and Bab Al Shargi (the Eastern Gate).

In 1940 we moved to a large house in Bab Al Shargi. The neighborhood was much closer to the river than the Old Jewish Quarter was and was adjacent to Abu Nawaas Street, a walker's paradise lined with coffeehouses and shopping. The Baghdad Casino—a popular café with no actual gambling—backed up almost to our house, and from our roof we could see the synagogue on the next street over. I remember getting our first telephone while in that house, connected to a central operator; our number was 6871.

The paved streets in Bab Al Shargi were much wider and smoother than the ones in Hart Al Yahud. Eliyahoo's bicycle was still an inseparable part of our adventures, and when I needed my own bike I could rent one down the street. Riding together on the wide-open Abu Nawass Street, which ran along the Tigris River, gave us more maneuverability than did the bumpy, beaten corridors of the Jewish quarter.

Our family rented our house from a provincial governor of Iraq. It was European style and, like our old house, was attached on either side to other homes. But instead of a central courtyard, this house had an open garden in the back. The garden wall was topped with chicken wire and shards of glass so that no one could jump into our yard.

I really loved that garden. It hosted an array of animal life—lizards, birds, and enormous rats, whose presence provided great entertainment for me and my siblings. On one occasion, we bought two deer and tethered them to a tree to supply us with meat for the holidays. One of the deer caught his horn in the rope. He twisted and turned, trying to untangle himself, and ended up choking to death. We decided not to buy any more deer after that.

At the center of the garden was a huge *tut* (mulberry) tree around three stories high that bore delicious small fruit. Whenever I would get in trouble for my ongoing shenanigans, I would climb up the tree and hide in its branches. I nailed together some planks of wood and built myself a platform up there and didn't mind staying for hours. When I disappeared into my treehouse, my worried mother would stand at the bottom and cry, "Come down, come down!" But I would stay there until dark, coming down when my hunger was stronger than whatever indignation I was suffering.

I climbed the tree often because my usual refuge—my Youmma's compassionate presence—did not follow us to the new house. My mother somehow convinced my father that Youmma would be better off staying in the Old Jewish Quarter with *Amu* Moshi rather than moving in with us. Though I went to visit Youmma often, I missed having her around to comfort and love me whenever I needed it.

My father assisted my uncle in Youmma's upkeep, and in other ways as well. When we lived in the Old Jewish Quarter, we visited *Amu* Moshi often. He was devoutly religious, and he had a store in the bazaar where he sold cloth that was used for the Muslim headscarves. It was in a poor neighborhood and he did okay, but his family was not well off. Now that we were doing better, my father regularly helped him out, continuing to play the father role in his family, just as he had as a teenager.

When it came time for Moshi's daughter Salima to marry, she needed a dowry. *Amu* Moshi had found a suitable husband for her, a man named Abdullah, who ran the kindergarten that I had gone to. It was the custom that the family of the bride paid money or goods to the bridegroom to start their new life together. Since *Amu* Moshi didn't have enough money for the dowry, my father promised an amount, but Shumail thought it was too much. He wanted *Amu* Moshi to beg so that he could throw his weight around. This argument between Shumail and my father lasted a long time, and I am not sure who prevailed in the end.

My father also helped support his other brother, my *Amu* Meir, who was an *attar*—a spice merchant. He was the most religious and poorest of the three brothers; he spent more time on his prayers than on his business. He had three daughters and three sons.

My father was very generous. He always gave money to poor people, remembering the charity he and his family had to live on after his father died when he was a boy. Now that we had more money, he gave more often and more generously.

When the weather warmed up in March and April, the scent of orange blossom filled the air. Spring was my favorite season, and I looked forward to our usual Passover preparations and celebrations, including spending time with my cousins.

Even before my family had money to spare, each spring I had always gotten a haircut and a new pair of shoes, new trousers, white shirt, socks, and underwear. And each spring the trousers were too long, the shirt was too big, and my feet were swimming in my shoes. I was happy as a lark and looked like a clown.

In our old house in the Hart Al Yahud, it took weeks to get ready for Passover (Pesach). The helpers scrubbed, cleaned, and washed drapes, sheets, and everything else. It seemed that the same was true now, but we had more helpers. All the cooking pots and cooking utensils had to be put in boiling water for a few minutes to make them suitable for use on Passover. My mother spent several days baking matzah at home. She scoured the *tanoor*, the clay oven, removing any vestige of the *laffa* and pastries she usually baked in there. Baking matzah, which we called *jradik*, was a whole operation, where she followed the strict timing of Jewish law to mix the dough, roll it out into thin sheets, and bake it on the superheated walls of the *tanoor*. The *jradik*, about twelve inches across, were delicate and crunchy, and she stored them with care in layers in a huge basket.

Rice was a staple, even on Passover, and my mother and her helpers would sift through each grain of rice to make sure there was no wheat or oats mixed in.

My uncles' wives, Rosa and Khatoon, and my Nana's friends used to get together to bake and prepare sweets and savories such as sugar-coated orange and grapefruit peel; thick quince paste with almonds (*luzina*); roasted almonds, pistachios, hazelnuts; and roasted watermelon, cantaloupe, and pumpkin seeds.

By the time the first night of Passover arrived, the house was sparkling clean. Even Khazna and Salima were dressed in their finest.

The table was lavishly set with an elegant tablecloth and with posh dishes and fancy cutlery that were used only on Passover and stored away the rest of the year. Each place setting had its own wine glass.

On Seder night, my siblings and I would gather around the table, usually with some guests. To start the Seder, my father blessed the wine and blessed us. We all kissed his hand and gathered to read the *Haggadah*, the story of the Jewish exodus from Egypt over 3,500 years before. We chanted together, "This is the bread of affliction that our forefathers ate in the land of Egypt." As the seventh of eight children, I was called on to sing the Ma Nishtana, the four questions that start the Seder, until my younger brother was able. I had a beautiful voice—at least, *I* thought so! I always sang with zest, and the adults seemed to enjoy it and asked me to sing more.

We read about the ten plagues and the parting of the Red Sea and always longed to celebrate the "next year in Jerusalem." We sang in Hebrew, which I didn't understand, and translated the meaning to Arabic.

I patiently waited for the *charoset*, made of date juice and crushed walnuts, in which we dipped romaine lettuce and matzah. I loved it and always wanted more. After the ceremony, we had a festive dinner and gorged ourselves on all the sweets my Nana and Youmma had prepared.

Pesach lasted eight days. When we lived in the Old Jewish Quarter, we went to visit my uncles' and aunts' homes on the first day. I had eleven first cousins from my father's side and sixteen from my mother's side. It was impossible to be together all at once, but Pesach was a time for visiting family.

We were closer to my father's side of the family. *Amu* Moshi had four boys and one girl: Shumail, Shlomo, Menashe, Aboudi, and Salima. *Amu* Meir had three girls and three boys: Salha, Habiba, Daisy, Shumail, Aboudi, and Elisha. Moshi's Aboudi was one year older than me, and Meir's Aboudi was one year younger, and the three of us liked to get into trouble together.

During the middle days of Passover, my family often took a train to Baqubah to have a picnic at a farm seventy kilometers outside of Baghdad—about two hours, which was a long trip for us. The white orange blossoms contrasted against the light red flowers of the pomegranate trees, giving me a sense of serenity and peace. There were plenty of palm date trees, and summer fruits were still green. The last day of Passover was another day for celebration. We threw green leaves at each other and waited to eat regular bread with *amba*.

Seven weeks later we celebrated Shavuot. On Shavuot, Nana cooked *kahi*—phyllo dough fried in butter and sprinkled with sugar or *silan*, date syrup. *Samboosak bil tawa*, fried turnovers stuffed with ground garbanzo, onions, and spices, was another of her signature dishes, along with *burekas*, phyllo pockets stuffed with cheese.

I knew that this year, our first Passover in Bab Al Shargi, would feel different. But I could not prepare myself for how different.

Buildup to the Farhud

In the days leading up to Passover in April 1941, I had none of my usual spring fever. My mother cleaned and scrubbed, but not with her usual gusto.

That year, the situation in Baghdad had turned precarious. A pro-Nazi, Arab nationalist coup sent our government into disarray. For weeks, my family sat in the small upstairs room huddled around the radio. We knew that we Jews were in danger of bearing the brunt of the explosive combination of Arab nationalism, Nazi propaganda, and government instability.

By the time we celebrated Shavuot seven weeks later, the reality had surpassed even our worst fears. None of us could have imagined that our city and our country, our own neighbors, could turn against us with such brutality.

On June 1, Baghdad erupted in the worst anti-Jewish violence and rioting the city had ever seen. This event would become known as the Farhud (which means violent dispossession).

At the time, I could absorb just bits and pieces of what was happening – the marauders packing the streets, the way we turned our home into a makeshift fortress, the terror in my parents' eyes. It was only later, after the events seared themselves into my memory, that I learned how it was that our secure and comfortable community became a victim of our fellow citizens during the Farhud.

The buildup to the Farhud was both a slow boil and a sudden eruption.

For centuries, Jews had been a tolerated minority in Iraq. Anti-Semitism had always been present, but we had learned to live with a regular level of discrimination and subjugation. Growing up in the Hart Al Yahud, we had always tried to avoid Muslims. I was taught never to fight back, because that could only make things worse. If a Muslim hit you, or took something from you, or did anything wrong, you were not supposed to fight back.

If a Muslim beat up a Jew, the Jew dared not go to the police. The Muslim could just turn the story around and say the Jew beat him up, and the police would of course go with the Muslim's story.

My father once told me a story about a neighborhood tailor. A prominent Muslim brought fine fabric to the Jewish tailor to have a suit made. The tailor took measurements and created an elegant suit. The customer came in for a fitting, and the tailor made all the necessary alterations so that it fit perfectly. When the customer came back to pick up the suit, he tried it on again, facing the full-length mirror. The tailor smiled, feeling proud of his masterpiece, but the Muslim pouted and gave a disgusted look. He started screaming and cursing at the Jew about what lousy work he had done to ruin his expensive cloth and began hitting the tailor. The tailor feared for his life, worried that the Muslim would draw his gun. He said, "Please, please, take the suit at no charge! It is a gift from me."

Typically, incidents like that were just occasional occurrences and were not the daily experience. Until the Farhud, relations between Muslims and Jews were generally congenial. Jews had learned to accommodate the whims of the Muslim society. It was the Jew who was subservient, and we knew we were better off accepting the status of second-class citizen rather than challenging the status quo.

Amid the occasional tension, many Jews were friendly with Muslims and many Muslims were friendly with Jews. My brother Elisha had Muslim friends, and they would go to the bars together on Friday nights, even though alcohol was supposedly prohibited for Muslims.

However, we always knew those friendships had limits. Because of the different rules regarding women, food, and prayer, Jews rarely went to Muslim homes, and Muslims rarely entered Jewish homes. We would play in the street and see each other around the city, but delving deeper and truly understanding each other's lives, customs, and religions was something that was, for the most part, out of reach. We were two different tribes, living in the same space.

But when in trouble, Jews did have one powerful weapon: bribery. If we wanted the police to act in our favor, we could always slip them a nice amount of cash. If a case was coming before a judge, the Jews would make sure the judge was well-greased before the trial started. Bribes had helped my brother Shumail achieve the success he had in business.

In 1940, Jews in Iraq numbered 135,000, about 3 percent of the total Iraqi population. Most lived in Baghdad, where ninety thousand Jews composed about 25 percent of the city and held high-ranking professional positions. Jews staffed nearly all the banks in Baghdad, were some of the best doctors, engineered city projects, and built strong businesses that significantly contributed to the economy. Jews were so integrated into daily life that most banks were closed on Saturdays for Shabbat.

In fact, for the most part, up until that moment, the modern era of Iraq had been one of the most free and prosperous periods Iraqi Jews had ever seen. While things were generally good under the Ottomans, the Jewish community began to flourish when Ottoman rule ended with World War I and the British installed the Hashemite King Faisal as the Iraqi leader in 1921. King Faisal realized how essential the Jews were to Iraqi commerce and society. He supported Jewish schools and opened up new professional pathways for Jews. As his first finance minister he appointed Sir Sasson Eskell, the only Jew ever to hold cabinet rank in modern Iraq.

In January 1918, when Faisal was *emir* (prince) of a small sliver of the Arabian Peninsula known as Hejaz, he entered into an agreement with Chaim Weizmann, who would become the first president of Israel and who at that time was representing the World Zionist Organization. Faisal agreed to support the Jews' return to their homeland as long as the British guaranteed Arab leaders sovereignty over a wider area of the Middle East and as long as the Jews of Palestine were supportive of the Arab population in the region. The Faisal-Weizmann agreement was meant to set the stage for the 1919 Paris Peace Conference, during which Britain and France split the Mideast into mandates they controlled as part of the broader peace agreement following World War I. But because of resistance among Arab nationalists, along with heavy-handed maneuvering by the French and British, the Faisal-Weizmann agreement never came to anything.

Of course, Faisal's tentative support of the Zionist enterprise was rare in the Arab world. The Balfour Declaration of 1917 enabled the Jews to continue the work they had started at the beginning of the century to build a modern state in the British mandate of Palestine—the ancient Jewish homeland in the land of Israel. But the more the Jewish settlement began to thrive in Palestine, the more anti-Jewish sentiment began to sweep the Arab world, including Iraq. In 1933, the Jews of Iraq lost their protector when King Faisal died.

Following the Arab revolt in Palestine in 1936, anti-Jewish sentiment in Iraq spiked. Jews were dismissed from government posts, were roughed up by gangs, and experienced attacks against their institutions. Three Jews were murdered in the streets of Basra and Baghdad over a four-week period.

Arab nationalists were also quick to grab onto the virulent anti-Semitism of European Nazism.

In the 1930s, Nazi ideology had spread to Iraq at the hands of Dr. Fritz Grobba, Germany's ambassador to Iraq. He helped bring Nazi propaganda such as Hitler's opus, *Mein Kampf*, to Middle East

In the 1920s, Sir Sasson Eskel, sitting second from left, served as the finance minister, and Menahem Saleh Daniel, sitting on the far right, was a senator in the regime of King Faisal I, far left.

audiences and broadcast Nazi propaganda over Radio Baghdad, the only national radio station. *Al Futuwa*, a premilitary youth movement heavily influenced by the Hitler Youth, grew rapidly.

I remember listening to Nazi broadcasts, with my family gathered around the radio in a small room upstairs, as Germany invaded Czechoslovakia in March of 1938. At that time, not only was I unaware of what was going on with European Jewry, I didn't even know there was this whole huge population of European Jews. I never knew there was such a language as Yiddish, or that there were Jews who didn't speak Judeo-Arabic. By the end of World War II, when I was around fourteen, I was more aware. We had seen newsreels of the concentration camps, and it was horrifying. But in the 1930s, I remained ignorant of the magnitude of the Jewish tragedy that was unfolding in Europe and how that racist ideology was rapidly filtering into Iraq.

After King Faisal died, his son, Ghazi, took over. Ghazi flirted with Fascism and Nazism, but in 1939 he died in a mysterious car crash. Every informed person knew the British had a hand in his death. Ghazi's son, Faisal II, was only six years old at the time, so his uncle, Abdul Al-Illah, was appointed regent and ran the kingdom for him.

Amid the power struggles, the German ambassador, Fritz Grobba, who was anti-British, inflamed pro-Arab nationalists and gained the support of Muslim Iraqis following these instances of British intervention. While Iraq was technically still connected to Britain when World War II broke out in 1939—it had become nominally independent in 1932—the country withheld its support of the British and simultaneously tempered its relationships with Germany and other Axis countries.

In 1941, just before the Farhud, the British were at their lowest point in the war. Most of Europe and North Africa were in Axis hands. On April 2, the military leader Rashid Ali Al-Gailani

carried out a successful coup against the British-supported government and formed a pro-Nazi government that had the support of
Grobba, along with a cabal of high-ranking military officers and
the former grand mufti of Jerusalem, Hajj Amin Al-Husseini, who
had arrived in Baghdad as a refugee in 1939 following a failed
Palestinian revolt against the British. The regent, Abdul Al-Illah,
took the young King Faisal and fled to the emirate of Transjordan,
a British protectorate.

I'm Coming Back for You

My family constantly listened to the radio, aware that Al-
Gailani's government was against the Jewish community. We heard
that some Jews were arrested, tortured, and imprisoned, but I didn't
understand what we had done to be singled out. As a ten-year-old,
I was scared and upset. My parents and brothers tried to keep the
information from me, but I could see and feel the tension in the
house, and I heard and read the news. After the coup, I often cried
myself to sleep at night.

Passover fell on April 12 in 1941, and our Seder was cheer-
less and gloomy. We lacked our usual guests, the food did not taste
as good, and the songs sounded somber.

However, the British were not willing to let the coup stand.
Concerned about access to oil supplies and trade routes to India,
as well as the prospect of more Arab nations following Iraq's lead,
the British sent troops into Iraq on April 19 to end the coup and
take down Al-Gailani. To aid in the fight, the British brought fresh
troops from Nepal, called Gurkhas, and additional soldiers from
India. The Gurkhas were famous for the knives strapped to their
legs, which they could throw to hit targets one hundred feet away.

On May 31, British troops had reached the outskirts of
Baghdad. Under pressure from the newly arrived troops, Al-Gailani's

صورة نادرة للفرهود في بغداد عام ١٩٤١
اليهود من فوق في بيوتهم ينظرون للمسلمين وهم يحملون الخناجر واليوف والعصي
التي فتكوا بها اليهود

Jews watch from the balconies above as Muslims with daggers and knives fill the streets of Baghdad during the Farhud in June of 1941.

pro-Nazi regime collapsed, and its leaders fled to Iran and to German-occupied Europe.

But the British decided not to deploy their troops into Baghdad. Instead, they waited on the outskirts and encouraged Iraqi forces loyal to the pro-British government to retake the major cities such as Basra and Baghdad to reestablish independent Iraqi rule. They wanted the Iraqi forces to enter first so that it would not be perceived as an invasion by the British.

Britain's foot-dragging left a dangerous power vacuum. The next day, June 1, 1941, Regent Abdul Al-Illah and the young King Faisal II returned to Baghdad and restored the pro-British government while British troops surrounded the city. Shavuot was traditionally marked in Iraq by joyous pilgrimages to the tombs of the prophets Ezekiel and Jonah and by visits to friends and relatives. We thought that with King Faisal II back in Baghdad, the danger was over. A festive crowd of Jews crossed over to the west bank of the Tigris River to welcome the returning prince. On the way back to the main street of Shaar'eh Al Rashid, a group of soldiers, who were soon joined by civilians, turned on the Jews and attacked them. They killed one and injured others.

Eliyahoo was around sixteen at that time, and his adventurous spirit nearly cost him his life. The day the Farhud erupted, he rode his bike to a friend's house; I don't know if he was just going for a visit or if he wanted to see what was going on. I am not sure why or how he left the house and why my parents didn't try to stop him.

On the way, Eliyahoo heard gunshots. He saw Muslim mobs stopping minibuses and dragging out the Jewish passengers. Jews were formally dressed in fine clothes for Shavuot, so it was easy for the rioters to spot who was Jewish. With his own eyes, Eliyahoo watched them rob, rape, and slit the throats of Jewish women and men. Eliyahoo got away with his life because the rioters took him for a Muslim—he had dark skin and spoke the Islamic dialect fluently because he attended an American high school with Muslims. He managed to return home safely, but he arrived deeply traumatized by what he had seen.

Many Muslim civilians in Baghdad and slum dwellers from the city outskirts joined the riots. The mobs incited widespread looting of Jewish shops, and with the British forces still outside the city, there was no one to stop them. Rioters swarmed the Jewish neighborhoods, crowding the streets of Hart Al Yahud, and my neighborhood, Bab Al Shargi, with their knives, swords, and guns raised above their heads. Pro-Nazi Iraqi soldiers and policemen, dressed in civilian clothes, along with *Al Futuwa* youths, entered houses and stole whatever they wanted. They raped women and girls and beat up or killed anyone who looked Jewish.

Amid that carnage, some Muslim men stood up in front of Jewish homes and businesses with daggers, swords, and guns to protect their Jewish friends with courage and loyalty. Some Muslim neighbors persuaded, or pulled, Jewish girls and women into their homes for shelter. Some Arab notables sent night watchmen to protect Jewish possessions, and many gave asylum in their homes.

My family locked and bolted our front door, stacking heavy furniture against it for a second line of protection. Eliyahoo electrified the chicken wire already mounted along the stone wall that enclosed our side garden. I carried buckets of water to boil on the roof, ready to toss on marauders who filled the streets below. In between preparations, we prayed.

We stayed up the whole night, barricaded in our house. My father sat reading the book of Psalms, but my brothers and I were too tense to join in. My older brothers, including Eliyahoo when he returned, maintained contact with the neighbors via the roof to share news while I watched the looting from our upstairs window and went up to the roof to help protect our family. For a split second, from my upstairs lookout, I locked eyes with a looter. He had an armful of my neighbors' clothes, and he stared right up at me. I could read the message in his eyes: "I'm coming back for you."

We found out later that the homes of my *Amu* Moshi and *Amu* Meir in the Old Jewish Quarter were ransacked. They told us how rioters broke down their front door and stole their furniture and everything in the house. The family escaped by jumping from roof to roof, terrified that the rioters would get to their daughters. Thank God, they were able to drag Youmma along with them.

The killing, looting, and raping ended at midday on Monday, June 2, when Iraqi and Kurdish troops entered Baghdad. The regent finally gave orders for the soldiers to fire upon the rioters, and dozens in the mobs were killed.

Historians believe that rioters murdered 186 Jews, injured six hundred others, and raped an undetermined number of women on June 1 and 2. While official Iraqi estimates were lower, Iraqi-Jewish leaders believed the numbers were actually much higher.

Marauders looted some 1,500 stores and homes. The community leaders estimated that about 2,500 families—up to 15 percent of the Jewish community in Baghdad—had suffered directly from the pogrom, but my guess is more. The disaster would have been even greater if not for the acts of heroism by the Muslims who protected and sheltered the Jews.

A mass grave, later documented by historian Avraham Twena, who lived through the Farhud, holds an estimated six hundred bodies; most are either Iraqi soldiers, policemen, or local Muslim rioters, as well as Bedouin tribesmen who came to the city to riot. Jewish victims are also believed to be buried in this mass grave—further desecration in a community that treats its dead with the utmost respect.

The Mass Grave holding Jewish victims of the Farhud; 1941

Other than those few protectors, there are no records of acts of resistance, nor of Jews fighting back against the Muslims. After the Farhud there were no arrests, trials, or convictions. The Iraqi government eventually paid out a paltry twenty thousand dinars in compensation.

Many in the Jewish community wanted to believe the Farhud was just a blip in an otherwise tolerated existence in Iraq. And, in fact, after the military restored order, things settled down pretty quickly. Our community was naively optimistic that things would go back to normal. We convinced ourselves that the worst was over.

In the days after the Farhud, my family helped *Amu* Meir buy new furniture and restock his house. I was still terrified, but my parents made me go back to school. I felt that I had to constantly beware. My father, Shumail, and Elisha went back to their businesses, and Jews all over Baghdad went back to their jobs.

But things were never the same for the Jewish community. Our reality had been turned upside down, and we would never again feel the kind of security we had enjoyed for 2,500 years. Even though Jews were doing well in the wartime economy and the remaining years of World War II were relatively calm in Iraq, the tension never fully disappeared.

Later in 1941, after the British restored order, a few Jewish people left Iraq to go to India, the Far East, England, or America. Some came back after the war, but many were gone for good. Some tried to get to Palestine, but the British White Paper of 1939 placed strict quotas on Jewish emigration into Palestine, capping the settlement of Jews to a total of seventy-five thousand over five years. Most of the Jewish community stayed in Iraq.

Shumail went to India for around a year to establish connections for importing fabrics. Eliyahoo decided to leave Iraq. He saw no future for us in Baghdad. Despite the obstacles, he was determined to go to Palestine.

After Eliyahoo graduated from the American missionary high school in 1942, my parents bribed officials to get him a passport and, with the recommendation of Dr. Stuart, the principal of the school, Eliyahoo got a visa to go to Palestine. That same year, he left to study at the Hebrew University of Jerusalem.

I was devastated. He was my partner, my protector, and my idol. I felt secure when I was with him. He knew Arabic and English, and he was strong and fearless. Whenever Muslim youth attempted to start a fight with Jewish boys, he was strong enough to fight back. Now I would have to learn to be strong on my own.

Fortunately for us at that time, Palestine was under British rule and Iraq was still under British influence, so the mail was pretty smooth and we could write letters to each other often.

I got to see Eliyahoo again in 1946, when my father and Shumail brought him back for a visit during the summer holidays. They tried to tempt him to stay in Baghdad by offering him cash and shares in the business, but he told them he had no interest in returning to Baghdad. He had already fallen in love with Ahuva, a girl born in Jerusalem to a Kurdish family, and felt passionate about his life in Palestine. A year later, when the United Nations decided to partition Palestine into Jewish and Arab states, he and Ahuva got married. Eliyahoo knew early on that the future of the Iraqi-Jewish community lay in Israel.

In October 1941, just a few months after the Farhud, my sister Marcelle, who was eighteen, got engaged to Sasson Ovadia, a handsome young man. I can remember the big engagement party for them in our house in Bab Al Shargi, attended by lots of family and friends, with plenty of food and belly dancers to entertain everyone. Marcelle's marriage was a priority and joy for my parents. Growing up with seven brothers, she had become a strong and educated woman. She alone mastered the daughterly duties of the house and

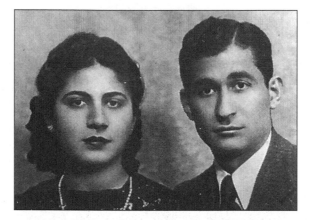

Marcelle got engaged to Sasson Ovadia in October 1941, just a few months after the Farhud.

became a fine chef under my mother's guidance. With my family's economic success, it was easy to provide her with a generous dowry for a good match.

Sasson immediately became part of the family textile-importing business. He was calm, ethical, and methodical and started handling all the bookkeeping and receivables. I had a positive impression of Sasson from the start. Despite a ten-year age difference, I really connected with him—more so than I did with my brothers Shumail and Aboudi—and we developed a strong friendship.

Sasson had the capacity to listen, and I was free to express my opinions without being belittled or stopped for being a foolish young boy. I, in turn, loved listening to him telling stories about his family and how he learned his moral values from his grandfather, a rabbi. Sasson deeply inspired me by explaining the supreme importance of being truthful and honest, even when no one was watching. I could see how a clear conscience helped him to feel good about himself. He became my mentor and taught me lessons that would last throughout my lifetime.

A New Normal

After the Farhud, we all became much more suspicious of our neighbors and of the government's ability, or will, to assure the safety of the Jewish community.

Like Eliyahoo and many young people of my generation, I was attracted to the message of Zionism—of establishing an independent Jewish homeland in Palestine, where we could live free and secure without the fear and humiliation of being Jewish. Where we could defend ourselves without relying on a foreign government for our well-being.

In 1942, the Mossad LeAliyah Bet, the Jewish leadership in Palestine promoting emigration, clandestinely sent *shlichim* (emissaries) to Baghdad to teach us Hebrew, help us defend ourselves, and prepare us to live among the growing Jewish population in Palestine. Some were part of *Haganah*, the paramilitary youth; some were part of *Tenuah HeChalutz*, the Pioneers Movement, which we called simply the *Tenuah*.

As young teens, we formed groups to study Hebrew to prepare us to go to Israel. In primary school we learned to use Hebrew only for prayer (which was still legal then), but with the *shlichim* I learned to speak and write in Hebrew, which was highly illegal. They taught us professions that could help build the state as soon as we got there—I chose electrician—and they trained us to use weapons to defend ourselves against any Muslim violence we might encounter.

This all had to be done underground, since it was illegal to express support for a Jewish state publically. As early as the 1930s, when violence between Jews and Arabs in Palestine was beginning to grow, the Iraqi government had begun to persecute all Zionist activity.

Iraqi Jews were mostly ambivalent about the new Zionist

movement in Palestine. Jews had felt secure in Iraq for thousands of years and identified as Iraqi nationals. But this new wave of negative treatment was stirring things up among the youth. In the wake of the Farhud and again at the end of World War II in 1945, the ranks of underground movements swelled. Many young Jews in Iraq were also attracted to the Communist movement, which was equally illegal. I was invited to join the Communists but declined. I had no interest; I was a follower of Zionism, and Communists were anti-Zionist.

I started playing with the thought of moving to Israel and meanwhile took my self-defense—and the defense of others—into my own hands.

One day, I saw a girl on the street with two Muslim boys. One boy was holding her by the arm and the other was fondling her, and she was trying to escape.

With horror, I realized that this girl was my neighbor—the more beautiful of two sisters who lived next door to us. She had fair skin and green eyes, and I used to look at her from our roof. The first time our eyes met, I was mesmerized. For weeks, I was wondering how to approach her or ask her name, and now these boys were assaulting her.

I knew we were not supposed to fight Muslims, but I was not going to stand by. I don't know if it was chivalry, hormones, or sheer stupidity that made me act, but I ran up to them.

"What are you doing?" I demanded of the Muslim boys. They looked at me in shock. "*Rouh ibn el chalib!*" one of them shouted, "Go away, son of a dog!" In the Islamic culture, a dog is considered an unclean animal and is used as one of the worst curses in Arabic.

So I punched him in the face.

The boys let go of the girl and began to chase me, one of them wielding a knife. I knew that my life was hanging by a thread. I ran and ran, with them following close behind. Around the corner

I spotted a man coming out of his house. I pushed him back through the door, ran inside, and pulled the door closed, screaming, "They're trying to kill me!" I climbed up to his roof and leapt from rooftop to rooftop to escape.

I couldn't believe I made it out alive.

A few years later, after I had started high school, I formed a gang of about fifteen boys to protect Jewish girls in our neighborhood. I was the leader, along with my best friends, Nadji Ambar and Haskel Katsab.

Ambar was tall and strong and did the hard work. If we spotted an offender, Ambar grabbed the boy while Katsab and I did the hero's job of kicking and punching. We'd beat him up, drop him down, and run away as fast as we could.

It was risky and stupid, but we were brave and reckless. And maybe a bit lucky; we should have known better.

My own family suffered a direct and serious anti-Semitic incident. One summer night around 1945, my brother Aboudi was on his way home when, unprovoked, he was assaulted by a mob of Muslims. They beat him so badly he almost died.

My parents were devastated, and this incident ruined Aboudi's life. The trauma crippled him psychologically, and he never fully recovered from the attack. He cried and hallucinated all the time and would wake up screaming in the middle of the night. After Aboudi recovered physically from his assault, my parents bribed officials to allow him to join Eliyahoo in Palestine, hoping he would get some treatment for his emotional problems and make a better life for himself. He was approved and moved to Jerusalem, but he was never the same again.

Aboudi's trauma was yet another sign that the era of Jews in Iraq was coming to a close. We had a few more years, but the Farhud had marked the beginning of the end.

Chapter 4

Shattered Dreams

Teenage Fun

My years in high school were marked by dramatic extremes.

On the one hand, I felt the weight of the Farhud and of Aboudi's trauma. The promise of Zionism was tantalizing, and I felt empowered by my work with the *Tenuah*. But the enterprise of building a Jewish homeland also made our current situation in Iraq feel more threatened. The future looked so uncertain.

At the same time, my family had made it, and I was living a life of luxury. We had maids, a chauffeur, and a country home where we entertained diplomats and businessmen. My mischievous nature turned to more grown-up fun—with my friends and with women. My life felt blessed, and I was a teenager ready for adventure.

Remembering the times when Shumail treated me to nights out with his friends on the islands of the Tigris, I went on the *jazra* with my own friends, Ambar and Katsab. We spent long evenings on the river, rowing out to the islands that emerged only in summer, roasting fresh fish, and singing around the campfire.

On one outing we decided to jump into the river for a swim. During the dive, Katsab managed to lose the gold watch and chain

Despite the growing tension around me, I remained a fun-loving and adventurous teenager, enjoying the streets of Baghdad. (Around 1947)

that his father, a jeweler, had given him. We searched and searched along the riverbed but couldn't find it. Katsab was afraid his father would kill him.

"Tell him we were held up by Muslims with a knife, and you had to give it to them," I suggested, always ready with a plan.

When Katsab told his father this story, his father was just happy we were all okay. "A *kapara*," he kept repeating, "an offering." The watch was a small price to pay for his boy's safety.

In 1946 my family moved to an even larger house in Al Aliwiya, an upscale neighborhood near the American embassy. Our house was quite grand, with a beautiful private garden. Unlike our first two homes, this one was a villa—a freestanding structure not connected to any other house. The whole building was just for our family. We had a full staff of a gardener, chauffeur, maids, and cooks—all of them Jewish, and everyone but our chauffeur from the poorer Kurdistan region. The license plate number on our

*Our chauffeur, Menashe, drove me around in our
1941 Plymouth, and also taught me to drive.*

Plymouth, 314, was an indication of how few cars were in the city
at the time.

We had really made it now, and I felt that we were wealthy.
We even purchased a *mush tamal*, a vacation retreat about thirty
minutes outside of Baghdad. The country home was on an acre
of land and had two bedrooms with a large kitchen. A high wall
surrounded it. There were clusters of rose bushes with amazing
colors and aroma. In the spring, the air was fragrant with orange
blossom. The summer ripened our trees of apricots, nectarines, and
plums—a miniature Garden of Eden. A live-in gardener also served
as cook, butler, and cleaner. He made kabob, *samak masgouf*, and
other delicious meals.

Shumail invited VIPs—well-known lawyers, government
officials, and members of the parliament—to the *mush tamal* for
evening parties as a way to build business connections, and sometimes he invited me as well. There was usually a Baghdadi music

band, and often belly dancers who serviced the guests later. I took advantage of the privacy of the house and brought girls there during the day. I told the gardener not to tell, but I am sure Shumail knew what I was up to.

It was not customary to have girlfriends. But somehow it was accepted, even by parents, for men to visit prostitutes. Nightclubs had belly dancers and showgirls—local women and many imported from Greece and Italy—who, after the show, would leave with the customers. There was a special quarter, Kalla Chia, for government-supervised prostitution, similar to the Red Light District in Amsterdam. But Kalla Chia was, as would be expected, seedy and grungy, and you would hear things about family members going there to murder sisters and daughters who had shamed the family.

Instead, my friends and I went to higher class prostitutes who were in private homes, where it was more hygienic and more expensive and you had to know a code to get in. One of the brothel madams, Um Bahij, had been the principal of a girls' high school. She started out by supplying her students to officers and government ministers, but after she was caught and fired from the school, she started her own brothel. This was the house we went to, because her girls were young and beautiful. Going to brothels was an accepted practice and common for teenage boys in Iraq, though looking back I understand that those girls were terribly exploited.

Girls and women in Iraq were the underclass, subservient to the men and expected to keep the households running. Women didn't have much say, even in their own homes. Muslim girls were generally not allowed to leave the house without the permission of their father or husband, and when they did they were entirely covered in their *abaya* (burka). Jewish and Christian girls had a little more freedom to leave the house, and they did not wear the *abaya*; they went *sufur*—dressed in European clothing. Many Christian and Jewish girls went to school, but only a fraction of Muslim girls could get their father's approval to attend.

After 1948, some of the prostitutes were Palestinian refugees. But sometimes even poor Jewish girls were sold into prostitution, as I found out firsthand on a school trip to the mountains of Kurdistan in 1947.

The class took an overnight train from Baghdad to Mosul, then piled into two minibuses, with fourteen or fifteen of us in each, to get from Mosul to the campsite while a truck with our gear and supplies followed us. We drove through Irbil in Kurdistan and stopped near the all-Jewish farming village of Sandor. It took us a whole day to get there because the roads were rough and quite narrow.

We camped in two large tents in a lovely setting surrounded by fruit trees and a lush valley with streaming water. For two weeks we hiked and explored the area.

Next we went to Zachu, a town with a Jewish population, close to the Turkish border. In the mornings we ate flatbread hot out of the *tanoor* dipped in freshly skimmed cream (*kaymar*) and topped with date syrup (*silan*). At night we were given fresh lamb and cooked our dinner on an open campfire while we played music and sang songs.

The Jews of Kurdistan were an ancient population. In 1947 they were impoverished but lived in relative safety. While we were there, we met some Jewish girls from Sandor and were able to become friends.

Some months later, when I went to the prostitution house in Baghdad, I learned that one of the Kurdish Jewish girls we had befriended on that trip was now working there. I chose her but refused to sleep with her. Talking with her, I learned that she and another girl had come to Baghdad to get a job. A Muslim man proposed to her and, after they were married, sold her into prostitution. This was a common scheme.

There was nothing I could do, and it made me feel terrible. She would likely never escape that fate.

Poor people had an exceptionally hard life—especially women. Once a woman was sold into prostitution, her family didn't want her back, even if she escaped by some miraculous event. She became the lowest class, suffering the worst discrimination and public shame.

Prostitution was a given in the culture I grew up in. One of my friends even went to a prostitute with his father. So I did what was around me, although now I am not proud of it.

A New Goal

It was only in my last few years in Baghdad that I began to take myself and my future seriously. For most of my boyhood, I was the class clown, the constant rebel, and was more interested in proving my independence or getting a laugh than in accomplishing much.

At Shamash junior high school, our English teacher was Mrs. Rahmat Allah, a British woman who was married to a Muslim. For some reason, I enjoyed tormenting her. Sometimes I put pins on her chair, and she would scream when she sat down. One day I put tobacco powder on top of the large ceiling fan in the classroom, and when it started spinning the tobacco flew through the air and everyone began to sneeze. My reward: some good laughs and another trip to the headmaster for punishment. I pulled so many pranks that summer school became the usual case.

I spent my first year of high school at the American School for Boys, a Christian missionary academy run by Dr. and Mrs. Stuart. I was exposed to a wide range of cultures there. I made a lot of Armenian, Assyrian, Christian, and Muslim friends at the school. Non-Christian students were not forced to participate in prayer or other religious activities, but I enjoyed singing Christmas carols. I also liked reading *Romeo and Juliet* and learning folk songs like Stephen Foster's "Oh! Susannah."

Even though my intellect was piqued in high school, I was still not motivated or committed to my schooling.

When I was around fifteen, my parents went to Palestine, hoping yet again to find a cure for my older brother Yaakub's cerebral palsy. With my parents gone, Shumail convinced me to quit school. He could see I was bored, so he asked me to join him in the family business. Desperate to change my environment, I accepted.

As my first business lesson, Shumail bought a bale of cloth in my name, then immediately sold it. He offered me the profit of ten dinars, which was big money for a teenager, but I didn't take it. I felt like he was bribing me—he had done all the work, and I didn't deserve the money. I was wary of working with Shumail. For my whole life, he had been a domineering influence and assumed the role of disciplinarian. It seemed this business relationship was no different.

When my father returned from Palestine, he was quite upset that I had left school. To get me back on track, he came up with a new plan to motivate me to study. He promised that if I worked hard at school and did well, he would send me to university in America.

Those words were like magic to me and changed everything. I switched to the Al A'adadiya high school in the Sinag district, a mostly Jewish school headed by Meir Zakaraya, the principal. It was here that my internal transformation began.

As a surprise to everyone, including myself, I committed myself to studying day and night and did well. I wasn't great at history and geography, but I began to excel in chemistry, physics, and math and mastered English quickly. I bought a little chemistry lab to use at home, and I was given the key to the chemistry lab at school so that I could complete my experiments after hours. I was

The atomic bomb that led to the end of World War II
inspired me to want to study nuclear physics.

progressing and learning quite a bit, with only a few minor burns to show for it.

It was then that I decided I wanted to be a nuclear physicist. This was just after America won World War II by dropping nuclear bombs on Japan, showing the world the powerful potential of nuclear energy. I wanted to harness the power of the atom to create new possibilities and advance technology for human use. Albert Einstein was my hero, and I dreamed of meeting him and maybe, someday, working under him.

Despite my turnaround, I still managed to use my growing intellect to create mischief. On one chemistry test, I allowed my friends to copy my answer, not noticing that I had made a silly calculation error at the end of the problem: somehow I totaled five plus six plus three as sixteen. The teacher failed us when he saw the repeated mistake, and he knew it had come from me.

Once a week we had open forums to practice public speaking. I used to translate Arabic passages into English in a literal way, making them quite humorous for my audience. In my second to last year in high school, I acted in a play. Since we were an all-boys school, boys played the parts of women, and I savored the comedic role of the cheating wife.

But even when I behaved and did well, my father and brother would not give me the satisfaction of telling me that I had done so. If I scored a 95 percent on an exam, my father wouldn't say anything, and Shumail wanted to know what happened to the other 5 percent. They never offered much encouragement, which took some of the joy out of learning.

In 1948, after I graduated from the Al A'adadiya high school with honors, my father gave me an incredible graduation gift: a trip to a five-star luxury hotel in the mountains of Kurdistan. Now that we had money, my father was grateful to be able to fully express his natural impulse of generosity. The hotel charged about two dinars a day—close to half of what a working-class Iraqi earned in a full month.

I invited my friend Menashe and his sister Katie to come on the trip. Menashe was a photographer who, after finishing high

By the time I graduated from Al A'adadiya
high school in 1948, I was finally a serious student.

school, opened a small photography shop in the Battaween district called Select Photo, so everyone called him Menashe Select. His sister was older, so it was considered acceptable for her to travel with her brother and his friend.

We took an eight-seat propeller plane to Kirkuk. It was the first time I flew in a plane, and I was terribly airsick. A car took us to the hotel, in Haji Amran, where we were greeted by the beautiful spread of green mountains and valleys. The hotel had marble floors, large rooms with modern bathrooms, and wonderful restaurants that served European-style food in addition to traditional Iraqi food. It was the first time I had creamy tomato soup. We also enjoyed steaks, the freshest of fish, and the juiciest of lamb kabob, along with plenty of fresh fruits from the local mountains. We played on the tennis courts by the pool while majestic mountains loomed over us.

The minute I came home, Shumail gave me hell.

Upon arriving in Haji Amran, I had sent a telegram home to tell my family we had gotten there safely and everything was in order. But the Mukhabarat intercepted the telegram. Shumail could not believe how stupid I was to send that telegram, and he let me know it.

This was in July or August 1948, right after the start of the Israel War of Independence, when tensions were extremely high. The Mukhabarat summoned my father and Shumail. They accused them of sending me to Kirkuk as an Israeli spy and demanded to know what the "secret message" of the telegram was about.

Shumail's mastery in negotiations served me well. I am certain he paid a hefty sum to convince them that my telegram was truly an innocent exchange. After he made sure I understood what an idiot I was, he instructed me to go to the Mukhabarat. He had paid the bribe, and all I had to do was sign a document confirming that I was not a spy.

I went to their headquarters, which was known as the place

where they tortured people into confessions. I was terrified, even though I knew that Shumail had already greased the wheels for me. I sat anxiously, waiting.

A man called me and took to me to Ibrahim, the officer in charge of my interrogation. After the formal questioning about my name, my father, and my home address, he began asking me specific questions.

"What was the meaning of the telegram you sent to your family?"

"Only what it said," I explained, trying to hide the shaking in my voice. "That I had arrived to my vacation safely and that I was happy. I did not want my parents to worry about me."

"What was the secret code? Were you sending messages about the Zionist activities?"

"No, sir," I answered firmly. "There was no secret code, and this telegram went only to my family. I was simply assuring my parents I was okay."

The investigator commanded me to sign the papers on his desk. Relief flooded over me when I realized they would not invent some reason to arrest me. I was free to go home.

In the months that followed, I focused on my vision for my future: studying nuclear physics at an American university. I went to the library at the American Institute in Baghdad, a project of the American embassy, to research colleges. I applied with help from the counselors at the American Institute and was accepted to three universities in the U.S.—one in Vermont, one in Seattle, and the University of Southern California in Los Angeles. I had my Iraqi passport, and did not have trouble getting an American visa, thanks to some well-placed bribes. All I needed was my *khurouj*, an exit visa to leave Iraq.

I didn't have to worry about being drafted into the Iraqi army. In Iraq, every eighteen-year-old male was required to serve three years in the army, but if you were a high school graduate you skipped straight to officer training. And if you could afford to pay fifty dinars, you would serve for only three months total. This all worked out well for the rich and educated but meant that the military ended up with an army full of the poor and illiterate.

I needed to pay no money, however. By the time I turned 18, the Iraqi army was not drafting Jews anymore. They no longer trusted us.

No Exit

In early 1947, UN delegates visited Jewish leaders in many Arab countries, including Iraq, to determine the level of support for the establishment of a Jewish state in Palestine. But Iraqi Jews were terrified of persecution for expressing Zionism, and many took a stand as Iraqi nationals.

The chief community rabbi, Hakham Sasson Khaduri, wrote an open declaration in the nationalist newspaper, *Al Istiqlal*, stating that "the community had no connection to Zionism" and was against the establishment of the Jewish state. "The Jews of Iraq are loyal citizens, who receive the scorn of their Zionist brethren and deserve the support of their fellow Iraqis."

Regardless of the community's public sentiment, on November 29, 1947, the UN adopted a resolution for a partition plan for Palestine, which would create two independent states—the Arab State of Palestine and the Jewish State of Israel. All Arab states rejected the proposal and warned that they could not prevent any violence that might be directed toward their own Jewish populations as a result of the UN decision.

With Israel on the brink of statehood, anti-Zionist and anti-Jewish hostility in Iraq became more pronounced and public, and we started hearing vitriolic radio broadcasts on a regular basis.

Iraqi Chief Rabbi Hakham Sasson Khaduri publicly opposed the establishment of the State of Israel, part of his effort to prove that Jews were loyal citizens of Iraq.

Muslim mobs gathered to protest the proposed partition of Palestine into Arab and Jewish states. The sign reads: "Down with the Palestine Partition Plan"

Newspapers were openly calling for people to get ready for war. Massive public demonstrations called for the liberation of Palestine.

The Jewish community continued to try to convince the Iraqi government that, although we were Jewish, we were against the idea of Israel. (In fact, some in the Jewish community, especially the Communists, were genuinely against the idea of a Jewish state.) My Jewish high school, Al A'adadiya, brought us to demonstrations against the Palestine partition plan to show solidarity with the Iraqi people. Though I was already secretly studying Hebrew and self-defense with Israeli *shlichim*, I would go to the demonstrations with all my Jewish friends and scream, "Free Palestine! Zionists are the enemy!"

But our show didn't work. Young people, my friends in-cluded, were arrested for being Zionists. And the fact that so many Communists were Jews further inflamed the Iraqi government and contributed to the wave of official anti-Semitic rhetoric. Many were tortured or simply never heard from again. I was terrified. I felt

Jews were hanged in the public square of Baghdad as punishment for supporting Zionism or Communism.

I could be next.

Sometime around 1947, I was on my way to school when I noticed a Communist had been hanged in the public square. Over the next few years I saw the brother of my English teacher and the brother of my cousin's wife both quietly swaying from the same gallows. The older generation did not understand how Iraq had become inhospitable to its Jewish citizens or why we were so eager to follow Zionism and stir up trouble with the Iraqi government. But we saw that their old reality of living in a submissive peace with the Muslims was a thing of the past.

Then it became official. The State of Israel declared independence on May 14, 1948. The following day, Iraq joined Lebanon, Syria, Egypt, Transjordan in launching an attack on the new Jewish democracy. This powerful Arab coalition was not fighting over land or resources; they were fighting to prevent the establishment of a Jewish state—of any size.

At home, we gathered around the radio and listened as claims of Israel being destroyed were broadcast on Radio Baghdad. In reality, the collective population of twenty million Arabs was failing to conquer the meager eight hundred thousand Israeli inhabitants. The Israelis had a secret weapon: *ain brera* (no choice). They fought because they had to win, or they would cease to exist. On the other hand, the Arab coalition was a paper tiger and had little personal investment aside from their resentment toward Jews. The tenacious goals of the Israeli army pulled them through tumultuous moments and after almost ten months of fighting left the Arab coalition humiliated in their defeat. It was a miracle. But as David Ben-Gurion, the founder of the new Jewish state, later professed, "In Israel, in order to be a realist, you must believe in miracles."

While the war was raging, in covert meetings and in our hearts, Iraqi Jews celebrated the establishment of the first Jewish state in two thousand years. But we were also terrified. We were uncertain if Israel would survive the aggression, and we were equal-ly uncertain what our fate in Baghdad would be if we stayed there. The Jewish population had suffered many blows in its extensive history, and our community had suffered hundreds of deaths and untold material and psychological damage during the Farhud. We knew we had to take this growing resentment seriously if we wanted to stay alive.

In July 1948, just after I graduated, the government passed a law declaring all Zionist activity treason, with a minimum sentence of seven years imprisonment and a maximum sentence of death. Jews were barred from civil service and government positions, had their businesses boycotted and confiscated, lost their jobs, and were arrested without explanation. Hundreds of Jews were put into Iraqi jails, accused of treason or other trumped-up charges. It was open warfare against Iraq's twenty-five-century-old minority.

The breaking point came in September, when Shafiq Ades, one of the most powerful Jewish businessmen in Iraq, was publicly hanged in Basra on false charges of selling weapons to Israel despite the fact that he was an outspoken anti-Zionist. Ades had longtime connections with the regent of Iraq and other powerful political figures, and most assumed the charges would be dropped. But within two days, he had been tried and charged as a traitor to the country.

On September 24, when I saw the photo of Ades' body hanging from a noose on the front page of the newspaper *Al Zaman*, I became hysterical. If this had happened to Shafiq Ades, I knew no one was safe and I had to get out. I loved my city, and I loved my family, but how could I stay?

The dark and ugly part of life in Iraq began to overshadow and swallow the good part, like a big fish swallowing a small fish. At best, we were seen as foreigners; at worst, we were seen as traitors.

America was beckoning, and I was ready to go.

Given the new laws, Jews were forbidden to leave Iraq for

The public hanging of Shafiq Ades, one of the most powerful Jewish businessmen in Iraq, was a signal to me that it was time to smuggle out. (1948)

fear they would go to Israel. However, I thought this wouldn't apply to me—I had a legitimate request to go to university in the United States. But after a year of waiting for my exit visa, I got the terrible news. Even though I had an Iraqi passport, had been accepted at three American universities, and had gotten my visa for entry into the U.S., because I was Jewish I was denied a *khurouj*. Without the exit visa, Iraq would not let me leave the country.

The officials offered me one impossible way out: my family could put up a three-thousand-dinar bond to guarantee I would return to Iraq after completing my education. This amount was the equivalent of approximately $1 million today, so the idea was out of the question. With all the bribing and greasing my family had done over the years, this they could not fix for me.

My dreams were shattered. I would not be going to an American university. I was almost nineteen, and I had no idea what my future looked like.

Shumail still wanted me to join him in the fabric business.

I had done more work for him while I was waiting for my exit visa, and that was further proof that we did not work well together. He wanted to monitor and direct my every move, and I knew I would have no independence under him. Plus, he was only interested in making money, and I was developing much bigger goals.

I finally decided that my only path was to Israel. I wanted to free myself from the mental slavery of fear and hopelessness and needed a new place to call home. Helping to build the Jewish State of Israel would give me a new sense of purpose. And it would give me a chance to be near my older brother Eliyahoo, who had been laying down the foundations of freedom since he moved to Jerusalem in 1942. I convinced my parents that Nory, who was sixteen, should come with me.

Elisha made contact with *Tenuah* members in Basra, knowing that they had begun to illegally bring Jews from Iraq to Israel via Iran. Iran was on relatively cooperative terms with Israel and still treated its Jewish population with some decency. Even when Iran joined the Arab states in opposing the creation of Israel, the country maintained quiet economic and political ties with Jerusalem and the West. This enabled the international Jewish community to operate out of Iran.

In 1942, the Jewish Agency for Palestine had opened an office in Teheran and was instrumental in moving refugees from Europe to Palestine. There was a whole apparatus, involving the Iranian and Israeli governments, the Jewish Joint Distribution Committee, and the local Iranian Jewish community, to help Jewish refugees, from both Europe and Muslim countries, escape to Israel. Hundreds of Jews—mostly young people like me—were being smuggled out of Iraq every month.

As Nory and I prepared to go, things continued to get even worse. In October 1949, fifty Jewish leaders were arrested and court-martialed—tried under military law—for claims of aiding the

Zionist movement. The community was terrified.

My childhood memories, my still-unaltered sense of belonging, and my love for my family were not enough to keep me
somewhere that had rejected me, somewhere that had no interest
in my future. In December of 1949, Nory and I were ready to leave.

I said quiet goodbyes to my parents but not to anyone else,
not even my beloved Youmma, my constant admirer and protector.
I had to keep my departure a secret.

Nory and I boarded the overnight train for Basra. Full of
anger, disappointment, and fear, I said goodbye to Baghdad forever.
The prospect of freedom was still an abstract idea, but what I was
leaving behind was real: my family, my home, and my history. I was
leaving behind my culture, a history of 2,500 years, and my place of
birth. I was leaving behind my faithful friends—Jews, Muslims, and
Christians. I was leaving behind memories of fun and fear, of hope
and despair. I was leaving behind my past and future dreams, never

The last photo of me and my mother in Baghdad. (1949)

wanting to look back.

I was sure of only one thing: I would be lucky to get out of that unpredictable heaven and hell. I had my youth, a love for living, and the determination to succeed. I refused to let the nightmare of the past enslave my bright future, no matter how uncertain it was at that moment.

To Freedom in Iran

Now, after our treacherous and terrifying journey on the Shatt Al Arab from Basra to Iran, Nory and I, and our fellow passengers, finally set foot on the eastern bank of the river, in Iran. We delivered ourselves into the hands of the three frantic men who had been waiting for us since the night before. They exchanged a secret code with the smugglers so that everyone was sure we were all part of the same operation. I found out later that the boat right behind us, also full of teenagers, never made it. The same men who met us were supposed to meet them, but that group never arrived. They were likely captured by the Mukhabarat and returned to Baghdad, and who knows what fate they met. My biggest fear may have become their reality.

Even before I found out about the other group, I knew how lucky we were to make it across. The three men escorted us, on foot, to the nearby homes of hospitable Jewish families in Khorramshahr. Our hosts welcomed us into their homes and fed us. We were still anxious for the future ahead, but they made us feel like we were part of their family. We stayed in Khorramshahr for two days until we were relocated to Ahvaz, about 125 kilometers to the north.

Ahvaz had an extensive operation set up to handle the influx of refugees. Many Jews from Iraq and Kurdistan escaped to Iran either through the northern mountains or across the southern river as we had. Our hosts and organizers, all of them Persian Jews, were proud of their country and were incredible people who went out of their way to comfort us in our most stressful moments.

Some of our group, including Nory, stayed in the big synagogue of Ahvaz, while I and some others were sent to a private home. I found out later that our hosts were paying the Iranian police per head, but the authorities only knew about the people staying in the synagogue, not about the ones in homes. We were cheating the police out of their bribe money.

Usually people stayed for a few days, then continued on the train to Teheran. From there, they were flown to Israel. Nory and the rest of our group left for Teheran soon after we arrived. But rather than going straight there, I assured Nory I would see him soon in Israel, and I volunteered to stay in Ahvaz to help for a few months. I became responsible for procuring supplies and food, getting someone to cook, and generally making sure everyone had what they needed and got where they needed to go.

In Khorramshahr, people speak Arabic due to the proximity to the Iraqi border. But in Ahvaz, as in most of Iran, they speak Farsi. I quickly learned a few conversational words in Farsi; I had a great faculty for languages and liked to use it. In the months between high school graduation and when I left Iraq, I had learned French.

One night, at two or three in the morning, a couple with a baby arrived at the house where I was staying in Ahvaz. They had come by truck through some treacherous mountain roads. This being January, in the dead of winter, the temperature was below freezing. The baby, just a few months old, had been crying throughout the journey but stopped right before they arrived. We did our best to warm him up with blankets and warm water. But in the morning we found that he had frozen to death. I can still hear the screams and cries of his mother and father. I cried along with them, and together we buried the baby.

I stayed in Ahvaz, helping out, until the end of February.

Then I, too, boarded a train to Teheran with other Jewish refugees. After a ride of more than eight hundred kilometers, we were met at the train station by the Jewish organization in Teheran. They had built bunk beds in the building in the Jewish cemetery to house the refugees on their way to Israel. The building was not heated, but there were plenty of blankets to keep us warm.

I was in Teheran only a few days, but I did have some time to explore. I walked down Pahlavi Street and stopped at a restaurant to enjoy an Iranian specialty, *chelo kabob*, a ground beef skewer dripping with fat, and rice. I was a foreigner in a foreign place, but the friendliness alone already made me glad I was far from the insecurity and brutality of my birthplace.

Soon it was our time to leave. Israel had arranged to pay for family visas, so I suddenly found myself the head of a fake household—a "family" of six. Israel had also made an arrangement with the American humanitarian and president of Alaska Airlines, James Wooten. As part of what was known as Operation Magic Carpet, Wooten converted salvaged wartime cargo planes to carry tens of thousands of Yemenite Jews from Aden to Tel Aviv in 1949 and 1950 after their country, like mine, expelled them following the founding of the State of Israel. Wooten had also participated in the Berlin Airlift and used his planes to ferry European Jewish refugees from Shanghai to Israel. It was on one of his refitted cargo planes that I made my way to Israel. Without luggage or seatbelts, we crammed together to fit four or five per wooden bench—the seats having been removed to allow for more passengers.

In theory, it's a quick and straight flight from Teheran to Tel Aviv. But we were not allowed to fly across Iraqi or Syrian airspace, forcing us to go northwest, over Turkey, and loop back around the Mediterranean to get to Israel. The flight lasted more than four hours, which, after all the anticipation, felt like an eternity.

I arrived at Lod Airport on March 2, 1950, a sunny and

glorious day. There was no fancy terminal; once we walked down the stairway, our feet were touching our Jewish homeland.

I knelt down and kissed the ground with tears in my eyes. Tears of relief.

This was our land. Our refuge. Our opportunity.

PART 2

❋ ISRAEL ❋

1949-1956

CHAPTER 5

EARLY DAYS IN ISRAEL

My New Identity

After the horrific experience of being smuggled out of Iraq, I was finally free, and my dream of being in the Promised Land was fulfilled. It was the most exhilarating feeling I had ever experienced. In the midst of the sadness of leaving my home and my family, and despite my dreams of higher education in America, I knew I was planting the seeds of our future as a part of the Jewish nation.

I had arrived in Israel with only the clothes I was wearing. I had no documents—no passport, no birth certificate, nothing. I had even lost the overcoat I left home with. We were herded into a tent set up at the airport with tables and chairs, where Arabic-speaking immigration agents sat waiting. They gave us tea and cookies, feeding us for the first time since we had boarded the plane in Tehran.

"What is your first and last name?" the agent asked.

It sounded like an easy question, but it was actually an early sign that I was coming to a foreign culture. In Iraq, some families had last names, but some didn't. In those families, people were given a first name by their parents, followed by their father's first name and their grandfather's first name. I was Yousuf Sasson Shumail, and my Iraqi passport, which was back in Baghdad along with all my documents, said "Yousuf Sasson." I told the agent, "Yousuf Sasson Shumail. He marked it down, but on my new identity card he put only "Yosef Shmuel." I had a new name.

Then came the question of my birthday. In Baghdad, we did not keep track of or celebrate birthdays. It wasn't part of our culture. I knew I was born in 1930 but didn't know the exact date, just that it was during the winter holiday of Chanukah. I looked at this as an opportunity, because in Baghdad we never had parties for our birthdays. I thought if I chose December 31, New Year's Eve, I would be guaranteed to have a party every year and could recapture some lost birthday parties I never had in Baghdad. Plus, I knew the whole world would always be celebrating with me.

Within a few hours of landing, I was a new person: Yosef Shmuel, born in Baghdad on December 31, 1930.

We left the airport on a bus headed for Sha'ar Ha'aliyah (the Gate of Immigration), an old British camp near Haifa that we would live in for a few days while we were tested for skills and health. As we drove through the diverse landscape of the State of Israel, I marveled at the idea that this all belonged to the Jewish people. It was springtime—in fact, we landed on the holiday of Purim, one month before Passover—and we drove by orange groves, the trees heavy with glowing fruit. The sky was bright, and the air was crisp. We ascended toward Haifa and drove through the verdant mountain town of Zichron Yaakov, then toward the shore, where the azure Mediterranean Sea sparkled in the distance.

The green of Israel's trees, the budding of fruit, and the glistening of the ocean awakened in me a sense of unlimited possibility. I felt an automatic kinship with everyone around me, and my opportunities seemed limitless.

There were no secret police to fear. No Muslims to run from. No threat around every corner. I felt freer than I'd ever felt before.

Herring and Steel Beds

But my romantic notions of Israel quickly turned into harsh reality.

When we arrived in Sha'ar Ha'Aliyah, medical staff performed a quick examination and sprayed us with DDT to kill any possible infections. Today, cleansing with DDT would be completely unacceptable, but at the time we felt that it was improving our health and safety.

They sent us to our barracks with two blankets, a towel, a tin plate, a fork, a spoon, and a knife. At mealtime I found the food was like nothing I had ever tasted or smelled before; I could barely eat it. In the morning they gave us herring, a salty, slimy, cured fish. We drank watery tea and ate hard black bread that tasted like sawdust. Instead of fresh butter we were given oily margarine, which I refused to eat. I dreamed of my mother's rich breakfast: fried eggs with *silan*, hard feta cheese boiled with onion, fresh fruit, sweet rice cooked in milk, and pillowy flatbread.

The food at lunchtime in the camp was even worse. They glopped some mashed potatoes on a plate and ladled washed-out soup into a bowl. I longed for a simple plate of rice laced with dill, maybe with some grilled mutton. But at that point I was quite hungry, so I learned to eat whatever they gave me. At dinnertime I encountered salami for the first time. In Iraq, cow's meat was considered a poor man's food, and most people only ate lamb, mutton, or chicken. I, along with most of the other Iraqis, tossed the salami in the garbage.

But in Israel, even bad food had a bright side. Standing in line I met Sara, a refugee from Romania. She was thin, blond, and beautiful, with aquamarine eyes that struck me from the start. We looked at each other and somehow connected. I didn't know Romanian, and she didn't speak Arabic or Hebrew. She taught me to say "*Ce face?*" (How are you?) in Romanian, and I taught her "*Ani ohev otach*" (I love you) in Hebrew.

Sha'ar Ha'aliyah was gated, but we were allowed to leave whenever we desired. On my second day I went to visit my mother's sister, *Khala* Salima. Her husband, Yosef Sourani (whom we called Safani), had imported kitchen dishes and crockery back in Baghdad but after some business problems with a Muslim client in the 1930s decided to leave Iraq for Palestine.

Khala Salima and Uncle Safani lived on Hassadot Street in Haifa with their three young daughters in a one-room tin shack on a *dunam* (about one thousand square meters) of land, where they grew vegetables and raised chickens. They had a well and an outhouse. When I told them that everyone was throwing away the salami, they said, "Please collect all the salami and bring it to us!" At that time, with the exception of fresh air, everything was scarce—rice, sugar, flour, eggs, chicken. Meat was rationed at four hundred grams per month per person, so they were happy to get the leftover salami. I guess they had gotten used to the food of the European Jewish immigrants who dominated Israeli culture.

We stayed at Sha'ar Ha'aliyah for four days. With Sara next to me, I forgot about the slimy fish and oily margarine and wished I could stay longer, but it was time to go. Sha'ar Ha'aliyah was just a pass-through for new immigrants, and we had been assigned to our temporary camps across the country.

I was transferred to Beit Lid, a refugee camp about five miles east of the coastal city of Netanya, north of Tel Aviv. We were housed in tents anchored to the sand and provided with steel beds with straw mattresses, a cotton blanket, and a candle. We used a putrid smelling outhouse, and we showered in corrugated metal stalls, where water dripped through a pipe from a huge, elevated metal tank that had to be refilled manually. Just a few months before, in Baghdad, I had servants, fluffy mattresses, soft blankets, and all the

In 1950, I spent a few weeks sleeping on a straw mattress in a tent anchored to the sand in Beit Lid, a tent encampment like this one.

food I wanted. This new life was not what I was used to. I felt sad, and I missed Sara after our short-lived romance.

The food at Beit Lid was no better than at Sha'ar Ha'aliyah, and here I had to wait in a long line for that same miserable tin plate. I was still wearing the clothes that I smuggled out with and had no money. There I was, a homeless, penniless refugee. I was grateful for the free food and accommodations, but I felt humiliated.

Lying down on the straw mattress at night, in the flickering candlelight, I heard a whisper of hope that lifted my spirits. It was the feeble voice of my Youmma, uttering the words she said when I ran to her crying and looking for comfort as a child: "*Ayuni,* don't cry, you are going to be rich."

Hearing her words in my mind made me confident that I could get through this. Allowing disappointments, failed dreams, and the nightmares of my past to control my thinking would render me a victim, and a victim's life is a life of rage, indignation, and voluntary enslavement. Instead, I was certain of one thing: I was

113

lucky to be alive and out of Iraq's unpredictable heaven and hell.

Standing in line for food, I understood better how Youmma felt. My grandmother had been a widow in her twenties with three boys, and while my father left school at thirteen to earn money, the family still had to rely on the *keren*, a community fund for widows and orphans. The *keren* gave them clothing and other household needs, as well as food. My grandmother never forgot what it meant to live in deep poverty, dependent on community charity.

Now, as I stood in a dirty refugee camp holding my tin plate out to receive a miserable pink chunk of salami, I was struck with the thoughts of all that I had left behind. I could not send word to my parents that I had arrived safely, as it was not safe to communicate with Iraq from Israel. A letter from Israel could expose my family to danger. Likewise, I could not get word of their well-being. I had to be content with the family I had nearby.

With the allowance of a few liras they gave us at Beit Lid, I got on a bus to visit my brother Eliyahoo.

Family Reunions

I celebrated my first Passover in Israel with Eliyahoo, Ahuva and their son, Yigal, in Jerusalem. Our feast was modest, and we didn't have all the Seder foods I was used to, but we sang the familiar songs together into the night, until we came to "Next Year in Jerusalem." I couldn't believe I was here, in Jerusalem, with my beloved brother, in total freedom.

I was still getting used to my own liberation. No fear of sudden arrest or torture due to false accusations of speaking against the government or of being a Zionist enemy of the state. No need for bribes when stopped by a policeman for no reason. No more Jewish corpses hanging in the public square. Liberated from the weight of that fear and anxiety, I felt like a bird fresh out of a cage, flying for

Eliyahoo and Ahuva, shown here in 1970, got married in 1947 in Jerusalem.

the first time.

Eli and Ahuva lived in a tiny, one-room hut that was attached to the back of someone else's house and covered by a tin roof. The hut served as both bedroom and living room, and a corner of the small, fenced-in area outside served as the kitchen. They shared an outhouse with a neighbor.

I was excited to see Eli and be reunited with him after all those years apart. My brother was more mature now that he was married and was a father.

Our reunion was joyous, and though we were worried for the rest of our family, we laughed at the fact that we had been assigned different family names. When Eli arrived in Palestine in 1942, he was given the name Eliyahoo Sasson, which was written on his Iraqi passport, while Nory and I were both given the surname Shmuel.

Before I left, Eli and I pledged to keep in touch and see each other often.

Nory had arrived in Israel directly from Iran two months before me. He first lived on a *kibbutz* and soon after joined the Air Force, working with the ground crew. He was adjusting well, but he was busy with his military duties, and it was hard to see him often.

My brother Aboudi had also been in Jerusalem since 1946; his new name was Ovadia Sasson. Aboudi found a wife once he moved to Israel, but they didn't have any kids and the marriage didn't last long. He was still married when I stayed with him for the first time. That night in his one-bedroom apartment, I was startled awake in the middle of the night by the sound of his screaming. He was still haunted by the beating he had received in Baghdad.

Like my brothers, I was trying to figure out my way to navigate this new life. It had already been a few weeks since my arrival, and I had nothing to do. Despite the overwhelming gratitude for my freedom, on a day-to-day basis I was beginning to feel aimless, disappointed, discouraged, angry, and confused.

CHAPTER 6

FROM KIBBUTZ TO THE NAVY

Hauling Stones

I had an easy time communicating in Hebrew, thanks to the underground lessons I took with the *Tenuah* in Baghdad, and I was quickly picking up more of the language. I hoped that would help me find a job.

The Sochnut, the Jewish agency responsible for refugee re-settlement, sent people to help us figure out what to do next. I knew I was not ready for the army; I was still too much of a spoiled rascal from my privileged teenage years in Baghdad to willingly sign up for unquestioning submission. As a refugee I did not have to go to the military right away, and the Sochnut offered two vocational courses instead: I could learn to cut diamonds or to be a ground surveyor. Considering I had wanted to be a nuclear physicist, neither option appealed to me.

The Sochnut counselor was an athletic-looking young man wearing a white shirt and blue pants. His tanned skin revealed that he had been working in the sun, and his radiant smile made me feel at ease. He was fluent in Hebrew and spoke Arabic too. He tempted me with a different kind of prospect—a *kibbutz*.

"No worries! Work, food, clothing, and accommodation are all taken care of."

"Where do I sign?" I replied.

"No signature needed. I'll pick you up tomorrow."

And like that, I was moving to a *kibbutz*, Israel's great experiment in socialist communal living.

The next day, the counselor took me to the southern shore of Yam Kinneret (the Sea of Galilee). The *kibbutz* was basically a farming commune where members worked for no direct pay but had all of their basic needs met by their collective work. There was no sense of individual ownership; everything was jointly owned, and everyone felt responsible for his or her contributions to the group. I had a nice barracks, and food was always available, especially vegetables. There were lots of young people, and at night we boys and girls got together to dance the *hora* and sing pioneer songs.

The first day at the *kibbutz*, I was assigned to be a shepherd. I went out to the fields with my staff and my flock and attempted to persuade the sheep to move. I was a city boy with seven siblings,

I enjoyed the social life on Kibbutz, but the manual labor didn't hold my interest for more than a few weeks.

used to always having people around. But the sheep didn't talk back. I felt lonely, like my mind had stopped working. I needed more stimulation.

After a couple of days, I was sent to the fields to pick lemons—but picking fruit was hard and boring work. A few days later I ended up in the barn, milking and cleaning cows—but the smell and the work disgusted me. Finally, I was assigned to serve in the dining room and kitchen, running back and forth with dishes and washing enormous pots. That was just as bad. I had hit my limit. I felt no challenge. Maybe some people considered it heaven to have everything prepared and decided for you, but *kibbutz* life was not for me. I lasted only three weeks there.

Back on my own, I went from one menial job to another—digging ditches, hauling furniture, working on a farm. I tried to make ends meet any way I could and worked for anyone who would pay me. I stayed in tents in different camps and even spent some nights in portable wooden structures. When I needed somewhere more comfortable or had the day off for Shabbat, I went back to my *Khala* Salima's shack in Haifa.

Along the way, I reunited with my childhood friend, Nadji Ambar, who now went by the Hebrew name Yechezkel Ambar.

The Sochnut trained me, and then I trained others, to cut stones for walls.

Ambar had been my accomplice in protecting our Jewish neighborhood when we were younger, and it was a relief to have such a close friend back by my side.

The Sochnut continued to provide work and sent Ambar and me to learn how to cut stones with straight edges so they could be used to build protective walls around homes. I guess we were pretty good at it, because soon they sent us to teach the craft in Zangariyye, a *moshav* (small agricultural village) for new immigrants from Yemen. Zangariyye was north of Yam Kinneret, on the road between Tiberias and Tzfat, only a few kilometers from the Syrian border.

Ambar and I joined with two others, so we were four *madrichim* (counselors), living with newly arrived Yemeni immigrants in tents with no electricity, no running water, and no road. Luckily, it was not the rainy season. We didn't use our cutting skills, but we taught the newcomers how to remove stones from potential farmland to prepare it for cultivation, a process called *sikul adama* (clearing the land).

There was a small *makolet* (bodega) in Zangariyye where we bought food to prepare our meals. The market had delicious Santa Rosa plums, the kind with the red flesh. But I guess they didn't have plums in Yemen, because the immigrants didn't know what to do with them. That only meant more plums for us!

One evening, I went out for a walk just as a bus full of residents was arriving back to the village. When I returned from my stroll, I found that I had missed a huge commotion at the camp. The Yemenites swore they had seen a *djinn* (a spirit) lurking in the evening's darkness as they pulled into the *moshav*. Some argued that it was not possible that there could be demons in *Eretz HaKodesh* (the Holy Land), but others felt certain of what they had seen. It took me a few minutes, but I realized it was I who was the *djinn* walking in the darkness. Luckily, they were reasonable enough to believe me.

While it might sound crazy to believe in *djinns*, I had heard such craziness before. My Youmma and my Nana used to always tell me stories about *djinns*. We were told on many occasions not to pour hot water on the floor, lest we hurt and anger the *djinns* living in the world underneath. And they claimed that people would be minding their own business, walking home at night, when they would suddenly be facing a cow, or a wall would unexpectedly block their path. Of course, they didn't account for how narrow and winding the poorly lit roads of Taht Al Takia really were.

Many of the Yemenite families remained in the *moshav* for years. The new Israeli government had difficulty handling the extreme influx of new immigrants, which had doubled the population in a few years. Eventually, the government built houses for the residents of the *moshavs*, and these settlements became permanent villages and cities. However, this was not the life for me. After a couple months in Zangariyye, Ambar and I were ready to move on to find different and, we hoped, better opportunities.

I started thinking again about my dreams of going to university. But I knew that before I could pursue my own goals for higher education, I had to serve my country first.

Serving My Country

I enlisted for my compulsory military service in September of 1950 and received my soldier number: 199087. We went through three months of rigorous training, where we were expected to get up early, run on command, carry guns, and go through grueling physical exercises to prepare us for potential combat. They took us on field exercises for three or four days at a time. We had to carry our packs and our guns and sleep in the open, going nonstop all day. My teenage years had not prepared me to take orders and push

After a few months in Israel, I was ready to join the Navy in 1950.

myself to the physical limit, and I found it challenging.

At the end of basic training, I was assigned to the navy, and placed on ship *Kuf-Shloshim* (30), a Canadian freighter that had been converted for military use. There, I was assigned as a waiter in the officers' dining room. But out on the water I was seasick and miserable—just as I had been as a boy on long car trips. I could barely make it to the tables. Once, while I carried dinner trays from the kitchen to the officers' table, I vomited right onto a tray.

I wanted to get off the ship, but you couldn't get reassigned for suffering seasickness. Instead, a friend told me that if you deserted the ship, they would kick you out and move you to another unit on land. I was willing to try anything.

One weekend I was given leave on Friday and was supposed to come back on Saturday night. Instead, I returned on Sunday. The captain called me to his office and demanded to know why I had gone missing. He tried to help me come up with excuses, asking if I had gone to help family or if I had been sick, but I was so arrogant and spoiled that I just said, "Because I did."

I wouldn't give him any explanation, even though he was trying to help me. I kept saying, "I did it."

I even refused to salute. They told me I had to salute, and I said, "I don't give a shit. I won't salute." It reminded me of when Shumail had tied me to the post and beat me because my mother told him I had used foul language. I didn't have trouble taking a punishment when I felt that I was standing my ground.

I understand now that this was a selfish cause and the fight was purely a symptom of my stubbornness, stupidity, and immaturity. But in the end, the plan worked. The army sent me to military detention at Bat Galim, a base that supported military ships, for a week. I didn't care; I was just thankful to be on dry land. At night I slept in the detention cell, and in the day I worked in the kitchen. After my detention was served, they assigned me to work in the stockroom at Bat Galim.

The military only paid us four liras a month, along with some chocolate and cigarettes. I'd eat the chocolate and sell the cigarettes. Still, the few liras weren't enough to afford any luxuries. So when I saw a private contractor building new barracks, I thought I could make a little extra money working for him. I offered my services, and the contractor agreed.

He first asked me to push a wheelbarrow of crushed stone, but it was heavy, and I spilled it. He then asked me to carry some cement bags; I couldn't handle that either. I lasted in that job for two or three hours before getting fired. Then I tried waiting tables on Hayyat Beach in Haifa on the weekends. Again, I lasted only two short hours, unable to deal with complaining customers. After I sat down to eat the meal that one table ordered instead of serving it to them, the owner rushed over to me, yelling, "You son of a bitch! What are you doing?" He couldn't believe it when I came back the next day to try to get paid for my few measly hours of work. "Get out! I'll break your bones!"

I finally landed an assignment I enjoyed: repairing military vehicles.

After a couple months of working in the stockroom at Bat Galim, I was fed up again and applied to be a driver. The military sent me to training, unaware that I already knew how to drive; I had been taught by our chauffeur in Baghdad, in my family's 1941 Plymouth. After completing the easy training course, I began escorting the military police. But I soon discovered that drivers could be awakened at any hour, and I had a rough time with that schedule.

Around springtime, I was relocated to the garage to be a mechanic. Learning about the inner mechanisms of the automobile appealed to my scientific side. In a short while, I became highly skilled at it and was promoted from apprentice to lead mechanic, eventually training two apprentices of my own. Finally, I had found something that I was interested in and that felt important. I enjoyed the challenge and got to help others along the way. As a bonus, officers were indebted to you when you fixed their vehicle or moved it up in the queue, so I was treated well in my new role.

It's no surprise that it took me so long to find a suitable job in the military. I had been a spoiled, haughty teenager, more focused on how I could have a good time than on how I could help others, and I was historically bad with authority. But now I was slowly getting used to the idea of hard work and being part of a team. I started following commands, cooperating with my comrades, and respecting my superiors.

I also began to appreciate and understand what the new State of Israel had been through just before I arrived. Israel won the War of Independence against five Arab states, but in doing so it lost nearly 1 percent of its eight hundred thousand citizens. With its hostile neighbors still blocking all land access to friendly countries, Israel's priority was to build an army to secure and defend routes through the Mediterranean Sea and to protect its very existence.

I had known all this before, but being in the navy, working alongside people who had fought and who had lost family and friends, I became even more grateful for everything Israel was offering me—even the strange food and meager shelter. Israel had saved my life and was offering me a taste of freedom, and I began to feel obliged to contribute to its future.

I was growing up.

Life in Bat Galim

Bat Galim is a neighborhood on the northern tip of the promontory where Haifa juts into the Mediterranean Sea to form the bay. From our barracks there, we gazed out at a sea view as we prepared for the ever-present threat of war on the Jewish state. The barracks fit twenty beds and housed soldiers from all over the world—Romania, Yugoslavia, Bulgaria, Poland, Argentina, Morocco, Turkey, Yemen—and I added Iraq. We spoke to each other in Hebrew, but we all learned a more important way to communicate: to curse in each other's mother tongue. We jibbed and jabbed at each other, having fun and enjoying our time.

My barracks and job were in Bat Galim, at the tip of the promontory on the Bay of Haifa.

I didn't feel a strong divide between Sephardic Jews (from the Middle East and northern Africa, also known as Mizrahi) and Ashkenazi Jews (from Europe). I was aware that some Mizrahi Jews felt they were not given equal opportunities by the Ashkenazim and, indeed, it became painfully clear later that the Ashkenazi-dominated government and social network discriminated against Mizrahi Jews in employment, dealings, and even camp placement. But I never personally experienced that discrimination. Perhaps that is because I never liked to see myself as a victim, and I didn't in this situation either. I made the most of any opportunity I got.

Not only did I not feel discrimination, but I believe that being Middle Eastern gave me certain advantages. I had been exposed to the brutally competitive atmosphere of Baghdad. At bus stops, for instance, no one stood in line to board in an orderly way, and at train stations Iraqis would stand on the platform and jump through the train window to be first to get a seat. If you went to the movies, it was a battle to get to the box office, and only the strongest and fastest survived. Some people would even buy a bunch of tickets and scalp them at a higher price. This ingrained culture

Me (far right) and my comrades from Argentina and Yugoslavia; our international group taught each other how to curse in many languages.

of chaos helped me to handle the rations and pressures of Israeli life and successfully push for what I needed, when I needed it.

I felt both empathy and camaraderie with my Ashkenazi cousins. We had all been terribly persecuted and traumatized in the lands we came from. As I learned more about the millions sent to concentration camps and murdered in Europe, I had nothing but sympathy. Coming from that horror, it was no surprise that they felt the need to look out for their own—for their *landsmen*, the people they knew from back home. They had lost everything and were clinging to what was left.

Ashkenazi and Mizrahi Jews may have had different cultures, but we all had a common purpose in Israel. I didn't care where a person came from, as long as he was there to keep our new country safe and free. In our first few months we established a strong sense of brotherhood and deep friendships. We would play cards and gamble our rations, trading cigarettes among ourselves in the name of a good time.

We often had a few drinks, but I remember one specific night when we celebrated one of our comrades' birthday and got especially wild. We bought cases of beer, and someone brought in a prostitute. I don't remember much of this party, because I drank so much that I passed out. When I woke up the next morning, I had such a terrible headache and nausea that I could not report for morning inspection. To avoid trouble with my commander, I went to the doctor and asked him for sick leave. While sick leave was granted, I hated the awful feeling of the hangover so much that I promised myself never to drink uncontrollably again—and I have kept that promise to this day.

As a mechanic, I often had evenings off. Some nights I would put on civilian clothes and go out to the city. I had a few girlfriends in my time there, but nothing serious. I wasn't ready to settle down or be responsible, so I floated.

One evening while I was in downtown Haifa, the smell of kebab filled the air and led me to a restaurant on Jaffa Street. Meat was rare in Israel because everything was still rationed at that time. But this restaurant was selling kebab. I stood in the long line of hungry people, placed my order, and savored every bite of that kebab pita sandwich topped with salad and pickles.

I went back to the base and told everyone about the restaurant, and the next day many of them went to find it, hoping to relish their own taste of kebab. But when they got to the spot on Jaffa Street, there was nothing there. No restaurant, no kebab. I swore I had eaten it the night before! They were so angry with me, they cursed at me in every language. I later learned the restaurant was shut down after health inspectors found cat skins in the back alley. Apparently, I had enjoyed my first—and, I hope, my last—helping of cat kebab.

My love of food had gotten me into trouble more than once before. On Yom Kippur afternoon when I was around eight, I was famished and saw a Muslim vendor in our Taht Al Takia neighborhood with a huge tray of *aloucha* (a sticky, stringy candy swirled onto a piece of wood). I ran inside, got my penny, and bought some. When Aboudi came home from synagogue and found me, he went crazy and started beating me. Not only had I bought nonkosher food, but I was eating it on the holy day of fasting.

As a child, I did not develop strong religious beliefs; I mostly followed the rituals out of tradition and respect for my elders. I was brought up in a religious home, but I was only taught *how* to practice, not *why* to practice or what the meaning of a ritual was. Bar mitzvahs in Iraq were not a big deal. For my own, my father and brothers were in synagogue with me, and I was called up to recite from the Torah. To celebrate, my mother made some fish and some sweets, but there was no big party or anything. Elisha gave me my only gift—gold cuff links with my initials in English letters, "JS," for Joseph Sasson.

Now, as an independent young adult in Israel, I rejected religion entirely. I was angry with myself, angry with my family, angry at my country of birth, and angry with God. I had dreamed of studying in America and of becoming a nuclear physicist. While I was grateful for what I had, I was disappointed with the constant reality of army life, the scarceness of resources, and the manual labor. The Shabbat I was used to in Baghdad had lost its serenity and become like any other day. I no longer snuck *aloucha* on Yom Kippur; now I openly ate *shawarma* in pita at Arab restaurants rather than fasting and praying the day away.

My rejection of religion gave me a sense of independence that I needed at the time. It eliminated the obligation to go to synagogue and celebrate holidays while providing me the freedom and time to enjoy new avenues of secular life. My heart became my only guide of right and wrong. I felt free, no longer restricted by the moral code of religion—or of my parents. I was the judge and the jury, the prosecutor and the defender of my actions and behaviors.

Rejecting religion did not mean I was ungrateful. I

appreciated my luck, especially when compared to others. I had arrived in Israel in the short window of time when the country was not at war—after the War of Independence and before the Suez Crisis in 1956—and I was never forced into active combat. And I was grateful to have Eliyahoo and *Khala* Salima nearby when I needed them. Some fellow soldiers felt just as uncomfortable in their new home and had nobody there for them to smooth their transition.

During those first few years in Israel, my aunt was a psychological savior to me, and I went to her house often. She and her three daughters helped me feel connected to family and were a source of emotional strength. She and Uncle Safani did not have a lot, but their tiny home was always open to me, and they happily shared whatever they had. I felt warm and welcome, which I needed to counterbalance all the unfamiliarity and discomfort I was experiencing.

I was especially happy to have my aunt when I had to have my tonsils removed. As a kid I suffered from frequent sore throats, and the doctors would put iodine directly on my tonsils to heal my infections. Now the infections had gotten more frequent, and I was told I needed surgery. When I got to the army hospital, the nurse injected me with an anesthetic. As I lay on the examining table, the doctor started to check my nose. He took a small rubber hammer and banged my nostril.

"Doctor," I said, as the effects of the injection were setting in, "it's not my nose that's the problem. It's my throat."

"It's your nose," he responded.

I insisted that he check the file, even in my hazy state. It turned out he had mistaken me for another soldier. I had the surgery a week later and was in the hospital for three days, surviving on ice cream and *Khala* Salima's soft cooking.

That ordeal was nothing compared with the terrifying

medical experiences I had as a child. When I was around nine, a doctor came to check the students in school. After the inspections, I was picked to go to the hospital, but I wasn't told why. The nurses took me to the operating room, laid me on the table, and tied my hands and feet. I didn't know what was going to happen, and no one from my family was there. We had no telephone, and nobody went to our house to inform my family. I was only told there was something wrong with my eyes. Without giving me any anesthetic, the doctor began scrubbing my eyelids with something that burned like hell. I screamed and used all my cursing vocabulary. I didn't know it then, but I was actually lucky. I had contracted trachoma, a blinding disease transmitted by flies. The doctors at Reema Khadouri hospital, a Jewish hospital just for eyes, saved my vision.

Later, in high school, I developed a horrible stomachache with unbelievable pain that kept getting worse. My mother's hot compresses and prayers could do nothing to soothe it. Shumail finally took me to the Al Saadun private hospital, where the doctor determined that I needed emergency surgery to remove an appendix that was about to burst. They called in Dr. Rogers, a British surgeon, who came from a party and still smelled like booze. I survived the surgery with a six-inch scar to show for it and stayed in the hospital for several days, with my mother waiting patiently by my side.

Now I was grateful to have *Khala* Salima with me at the hospital in Israel, but I still missed the comfort only my Nana and her presence could offer. I hadn't heard anything from my parents since I had arrived in Israel, and I knew the situation for Jews in Iraq was getting worse.

CHAPTER 7

FINDING MYSELF

My Family Arrives

Jews in Iraq were being persecuted, but they were also prevented from leaving the country. So thousands, mostly young people like myself, made the same illegal and dangerous journey I had undertaken in 1949.

Realizing that something had to be done, in March 1950 the Iraqi government issued a decree stating that, for one year, Jews would be allowed to leave if they relinquished their Iraqi citizenship. In Arabic, it was called *Al Taskit* (renunciation of citizenship). Both the Iraqi government and the Israeli immigration agency expected a maximum of ten thousand Iraqi Jews to take up the opportunity. But they vastly underestimated. Like me, most Iraqi Jews remembered the murders and looting of the Farhud and could see that there was no future in Iraq.

That Passover, the Zionist organization opened registration centers for *aliyah* (immigration) in major synagogues. They were inundated with people: nearly one hundred twenty-five thousand of the one hundred thirty-five thousand Jews in Iraq—almost 93 percent—registered. Neither Israel nor Iraq was prepared for that kind of response.

After the year was up, the Iraqi government extended the *Taskit* and froze all assets of Jews who had registered—both those who had already left and those who were still waiting. Anyone who was planning to leave had their property confiscated and could not legally transfer their money. Each person was allowed to take only one suitcase out of the country, which was likely to be stripped of anything valuable at the airport.

In March, Israel mounted Operation Ezra and Nehemia, which sent agents to urge people to register as soon as possible and helped the remaining Iraqi Jews get to Israel. By the end of 1951, one hundred twenty-one thousand Jews—almost the entire Jewish population of Iraq—had left the country. Fewer than ten thousand Jews remained from our once proud and successful Iraqi-Jewish community.

In the course of just a few years, twenty-five centuries of Jewish life had disappeared. Persecution, arrests, and trials continued in Iraq, and Jews were publicly hanged after being falsely accused of Zionism. By the end of 1952, emigration for Jews was again banned.

My mother and Yaakub came during *Al Taskit* and were among the first to arrive with Operation Ezra and Nehemia. On the way, my mother was stripped of all her jewelry, with the exception of her wedding ring. My entire family—aunts, uncles, grandmothers, and cousins—left Iraq that year with just their suitcase, leaving behind everything else.

Though I was now an independent adult, it was a huge comfort to have my mother back. When she arrived, Nana moved into a small apartment in Jerusalem close to Eliyahoo. Those were hard times in Israel, and even though she was fortunate enough to avoid living in the transitory camps, it was a rough transition for her. Rice, sugar, and meat were all still rationed, and powdered eggs or smelly eggs imported from Poland replaced fresh ones. Nana had to make due with the little she could get her hands on until my father and Shumail arrived.

My Youmma also came and moved in with *Amu* Moshi in Jerusalem. After a short time at the refugee camp, *Amu* Moshi had found an abandoned warehouse facing the walls of Old Jerusalem, where an armed Jordanian border patrol stood atop the wall. There were no windows and only sheets dangled in the openings, but he and his four children cleaned the place up and made a home.

My mother's mother, Nana Simha, also came during *Al Taskit* and moved to Haifa to live with *Khala* Salima. Growing up, I wasn't as close with Nana Simha as I was with my Youmma. Nana Simha and Baba Sion, my mother's father, had also lived in the Hart Al Yahud district of Baghdad, not far from us. Baba Sion had a scruffy beard that scratched my cheek when he kissed me, and he used to pinch my cheeks, which to me was a bit of torture. He died when I was still a little boy, but I enjoyed my time with him, especially since I didn't have another grandfather.

Nana Simha knew how to read Judeo-Arabic (written in Hebrew letters), which was unusual for women in Baghdad. Her favorite book was what was known as the *Ben Ish Hai* by Hakham Yosef Hayyim, who was a leading halachic and kabbalistic scholar in Baghdad in the mid- to late-1800s. He wrote *Qanun-un-Nisa*, a book of Judeo-Arabic parables on self-improvement aimed at women. The book contained many stories, which my Nana Simha used to read to me.

Khala Naima, my mother's sister, moved close to Tel Aviv. She and my mother did not get along. Back in Baghdad, they had a silly fight and never got over it. My mother was convinced that Naima was jealous of her because we had more money. When *Khala* Naima came to visit our home, my mother, who was ridiculously superstitious, worked to ward off any evil eye her sister might throw her way. She wove the numbers five and seven, thought to offer talismanic protection, into the conversation as much as she could. Naima noticed that my mother said she had five chimneys when she clearly did not, and seven tables, which was also not true. She caught on that my mother was afraid she was trying to curse her and accused Nana of assuming the worst. I can still remember the yelling. They never made up. When the family would get together at *Khala* Salima's house, my mother and Naima did not speak to each other. But somehow their children stayed close. I always stayed in touch with my cousins, Shalom, Daisy, Shoshana (who used to be Juliet), and Shulamit (who used to be Latifa).

By the end of 1952, my father and Shumail smuggled themselves out of Iraq and arrived in Israel. While they had held out in Baghdad longer than most, they knew it was finally time to leave when a Muslim customer taunted them, "I will pay you what I owe you, but don't ever ask me when." In other words, he was not planning to pay. They felt that their life was threatened—and certainly their ability to run a business—and they saw no future in Iraq. They left behind all their properties—our car, our furnished home, the *khan*, and everything inside. They couldn't sell anything. But we had what was most important: each other.

My father and Shumail did manage to get some cash out of Iraq through an ancient but risky system called *hawala*. A *hawala* is like a bond: my father deposited some money with someone in Baghdad and was given a code word. When he and Shumail arrived in Israel, they gave that code word to another person, who then gave them the same amount of money they had deposited in Iraq (after taking a cut of it, of course). Besides being illegal, it was exceptionally risky because it all depended on trust. You had to trust the person you deposited with, and the person on the other side had to trust that he would be paid back for the amount he gave you. And in this case, my father had to trust that his contacts wouldn't reveal that he was planning to leave Iraq. Luckily for my family, the system worked in our favor.

My father bought a semidetached house at Rechov Hasneh 5 in Ramat Yitzchak, a neighborhood of Ramat Gan, just a few kilometers east of Tel Aviv. A one-story, two-bedroom home with a small kitchen, it was compact compared to our villa in Baghdad, but it had everything they needed. My mother and Yaakub moved into the house, and a new life for my family began.

But Baba's life in Israel was difficult. Although financially he was okay, he found it burdensome to converse in Hebrew (even though he was fluent in reading it) and had difficulty making friends who were not Iraqis. And even with money, most basic foods were hard to buy. To combat these shocking changes, he found comfort in praying and attending synagogue regularly.

Shumail had gotten married soon after I smuggled out of Iraq. At age thirty-nine, he had married Albertine, a slim nineteen-year-old blonde with beautiful green eyes. It was not uncommon in Baghdad for a bride to be twenty years younger than her husband, and she was from a poor family that desired a wealthy match. Their children—Freddie, Olivia, and Nasi—were born in Baghdad, and now they were all living in a two-story house in Ramat Gan near my parents.

Marcelle and her husband, Sasson Ovadia, along with their children Myrna, Yudit, and Yousuf (in Israel he went by Yosef or Yossi), arrived with the *Taskit* and were cooped up in a one-bedroom apartment in Kikar Hayeshuv, a neighborhood in the center of Ramat Gan.

Last to arrive, Elisha made it to Israel in 1955 after traveling and working in France, Denmark, and other countries.

Eliyahoo, who had been here the longest of anyone in my family, was doing well in Jerusalem. He had finished college and become an assistant professor in the physics department at the

Hebrew University, specializing in optics. He was inclined toward the sciences, like me. While he didn't make a lot of money, it was enough to live on, and he was happy with his life. Ahuva was his true love, and together they had three children—Yigal, Yalta, and Yifat.

We were all grateful that we had made it, and we realized how fortunate we were. Most refugees lived in tent cities or temporary absorption centers in the middle of nowhere for months. But this new life in Israel was accompanied by new challenges: a different language, new customs, buses instead of cars, scarcity of food, and the need to find education for the children. Each of us faced different trials as we adjusted to our new lives, and each of us had our own vision for the future. While we were there to help each other, we learned to do things in our own ways.

My father and Shumail set up a new business together, a small money-lending operation. In addition, they owned prime property in Tel Aviv. On a trip to Lebanon and Palestine in the 1930s, my father purchased a building at Ben Yehuda 5, right outside Shuk HaCarmel, the main outdoor bazaar of Tel Aviv. In addition to seven residential units, the building had three retail spaces on the ground floor. My father and Shumail were now managing this building, which provided income to the family for years.

My parents never really learned Hebrew outside of the few words they needed. My mother would go to the *shuk* and pick out the fruits and vegetables she wanted, but she needed Yaakub to go with her to read the signs and to translate. My father relied on Shumail to do business and help him converse in Hebrew.

The last time I saw my Youmma was in 1952 at an old-age home in Jerusalem. I was twenty-two years old and still serving in the navy. Though she couldn't have been much more than seventy, she was bedridden, skin on bone, and nearly blind. When I uttered, "Youmma," she turned her face slowly. She touched my arm with her shriveled hands and extended both arms. Her thin and shaky fingers meandered around my cheeks, my forehead, my eyebrows, and my lips. In a feeble, shimmering voice, she whispered, "*Ayuni.*"

She pulled me close. I knew she wanted to hug me. I felt her heart bursting out of the wall of her paper-thin chest. She pressed my face to hers, and with her toothless mouth she pounded me with kisses. She smelled me and held me tight. I felt warm, wet drops on my cheek. I cried too.

The next time I came to visit, a month later, I was told that a few days after I had last seen her, she had passed.

Post-Army Struggles

The closeness my family had in Iraq was never the same after we arrived in Israel. Everyone was grown up and trying to establish our own life, which kept us busy and made it difficult to get together. It was a hard time in Israel—the population doubled in just a few short years, and the infrastructure and economy needed some time to catch up. In my family, everyone was figuring out how to make a living and create a future.

While my father always stayed religious, my siblings and I all became secular like many of the Jews in Israel. None of us had time for religion when there were big worries at hand, like bringing food to the table. We still celebrated Passover together, but none of us had strong religious inclinations.

Day by day, I completed my compulsory military service of two years, looking forward to being able to start university. When I had just four months left, the government decreed that compulsory army service would be extended to two and half years. Anyone who had less than six months left would double the time remaining, which added an extra four months to my service—and meant I would not be able to start university until the following year. I was

In the spring of 1953, I was ready to leave the Navy and start the rest of my life.

discharged from active duty in the spring of 1953 and left Bat Galim to move into my parents' home in Ramat Yitzchak.

In retrospect, in spite of all the difficulties of adjusting to life in the navy, I can see that the military straightened me out. I wasn't the mischievous boy I had once been; I had a new sense of maturity and responsibility, not only to myself but also to others. Now I was again confronting the question not only of what I would do for the next year, but what dreams I had for my future.

My father was a wise man and sensed that this question was on my mind. I had become close to my father. We lived in the same house, and I knew he wanted me to succeed. He felt bad that I had not gone to college in America as he had promised, and that now I had to wait even longer to start Israeli university, so we had a conversation about what my next steps would be.

I drove cars and big trucks in the navy, so I told him I wanted to buy a truck and work as a hauler. My father asked Shumail to use his connections to help me get started. But each time I found a truck, Shumail found something wrong with it. It was too old, too big, or too expensive. Finally, after nearly six months of this, he couldn't find any more excuses and he asked me, "You want to bring shame on our family and be a truck driver?" I felt disappointed and angry. Shumail had built up my hope, then knocked it down. Why did he have to waste my time? Couldn't he have told me this at the beginning? My older brother was again continuing his domineering and manipulative ways.

I still had no clear direction. My friends sat around in the evenings drinking coffee and playing *shesh besh* (backgammon), but I did not want to idle my life away. Shumail asked me to manage the property in Tel Aviv. I didn't want to work with him again after the few experiences I had with him in the fabric business in Baghdad, but out of desperation, I convinced myself that maybe this time would really be different, and I took on management of the building on Ben Yehuda Street.

Once again, I should have stuck with my first instinct. Shumail wanted me to report every detail to him—how I spoke to tenants, what words I used, how I collected the money, how I handled any problem. I couldn't do anything on my own without being criticized. His authoritarian attitude rekindled my resentment toward him.

I told Shumail, "I would like to learn, and you can correct me, but please let me feel like I am doing something on my own." But he couldn't change. He was too insecure to trust anyone else, and I would never have independence under him. "Here are the keys," I told him. "I am done with this job. I feel like I'm your puppet, and I cannot take it."

I told my father I had decided to study. I enrolled in evening classes at Beit Sefer Mishpat V'kalkalah (the School of Law and Commerce), which was eventually integrated into the newly established Tel Aviv University. I didn't think being a lawyer or an accountant was for me, but it was a good way to occupy my mind and to meet other young people. I even took some classes in Italian, which I learned to speak pretty well. (It was there that I learned the song "Mama Son Tanto Felice," about a soldier longing for his mother, which I still enjoy singing today.)

Life was not bad at that time. Between the navy and law school, I had made good friends. We used to go ballroom dancing in the evening in Ramat Gan, where I also assisted in teaching dance, and we traveled, hiked, and picnicked in different parts of Israel whenever we could.

We had giant celebrations for Yom Ha'Atzmaut, Israel's Independence Day, and I always hosted or went to a big party for New Year's—my adopted birthday. With Jacob Bar-On, a university friend, I rented a room at the back of Elite Restaurant near the Elite Chocolate Factory, which served us both as a place to study and as a love nest. We used to throw small parties there, inviting my friend Ambar and my cousin Aboudi to bring their girlfriends. I was living life on my own terms.

The only sour moment came on one of my trips to the Galilee, at *Kibbutz* Kfar Giladi near the Lebanese border. While walking back to a table to eat dinner in the communal dining hall, my heart nearly popped out of my chest. I couldn't believe who was in front of me. It was Sara, my first love from when I had stayed at Sha'ar Ha'aliyah upon arrival in Israel three years before! With her green eyes, blond hair, and bright smile, she was even more beautiful than I remembered. I nearly dropped the tray out of my hands. But when she saw me, she acted as if she didn't recognize me. I approached her.

"Do you remember me?" I asked, my voice shaking with excitement. I quickly came crashing down when I was met by her answer, "Oh. Yes. Yosef. Meet my husband." It was a hard reality to deal with, but life marches forward.

In the summer of 1954, Shumail had a heart attack. He was short and heavy and always tense, but no one knew about cholesterol or healthy eating at that time. He survived, but his heart condition stayed with him.

Shumail's health issues made my father worry about who would take care of Yaakub in later years. While Yaakub had learned to manage his own health problems on a day-to-day basis, he was incapable of supporting himself. Deciding I was the right choice, Baba transferred his 51 percent share of the Ben Yehuda building to me and asked me to hold it for Yaakub's security. I didn't get any benefit from it; my father was just putting things in place to ensure that Yaakub would always be taken care of.

My father still felt bad that I had not gotten a truck, and he wanted to help me achieve my independence. In the spring of 1955, he gave me a gift of twenty thousand liras (about $5,000) to help me get started in life.

Moving in, Then Moving On

I wasn't quite ready to settle down yet, and the cash in my hand tempted me to seize a different kind of opportunity.

The travel bug had bitten me when I was a child in Iraq. My mother sometimes traveled with Yaakub to Hamam Al Alil, a mineral hot spring in the mountainous north near Mosul, where the sulfur waters were supposed to be good for your health. When I was around nine, she took me along. It was my first trip on a train, and I was hypnotized. I sat by the window for the whole ride, watching the scenery roll by as we journeyed from station to station. I knew

*In 1955, I sailed on the SS Jerusalem from Haifa to Naples,
and from there traveled through Europe.*

then that I wanted to see more of the world—and now, with my father's gift, I had the chance.

Nory was now twenty-two. After he had finished his Israeli army service, he went to study in London, where he lived with the Myer family, Iraqis who moved from India to London after India got independence in 1948. Shumail met the Myers when he was in India in 1943 on business and sent Nory to board with them when he decided to go to London. Nory had fallen in love with their daughter, Rachel, and they planned to be married in London in June of 1955.

This was a perfect opportunity for me to travel. I embarked from the Haifa port on the ship *SS Jerusalem*, stopped in Cyprus, passed through the Greek isles on the way to Athens, and finally docked in Naples. My dark complexion, along with my new fluency in Italian, opened many doors as I wandered through the streets and markets of Napoli. Unlike in Israel, fresh produce and meat were everywhere. I'll never forget how many peaches I ate while I strolled

I attended Nory and Rachel's wedding in London in 1955.
Left to right: Rachel's cousin, me, Rachel and Nory.

though the flea market. I finished a full kilo and paid for it in many trips to the bathroom the next day.

After Naples, I toured other parts of Italy. I saw the ruins of Pompei. In Rome, I was impressed with the catacombs and the Colosseum and overwhelmed by the size and sights of the Vatican. On one of the guided tours, I met a couple of Scottish girls and traveled with them to Geneva, where we spent about three days. Next, we made it to the Latin Quarter of Paris. I loved the French food and wine and the beauty of the city. Finally, I arrived in London and was overjoyed to attend Nory and Rachel's wedding.

It was the first time I had been present for one of my brothers' weddings. The excitement of the room was infectious, with everybody in beautiful outfits, dancing, drinking, and laughing together. Nory looked debonair, wearing a tuxedo and bow tie—clothes that were not traditional in Baghdad. I was proud to be there. The smile on Nory's and Rachel's faces as they walked down the aisle filled me with joy for their happiness. I respected their maturity to make such a decision at the young age of twenty-two. Marriage was the last thing on my own mind, but seeing their commitment truly pulled at my heartstrings.

From London I went to Marseilles and from there sailed back to Israel on the SS *Filippo Grimani*. On the ship I befriended two girls: Elisa, whose father owned the chain of Richstone's bakeries in Montreal, and Faigele. My Israeli friends came to greet us at the port of Haifa. "Everyone kiss the girls!" I said, and they all stood in line. Elisa and Faigele would mention this warm welcome for years. We brought the girls to Ramat Gan and showed them around Israel. We took them dancing, and I invited them to celebrate Shabbat with my family, where they were impressed with my father's all-white attire.

When I began my trip, I thought I was going to get the travel fever out of my system. Instead, it rekindled my flame of adventure. However, the reality of life was awaiting me, and it was time to get serious about figuring out my future.

I had saved enough money from my father's gift to do with it what he intended—to make something of myself. I started a real estate partnership with Aharon Yitzhaki, a family friend who had lived in Israel for more than ten years and had become an experienced broker. We bought a storefront in Ramat Gan at Rechov Yahalom 8 and started a real estate brokerage house called Makor Hadirot Yaeel—the Apartment Source. You didn't need a license to practice real estate, so we were able to start immediately.

To drive customers around, I bought a car, a Hillman '47, for three thousand liras. It wasn't in great shape—to open the passenger door you had to put your hand through the window and grab the inside handle—but it served my needs. Prospective customers just needed a way to travel, not luxury. And on weekends, a bunch of my friends and cousins piled into the car and took trips around Israel: Haifa, Nahariya, Tiberius, Jerusalem, or a long trip to the Negev.

Aharon and I would first go to the developers and get

permission from them to sell their property, then we'd advertise the apartments in the paper and show potential buyers the units. Most customers who had money to buy apartments were newly arrived European Jews who had received reparation payments from Germany.

At one point, we took clients to a property where the owner was present, and they started talking to each other in Yiddish. Since neither Aharon nor I spoke Yiddish, we had no idea what they were saying.

We didn't hear back from the couple, but a few weeks later we saw that they were living in the apartment we had shown them.

"What happened?" I asked. "I thought you weren't interested."

"Oh. I was friends with the builder before, so I just worked it out with him directly," he answered unabashedly.

I could see what was going on. Since brokers worked on commission—2 percent from the buyer and 2 percent from the seller—it was in the interest of both buyer and seller to screw the broker. Not one to be outsmarted, I decided to turn to my faculty with languages.

The next day I put an ad in the paper: "Wanted for immediate hire: Yiddish-speaking secretary." I hired a woman and sat with her for hours, practicing Yiddish. In particular, we worked on all the phrases that related to housing, pricing, negotiations, and figures. I had not even known that Yiddish existed when I lived in Iraq, but I picked up the necessary words fairly quickly. From then on, when clients and their builders started conversing in Yiddish, I would chime in. They would suddenly stop talking and look at me in shock. Now I was in on the game, and there was no more funny business. I would get my signatures, make the sale, and get my commission paid. In 1950s Israel, understanding Yiddish was my survival tool.

Meanwhile, life in Israel was becoming more challenging.

Egyptians and Jordanians had been training infiltrators to enter Jewish settlements from the Gaza Strip and West Bank and cause violence and unrest. Terrorists maimed and killed adults, children, and animals in attempts to create fear and chaos. Israel had an air of anxiety that permeated daily life.

The challenges of living in Israel really got to my mother. The daily stress, her inability to understand the language, and the absence of friends began to add up, and she suffered a nervous breakdown. She would ask about Khazna, who helped with the cleaning and cooking in Baghdad. "Where is Khazna? Why hasn't she come today? She knows we will have the whole family for Shabbat." And Nana talked about Esther, who used to wash our clothes. She was regressing back to her life in Baghdad. At the recommendation of Dr. Fink, she spent five days in the hospital and was given medication to improve her condition. It hurt me deeply to see her this way, and I had no one to talk to about it. Like my mother, most everyone was dealing with his or her own problems. I was truly on my own in terms of emotional support.

In fact, I was having a hard time seeing my future in Israel. Even with my successful business, the desire for a higher education still burned in my heart and in my mind. I could not imagine that I would be able to pursue my own intellectual blossoming in such a tense and distracted atmosphere.

While I was honored to be part of building the Jewish homeland, and I loved being close to my parents, I felt that I needed my own space to accomplish something. I decided that it was time to leave Israel and pursue my education in North America. My father was supportive; he always wanted to see me reach my potential and achieve goals.

I started to make concrete plans to move toward my future. I considered Argentina or the United States, but it was hard to get a student visa, so it seemed my best route was to Canada. A few months later, I applied to McGill University in Montreal and received my visa. I sold my share of Makor Hadirot to my partner, along with my car, and bought a ticket going west.

I had arrived in Israel six and a half years earlier under dire circumstances. I had smuggled out of my homeland in the hay-covered crawl space of a boat, trying to avoid the torture of the secret police. I had suffered the indignities of being a homeless, penniless refugee, accepting handouts of food while learning to work hard and follow commands.

When I left Iraq, my future was ripped from me. Now, as I left Israel, I was taking my future into my own hands. In August of 1956, I took a boat from Haifa to Marseilles, then a train to Rotterdam. There, I boarded the SS *New Amsterdam*, bound for New York City.

PART 3

☰ MONTREAL ☰

1956-1978

Chapter 8

My Winter Wonderland

Starting from Subzero

Opening my eyes, I looked out my window at the blank canvas the blizzard had created and wondered if this time I would be able to find my car. Just a few days before, I had spent energy and time shoveling, only to realize I had dug out the wrong vehicle. With only antennas poking up through the white bank of snow, I had gambled on the wrong parking spot.

I wasn't sure I would ever get used to these winters. The stony, damp cold of Baghdad's winters didn't even compare, and the Mediterranean climate of Haifa and Ramat Gan had done nothing to prepare me for this deep freeze.

The first time I saw it snow in Montreal, I was awed by the natural beauty. I had never seen snow falling before, and I was mesmerized by the fairy dust wafting to the ground, creating a pristine sheen over the streets.

But after just a few weeks, the wonder wore out its welcome. I lived in a cold-water flat where the only oil furnace faced the room of my roommate, a law student named Bill Miller. I slept in layers of clothing under coats and blankets, longing for the *jafoof* and the body heat that had warmed me and my brothers on cold Baghdad nights.

On mornings like these, I had to will myself out of bed. I summoned the words of my Youmma: "*Ayuni*, you are going to be rich." I wasn't sure when I would be rich, but I knew that right now, the first step was to get up and go to work to earn some money to support myself. I knew I had to leave part of my day to study, to pursue the education that had pulled me away from my family and the warm sun of Israel to this frozen, foreign land to begin with.

I was proud of the social and professional connections I had made in the few months since arriving in Montreal, when I went from being Yosef Shmuel to Joseph Samuel—called Joe. Despite my complaints about the cold, I was optimistic about what I could accomplish.

I arrived in Montreal on Aug. 26, 1956. Before I boarded the *New Amsterdam* from Rotterdam, I spent a few days in Amsterdam, cruising the canals, touring the city, and exploring the Red Light District.

I shared a cabin with two strangers on the five-day voyage to New York. It was a journey of curious anticipation and seasickness. By the time we arrived at New York Harbor, I was hopeful, but I was not ready for the overwhelming vision of modernity in front of me—the towering skyline, the many ships and boats in the harbor. As the ship passed the giant lady with the torch, I was told that she was the Statue of Liberty, welcoming people like me.

In the days that followed, I walked through the pulsing heart of Manhattan. The skyscrapers towered over me, making me feel tiny but exhilarated. The bustling streets were nothing like the un-paved, winding roads of Taht Al Takia. I joined the masses of people streaming along the sidewalks, visited the Empire State Building, rode the subway, and looked out at more buildings and cars—par-ticularly the yellow taxicabs—than I had ever seen in one place. I

My ship landed in New York in August, 1956, and I was sure I had never seen anything as spectacular as The Rockettes.

tasted my first hot dog under the neon lights of Times Square, amid the endless choices of cuisine. I went to see *High Society* with Bing Crosby, Frank Sinatra, Grace Kelly, and Louis Armstrong at Radio City Music Hall. The Rockettes, with their perfectly shaped legs, performed their famous "eye-high kicks" before the movie and I was sure that, even in my European travels, I had never seen anything so elaborate.

I arrived in Montreal six days later, via overnight train from New York. It was August, and Montreal offered a more European picture than New York: the pace of life was slower, the neighborhoods were quaint, and the boulevards were wide, with frequent electric cable cars filled with people. Montreal, like Manhattan, is surrounded by water, built on islands in the St. Lawrence River. This river was nothing like the Tigris, but it still somehow gave me a sense of belonging. People sat and drank coffee late in the evening, and the residents seemed to be enjoying life. On those late summer days, the lingering sun lit up the trees in a way that made me feel welcome.

Nory and Rachel had moved from England to Canada soon after they were married. Rachel's brother, David, was already living in Montreal and had encouraged them to come with promises of better opportunities and employment. Even though Rachel was pregnant with their first child, Michael, she and Nory generously opened their home, a one-bedroom apartment in Côte-des-Neiges, and allowed me to sleep in the living room until I could find my own place. Their open heart and open house provided me my only rock in a new environment.

Aside from them, I knew no one in Montreal. But I love social interaction, so I immediately began meeting nice and helpful people. The first of these was Harone Kattan, twenty years my senior, who was a real estate broker and a well-spoken leader of the Iraqi-Jewish community. Harone and his wife, Suzanne, had big hearts and were always helping new arrivals. They invited me into their home regularly.

Harone was well acquainted with the challenges of being an immigrant. As a young boy, he was sent from Baghdad to Bombay, India, to study at a boarding school. A few years later, when his father's business failed, Harone's education was cut short and, although still a teenager, he was brought back to Baghdad to help support his family. He soon married Suzanne Khalaschy (from a family of prominent landowners in Iraq), and the two of them moved to England and later to Canada.

Harone's multiple experiences of being a newcomer made him an adaptable person, and he enjoyed guiding me through the problems I encountered in adjusting to my foreign surroundings. He became a close friend, a mentor, and a father figure. His first advice to me: Join the Young Israel Synagogue.

But my life in Israel had left me disconnected from God. I had left religion behind and felt free of its limitations. Why would I want to return to that which I felt constrained me? I struggled to imagine myself following religious tenets once again and was hesitant to follow Harone's advice. Eventually, I decided to see it as a great social opportunity and to expect nothing more than meeting new people.

After a long struggle to get myself through the door, I joined the Young Israel Synagogue of Montreal and began mingling with the city's Iraqi-Jewish community. I met newcomers, just like myself, with whom I would build long-lasting relationships. I introduced myself to the Lawee family, who had owned Chevrolet agencies in Baghdad and were already active in Montreal's real estate scene. Rachel's brother-in-law, Emil Liefschitz, introduced me to his insurance agent, Morton Kitaeff, who urged me to join the B'nai B'rith Lodge, a Jewish social and charitable organization. There I met Ronnie Singer, president of the B'nai B'rith chapter, who would later become my great friend and accountant.

Through B'nai B'rith, I also made the acquaintance of Bill Miller. Bill was a law student looking for somewhere to live, and together we found a cold-water flat at 4611 Linton Street for $65 a month. I arrived with $3,000 in savings after selling both my car and my share of my business, but I knew I would run through it quickly if I didn't find a steady source of income.

At the same time, the fantasy of university was still buzzing in my head. In order to leave my daytime hours open for work, I enrolled in night classes at Sir George Williams University (now Concordia University) and started taking economics, English, physics, and chemistry. It was tough; I was getting by with my French in the city, but classes were in English and I was still pretty weak in that language.

I was thrilled to be studying, but the desire to provide for myself kept me anxious. The traumatic memories of standing in line for food were too fresh for me to risk going back to that kind of indignity. Although other students applied for assistance while they were in school, I didn't want to take welfare or subsidies, so I started looking for a job.

Back to Work

Without a specific talent, profession, or education, I knew I had to consider my work options carefully. Emil, Nory and Rachel's brother-in-law, offered me a job at his nylon-stocking factory. Working with my hands would provide me with immediate income, but the long-term salary prospects did not appeal to me; I was searching for a future of financial independence. I concluded that I had to work with my head, not my hands, to make a comfortable living. The only way this seemed possible was in sales. I decided I needed to find what people needed. This would not only enrich myself, but enrich those I served.

Real estate had worked well for me in Israel, and it was a business I felt I understood, so I decided to try it in Canada. Morton Kitaeff recommended I apply for a sales job at Sullivan Realties, a

My 1953 Monarch, parked in front of my flat on Linton Avenue, helped me look the part of a real estate agent.

real estate firm that specialized in selling large plots of land. There was no need for experience, a license, a special education, or a credit check to become a real estate agent.

I got the job and bought a 1953 Ford Monarch for $1,000 to fit the part of an agent. It didn't take long for both the buyers and sellers to realize that I didn't know what I was doing. In Israel you met with the buyer, you met with the seller, you got them together, and you made a deal. But selling vacant plots of land to sophisticated developers and investors is different than selling apartments to average people who want to live there. And in Canada the process was more formal than what I was used to—the buyer had to submit an offer, the seller could accept or reject it, and negotiations happened through the agents. This new way of selling real estate turned my Israeli experience on its head!

Despite my best efforts, I started feeling overwhelmed: a new city, new classes, new customs, new language—it was all too much. How could I work all day and take courses at night, in a language I wasn't yet fluent in? I tried hard at Sullivan Realities, spending time and gas, but didn't earn a penny. At school, I struggled to keep my eyes open in the classroom, and certainly had no time to study.

I could not keep up. I realized that I would have to choose between studying and working, and I had to support myself. With great sorrow, I put my dream of higher education on the back burner and dropped out of college. At least this time it was a choice I made, not one that a tyrannical government made for me.

As the temperature dropped and fall approached, I observed the spectacle for the first time. The changing color of the leaves fascinated me, filling my eyes with beauty and my mind with wonder. Then suddenly, without proper notice, my first Montreal winter set in. The conditions were like nothing I could have imagined. I had to learn how to shovel snow, drive on ice, and pile on layers and layers of heavy clothing. To add to my misery, the subzero temperatures

During my first winter in Montreal in 1956, I learned how to handle giant snowdrifts, sleek ice, and subzero temperatures.

froze the gas pipe in my car while I was driving one night. How would a guy coming from the desert oasis of Baghdad know that he needed to add antifreeze to his gas tank?

At the hardened age of twenty-six, I did not let the cold freeze my ambitions. After working tirelessly at Sullivan Realities for months and still earning no money, I noticed a small ad in the *Montreal Star*: "Train 4 Days, Earn $40." That sounded good to me. I responded and found out I would be learning to sell health insurance for Mutual of Omaha. At the training we watched a Dale Carnegie slide show where the instructor taught us, "Act enthusiastic, and you will be enthusiastic." These words resonated with me and served as a lesson that would prove priceless as I continued to shape my life: Behavior changes feelings.

After I completed the training, those first few dollars warmed my heart and melted my despair. I treated myself to Ben's Deli, famous for their delicious smoked meat sandwiches—nothing like the salami I had tossed away in Israel—complete with French fries, a Coke, and a dill pickle. My confidence level shot up.

To get myself started, I went into the field with a manager to learn to sell health insurance policies. We did some cold calling, knocked on doors to talk with residents, and met with potential clients who had responded to promotional flyers. At that time there was no nationalized health care in Canada, and the market was ripe for business opportunities.

I would wake up in my freezing apartment, see the snow outside, and give myself a pep talk: "I'm going to make a sale today! I'm going to do it! Act enthusiastic, and you will be enthusiastic." I mustered all the gusto I could and pumped myself up each day. And I did pretty well; in three weeks I made more than $300—big money for the times.

Yet I was not totally happy. It was hard for me to find joy in selling a piece of paper. But my English was getting better, and the job was giving me some sales experience. Spring was coming when I went to Harone, asking for words of wisdom. He gave me blunt but excellent advice: selling those big plots of land at Sullivan had been the wrong choice; I needed to start back at the bottom, selling homes.

Making the Sale

Harone recommended Lew Kozlove and Company, one of the largest Jewish-owned residential real estate brokerage firms based in Montreal.

I put on a white shirt with a starched collar, a tie, and my best suit to face Mr. Leopold, the manager at Lew Kozlove's. Mr. Leopold, a successful, well-dressed man in his thirties, was impressed by my appearance, energy, and eagerness. The firm had about thirty salesmen who worked on commission only but got no training.

By the next day I had a desk, a chair, and Rudner's telephone book, which was organized by neighborhood rather than name. Addresses were listed first, followed by the names and phone numbers at that address. So with no training, I sat down and called every house in Snowdon, a middle class suburb of Montreal composed of primarily two-story single-family homes and duplexes.

"Do you want to sell your house?"

"No."

"Home prices are at their highest. Do you want to sell your house?"

"No."

"We just sold a house in your neighborhood, and we have many potential buyers who are looking in your area. Do you want to sell your house?"

"No."

I kept my spirits up. The more no's I heard, the more determined I became to get a yes.

But after three weeks, I had listed only one house. The most experienced agents got leads when buyers or sellers called into the office, but I was a "greener" and didn't speak English well. The other salesmen, who were all Jewish, mocked me with names like "the Arab" and didn't trust me to handle their customers yet. I just smiled and laughed and continued cold-calling and knocking on doors. That's just how it is in real estate brokerages: veterans get the first break.

During this time of inactivity, I met Steve Acre, a new agent who had also smuggled out of Baghdad, served in the Israeli army, and eventually made it to Lew Kozlove's in Montreal. We became friends in our fight for success and provided each other with encouragement when we needed it most.

Still, I was getting desperate financially. Plan B was driving a taxicab, but I remembered how my brother Shumail scorned the idea of my being a truck driver in Israel. I knew I had to figure something out.

"I need an advance to carry on, Mr. Lew."

I stood upright in front of Lew Kozlove, a tall, heavy, self-confident man in his fifties. He had the aura of wealth and power. He looked at me, his tiny reading glasses drooping from his nose.

"My boy, is $50 a week okay?" I was shocked and thrilled that my chutzpah would pay off.

"Thank you, sir! I will pay back every dollar very soon, Mr. Lew."

I felt resuscitated, rejuvenated, and grateful. Fifty dollars a week was not enough to cover my rent, food, electricity, and gas, but it would help. Besides the advance, my natural optimism kept me afloat. I looked at the successful people I had met in Montreal and found that many of them had started with nothing and still made it, even without a college education. As I forged friendships, I talked with my friends about how they had succeeded and heard some things repeated over and over:

"I started with zero."

"Use your head, not your hands."

"Investors will provide capital for a viable idea with a profitable concept."

"Success is a combination of preparedness and opportunity. Be prepared when opportunity knocks."

I absorbed every word like a sponge.

At night, lying in bed, I remembered how my Youmma made me feel wanted and important whenever I was feeling alone

The day I closed my first sale, in March 1957, my heart was filled with confidence and hope.

and desperate, and I thought of her soothing words:

"*Ayuni*, don't worry, you're going to be rich."

Thinking of her words gave me strength to believe and act on the lessons I was learning. "I guess I'm starting out right," I thought. I had all the ingredients of the rich people I'd met: no money, no education, and no special talents, but I trusted my mind and my persistence. I assured myself that I was a member of the rich club, and I felt and acted like one.

The sunny days of spring brought welcome change into my life. I closed my first house sale, earning $235 in commission. That day, I tipped the gas station attendant ten cents. My heart was re-filled with confidence, and my mind was racing through possibilities to apply what I had learned.

A few weeks later, I spotted a listing on Baily Road in Côte-Saint-Luc, a suburb on the west side of Montreal. The owner was asking $16,000 for a well-maintained three-bedroom house, but no salesman wanted to touch it because of a major drawback—its back-yard was smack up against the railway tracks, where freight trains rumbled past day and night. The owner was rushing to move to Toronto, and his company was willing to absorb the loss on the sale of the house. I saw an opportunity. It was time to prove my chutzpah again.

"Are you willing to take $12,000?" I asked the owner. That was 25 percent less than his asking price.

"Do you have a buyer?" he asked.

"Yes."

The buyer I had in mind was me. I needed $2,000 cash for the down payment, but I had only $65 in the bank. My friend Albert Shahin introduced me to his older brother Nadji, who liked my plan. Nadji agreed to fund the down payment if we split the profits on the sale. We shook hands, and I signed the contract for $12,000. I immediately flipped the house back onto the market for $14,000, which was still underpriced and a bargain for any buyer. Through aggressive fire-sale marketing, I sold the property within a couple of weeks. Everybody was happy: the seller, the buyer, and Nadji. And I was personally thrilled to repay Nadji's investment and split the $2,000 profit.

This was quite an epiphany for me. I had no money, no credit history, and no one to vouch for me, but I had made $1,000 with someone else's money. Once again, the words of the wise had proved correct: Investors will provide capital for a viable idea with a profitable concept. If you had creative ideas and a good product, worked hard, and spiced it with chutzpah, you could make your fortune by using other people's money.

Another few months passed with no sales, no listings, and no customers. My only income was Mr. Lew's $50-a-week advance. I was getting desperate once again, but I had new ideas to go forward.

Marvin Kane, a cousin of one of the managers, was a top

seller and was always getting the leads. He was a handsome college graduate and engaged to a daughter of the Bronfman family, who owned the Seagram Company and was one of the wealthiest Jewish families in North America.

"You and I are going to be partners," I said to Marvin.

"You?" he sneered.

"Listen to my offer," I replied. He was surprised I even had an answer.

"From today on, whatever I sell, I will give you 50 percent of my commissions. Whatever you sell, you will keep 100 percent."

The look on his face was easy to read: "What an idiot." But I knew what I was doing; half of something was better than all of nothing.

Marvin gave me the leads he didn't want—small deals, hard-to-get listings, anything he thought was not worth his precious time. I was running all over the place, qualifying leads, listing properties, and doing any errand he needed. I was his gofer, but I was excited to be busy. I was always open to new things, and I was learning quickly. I even took a Dale Carnegie public speaking course to build my confidence and improve my communication with coworkers and customers. Within a couple of months, I started closing deals and making money.

In early 1958, the manager put Marvin on a new housing development in the city of St. Martin (which merged with two other towns in 1961, becoming Chomedey) north of Montreal on the suburban island of Laval. The houses were selling from $13,000 to $17,000 with a 1 percent commission for the salesman, and I was a part of Marvin's sales gang. There were four of us who would alternate showing houses seven days a week, competing with each other to get the most sales. After one too many feuds, I proposed that we become partners; rather than undercutting each other, we would work together to make as many sales as we could and split all commissions four ways. I was there every day, selling more than all of them combined, but I didn't care. All I was interested in was that the boss would see my signature on the most sales. I worked day and night, through sunny skies and stormy weather. I was eager to continue mastering the art of negotiation.

After a year, the boss recognized my high rate of sales and gave me a bonus of $500. That was big money; if you earned $100 a week, you could qualify for a mortgage. Soon after, I was able to pay back all the advances that Mr. Lew had given me.

Now that I was recognized in the office, I was developing leads without Marvin's help. I no longer needed the one-sided deal with Marvin, but Marvin wasn't interested in changing the terms into a full fifty-fifty partnership. So we parted ways as friends, and I began working on my own.

As soon as I started making money, I began sending some to Israel. The family had to move Nana Simha into an old-age home in Jerusalem, and I helped provide the funds for her placement at the home. At the same time, my father realized I had no plans to return to Israel and requested that I transfer my share of the Ben Yehuda building in Tel Aviv. He had trusted me with his 51 percent ownership in hopes that I could later use the money to support Yaakub. But now that I was so many miles away, this arrangement didn't make sense. I went to the Israeli embassy and arranged to transfer the building back to Yaakub's name, leaving Shumail to manage the building.

I kept in touch with my family by letters, since trans-Atlantic phone calls were a rare luxury at that time. I also spent a lot of time with Nory and Rachel in Côte-des-Neiges. Their first son, Michael, was now almost a year old.

My first couple of years in Montreal were difficult, but my persistence and hard work were starting to pay off. I had a promising career ahead of me, I was making new friends, and things seemed to be falling into place. I sold my old Ford Monarch and bought a new 1958 Chevrolet Delray for $2,000 cash. And at the very top of my list of reasons for joy in my present and optimism in my future was an enchanting woman named Ruby Isaac.

CHAPTER 9

MEETING RUBY

Finding My Treasure

"Would you like to dance?"

I offered my hand to the elegant woman sitting next to me at Nory's brother-in-law's wedding. She was beautiful, charming, and warm. She had the most adorable British accent and could even throw out a few phrases in Arabic. I silently thanked Nory and Rachel for putting us at the same table—a purposeful decision, I was sure.

Ruby Isaac had arrived in Montreal just three days before, on June 20, 1957, having moved from London to be close to her brother, Alex. Ruby, whose family was Iraqi, had grown up with Rachel in India.

Ruby allowed me to give her a ride home, and I asked if I could see her again. We started dating and talked a lot about our backgrounds, which had many similarities. We enjoyed the sheer presence of each other's company.

That summer Ruby and I explored Montreal together. We went on long car rides, where we traversed the countryside and I taught her how to drive. We went to the movies, swam in the local public pool, danced the nights away downtown, and dined on

Ruby Isaac arrived in Montreal from England just a few days before we met at a wedding in June, 1957.

Montreal's famous smoked meat sandwiches.

Life was going well. At work we were selling in St. Martin, and I had earned enough to move into a modern one-bedroom apartment, complete with central heating. Another salesman needed a place to live, so he rented space in the living room from me. Although I was still constantly learning lessons, daily life seemed to stabilize.

Ruby quickly found a well-paying job as a secretary in a bridal gown company, and after long days at work it was a pleasure for both of us to spend time with each other. The $70 a week she earned was more than double the ten pounds she had been earning in London at a similar job. The first day at Bride Beautiful, her boss asked her to dial a client. When she didn't send the call to him, he asked her why. With her British customs still in effect, she replied, "The line is engaged." "Engaged to who?" he asked. Ruby quickly learned the right answer, "The line is busy."

I had run around with many girls in my time, but I was never in a serious relationship. I always wanted to have a good time and enjoy the moment, and marriage was far from my mind. With Ruby, it felt different. I was older and more focused on my future. I could imagine spending my life with Ruby, and I sensed that she thought the same about me.

As we spent more time together, I learned about her family and her childhood. Ruby's given name was Rebecca Isaac. She was born on January 30, 1931, in Bombay, India, and her family lived in the Fort area, a wealthy Jewish enclave with beautiful homes. Her mother, Hannah Bilbool, had come from Baghdad to Bombay at the age of fourteen for an arranged marriage to Nissim "Nunu" Isaac. Nunu was an Iraqi Jew whose family had moved to Bombay in the late 1800s. There was a lot of trade between the Jewish merchants of Iraq and India, and immigration had become fairly common.

Like my mother, Ruby's mother was illiterate. When she arrived in Bombay she knew no one. It took her about eight years to get pregnant after she and Nunu were married—a fact that could have broken up a marriage in traditional Iraqi culture. But they stayed together, and she eventually gave birth to five children: Aaron, Eliza, Ruby, Ezekiel, and Victor.

Ruby's mother was often on her own while Nunu traveled to Bahrain for his pearl-importing business. In 1938, when Ruby was seven, her father went to Iraq for a business trip. While there, he got caught in the country's anti-Semitic policies and was told that he could not leave. For nearly ten years, Hannah was forced to raise their children on her own. It was an extremely difficult time. Ruby's uncles in Bombay helped support her family, and her mother had to slowly sell off some of her jewelry and other possessions to feed the kids. Seeing her mother struggle under such financial strain and missing her father for so many years left Ruby with long-lasting emotional scars.

Ruby (right) with her sister Eliza in Bombay, India.

Ruby's family, like mine, was quite observant, keeping Shabbat and keeping kosher. Jews in Bombay generally did not socialize outside of Jewish circles and, in fact, most of the people in the Isaac family's social circles were other Jews who had come from Iraq and were relatively well off. Ruby and I both have memories of our mothers spending the afternoon gossiping with friends.

Ruby's family belonged to Knesset Eliyahu, an Orthodox synagogue in the Fort area, and she and her siblings were all active in the *Habonim*, a Jewish youth group, from a young age. But to get the best teaching possible, most of the Indian Jews went to Catholic school, although they were not required to pray. Ruby attended the all-girls school, the Convent of Jesus and Mary. It was only outside of school that they could learn Hebrew and study Judaism. The boys were expected to get tutors to help them, but the luxury of a personal teacher was not given to girls.

After passing the Senior Cambridge exam to graduate high

school, Ruby took a course in shorthand and typing and worked in Bombay. Her brother Aaron had left for London in 1939 at the start of World War II. He was an engineer and found that there was quite a bit of anti-Semitism in the job market. He changed his name to Alexander Vivian Wyvan Stenson and was then able to get a job.

Nineteen forty-eight was a tumultuous year for Ruby, both personally and in world affairs. For a decade, her family had been trying to get her father out of Iraq. Her brother was finally able to have him sent to England in 1947, but he was in extremely poor health. When Nunu arrived in India in 1948, he went straight from the boat to the hospital. He died a short time later. Because her father had left when Ruby was so young, she really never knew him.

In 1947 India had gained independence from Britain and split into the primarily Hindu India and Muslim Pakistan. Ruby had grown up amid constant riots between Hindus and Muslims, and independence brought little respite from religious strife as the two groups, as well as Christians and Jews, attempted to find their places in the newly created countries. As more uncertainty settled over India after the assassination of Gandhi in January 1948, Alex encouraged Ruby to come to England, and later that year she left Bombay and moved to London.

She found a job as a secretary five days after her arrival in London, working first for a company that sold exercise equipment and then for a fabrics firm near Buckingham Palace. She moved in with Alex, then got a flat in Hurlingham near Putney Bridge, where Oxford and Cambridge held their boat races.

Alex left London for Ottawa, Canada, in 1956. Soon after, he summoned Ruby, telling her how much better life was in Canada. She moved to Montreal, and we met three days later.

We often took day trips to Quebec City or to Ottawa to see Alex, and on one of those trips, I told Alex I wanted to marry his sister. Alex thought I was a flaky playboy, but I convinced him I was

Ruby and I enjoyed day trips around Quebec.
We didn't need fancy dates or expensive presents to show our love.

Two natural beauties, Niagara Falls and Ruby, on a trip we took in 1958.

honorable, and ready to settle down.

I had no ring, but in the summer of 1958, a year after we met, I proposed to Ruby. We celebrated our engagement with a small gathering at Nory's house, and I wrote a letter to share the good news with my family in Israel.

I knew we needed to save some money before we could start our lives together, so we waited another year before we got married.

We loved being together. We didn't need expensive dates or fancy presents to show our love. We would go for drives downtown and dine on ten-cent hot dogs and five-cent fries on St. Laurent

We purchased our first home in the St. Martin development I was representing.

Boulevard. Sometimes she came to the synagogue with me, and every once in a while I would treat her to a nice restaurant. We continued to take day trips to Ottawa and Quebec City, and some short weekend trips to New York City, Niagara Falls, and Toronto.

In the two years since we met, we managed to save about $6,000 between us, and we set our wedding date for June 30, 1959. I bought Ruby an inexpensive gold band—she would get a nice diamond years later—and she was gifted a stunning wedding dress by her boss at Bride Beautiful.

We had a small, traditional Jewish wedding in a modest hall on the second floor of a building on Avenue Van Horne, where we celebrated with forty guests and an orchestra composed of a single violinist. Among our guests were Nory and Rachel, Alex, and friends we had made over the last couple of years in Montreal, like Joe and Evelyn Azar. My best man was Edward Obidiah, my high school friend from Baghdad whom I had recently sponsored for immigration to Canada.

Before the wedding, we put a $700 down payment on an 1,180-square-foot house in the St. Martin development where I was selling. The house had three bedrooms, one bathroom, and a garage. It was a model home, and as a salesman for the company I was able to get a good deal on it—$14,000. My monthly mortgage

payments were $103.52.

Ruby put all of her savings into furnishing our home with wall-to-wall carpets, brand-new living room and bedroom furniture, kitchen appliances, and a dining set. Our new home was ready for us.

But first, the honeymoon.

Honeymoon on Wheels

The day after the wedding, we packed up the car, took the rest of our savings, and left for a four-week honeymoon on the roads of North America. I was eager to share with Ruby my love of travel, which had taken root so many years before on that trip to Mosul, and to show her how amazing it is to see the world and encounter other cultures.

But our trip almost ended before it began. U.S. customs officials at the border at Plattsburgh, New York, discovered that my Israeli passport had expired. We were forced to return to Montreal. Luckily, a friend at the Israeli consulate was able to renew my

Our U.S. honeymoon took us to the Petrified Forest in Arizona.

The place made for me: Point Joe in Pebble Beach, California.

Throughout our honeymoon, I couldn't stop looking at the woman I loved.

passport that evening, and we were back on the road the next day.

This time, we went through Toronto and crossed into the U.S. near Detroit. From there we headed to Illinois, picked up Route 66 in Chicago, and drove southwest through Oklahoma and New Mexico, making a stop at the Grand Canyon in Arizona. We stayed at Travelodge motels for $7 or $8 a night. We were newlyweds, so contrary to the wisdom of experienced travelers, rather than getting an early start and resting during the hottest part of the afternoon, we took our time in the morning, enjoying a late breakfast before we got on the road.

My 1958 Chevy Delray, however, did not have air conditioning. This wasn't much of a problem through the northern states, but the further southwest we got, the hotter it got. Then we hit the desert. On the way from Phoenix to Las Vegas, the air felt like we were standing in front of a fireplace. If we closed the windows, we boiled. If we opened them, hot air blasted into our faces.

"Can you open the window?" Ruby asked.

"I just did a few minutes ago," I answered.

"Open it again. I'm going to faint."

"Honey, the temperature outside is a hundred and ten degrees."

I just wanted to make my new bride happy. I stopped at a gas station, bought a block of ice, and placed it right under Ruby's feet. She had her own personal cooling system.

When we got to Las Vegas, Ruby got lucky at the slot machine—she put in a dime and won $15 and got to ring the "Jackpot" bell. At that time, there were only two or three hotels on the strip. One night we went to the Tropicana and saw a burlesque show starring Jayne Mansfield.

From Las Vegas we continued to Los Angeles, where we found a room at the Travelodge on Hollywood Boulevard. Ruby's cousin Norman had moved from England to Hollywood a few years before. He was a waiter at an Italian restaurant and treated us to the house specialties and family extras. We stayed in Los Angeles for about a week, then went north to San Francisco on the Pacific Coast Highway, stopping in Monterey. The scenery was breathtaking, and to my great delight we found Point Joe, a scenic lookout on the 17-Mile Drive near Pebble Beach. Finally, we made it to San Francisco and marveled at the Golden Gate Bridge, the curvy slopes of Lombard Street, Fisherman's Wharf, and Telegraph Hill; it was all such novelty to us.

From there, we drove north to Oregon; Washington; and Vancouver, British Columbia. We took the ferry to Vancouver Island and visited Butchart Gardens in Victoria. My plan had been to sell the car in Vancouver and take the train through the Rockies to get home, but no one wanted to buy the car because of body damage from the salt used to melt ice on Montreal streets. So we changed plans and continued our road trip on U.S. Highway 2 through the northern states of Washington, Idaho, Montana, North Dakota, Minnesota, and Wisconsin, and eventually made it back to Chicago, where we stopped and bought a set of pots to help feed us in our new love nest.

As we came to the final leg of our trip through Indiana and Michigan back into Canada, we couldn't help but reflect on our amazement at what a wide, wondrous country we had just visited. There was so much to see, so much to do, and the freedom to move across wide open spaces. It was a feeling I wasn't used to—not in Iraq, not in Israel, not even in Canada—but quickly embraced. When we got home, our odometer showed we were just twelve miles shy of hitting eight thousand miles on our drive. We had spent almost all of our cash on the trip, but it was worth the memories, and we knew we had a great future ahead.

And, Ruby was pregnant. When we told people, you could see all the neighbors counting backwards in their heads to our wedding date.

On April 11, 1960 (which was, for the record, more than nine months after the wedding), Ruby felt her first labor pains, and I immediately drove her to Montreal General Hospital. The doctor admitted Ruby and told me that it would be a while and I should go home and come back the next day. I went home, but just as I was getting to bed, I got a call from the hospital. Ruby's delivery had been quicker than expected, and she had given birth to a healthy, six-and-a-half-pound baby girl. We named her Sharon Linda (Shahron in Hebrew).

In just one year, Ruby and I had taken on the "3 M's of maturity": marriage, mortgage, and munchkins. Our family was beginning to blossom.

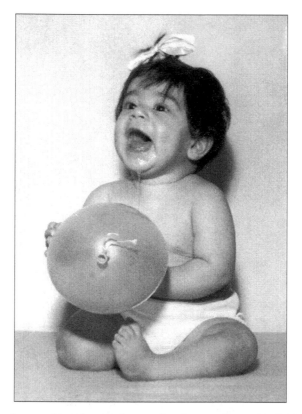

Sharon, the sunshine that made us a family, was born April 11, 1960.

CHAPTER 10

FOR FULL SATISFACTION

Taking Charge

After we got married, Ruby left her job at the bridal dress company. Just a few months later Lew Kozlove died of a heart attack, and his firm quickly began to disintegrate without him. We had spent all our savings on our home, our car, and our trip, and I couldn't afford to lose my income. With experience in hand, I joined a midsized brokerage firm, Town Realty, in the upscale town of Mount Royal.

At Town Realty I ran into Emil Sayoun. He had been the manager and instructor at the Mutual of Omaha training program I went to a couple years before—the same program that put the first $40 in my pocket when I was a newcomer to Montreal—and had taught me some valuable lessons. Emil was a Palestinian Christian born in Haifa who had moved to Canada after Israel's independence in 1948. He was smart and charming, with an aggressive personality and a good command of English, and had quickly become a manager at Town Realty.

After I had worked there for a few months, Emil approached me about starting our own firm. He was aware of my experience

selling homes in new developments and knew that I had good connections to acquire the selling rights. I thought he was a capable
salesman and liked the idea of having my own business, even with
a partner. We quickly became friends and often spoke to each other
in Arabic.

In a short time we started a firm called Better Home Realty;
I was in charge of listing and selling new homes, while Emil managed investment and expansion. Between us, the company grew
rapidly. I connected with a successful developer, David Zapp, whom
I'd met at Lew Kozlove's firm. He built large housing developments
of single-family homes and duplexes. His houses sold for around
$20,000, which was considered expensive at that time.

But after just a few months, salespeople started coming to me
complaining that Emil was not giving them their fair commission.
I found out they were right; he was cheating them. As a salesman
myself, I did not like that. I started poking around and learned that
he had left Mutual of Omaha after he was found to have misappro-
priated funds.

I knew that if Emil was cheating the salespeople and had
stolen from his bosses, he would likely cheat me too. I had to get
out of the arrangement quickly. Honesty was important in dealing
with others; I had no desire to be involved with people or deals that
would stir up trouble or drama. So I told Emil that although we were
doing well, I had decided that I didn't want a partner and I had
promised myself I would go out on my own. I didn't get my fair share
for the business when I sold it to him, but I didn't care; my priority
was just to get out of there. It wasn't worth my energy to go to court
to fight him to the last penny.

Even though Emil and I parted under bad circumstances, I
now knew what I was capable of. Soon after Sharon was born, in
April of 1960, I started my own firm, Fulton Realty. I came up with
the name, complete with a slogan: Fulton, for Full Satisfaction.

I started selling houses in new developments and hired a sales force. Business grew rapidly, thanks to my unique approach to selling new homes. In most projects the developer paid the real estate firm 3 percent of the sale price, and the firm was responsible for advertising, finding customers, and selling the home. But that created conflicts of interest because the developer demanded more advertising than the realtor wanted to pay for.

To increase the incentive for both sides, I asked the developer for a 2 percent net commission and left the developer responsible for all advertising costs. We would help develop the angle and design the ads, but it was up to the developer to spend what they needed to get the message out there. Costs remained about the same, and everyone got what they wanted.

I rented an office on Avenue Van Horne near Victoria Avenue in the Snowdon area, above a Chinese restaurant called Yung Tzee. The smell of Chinese food constantly permeated our offices as we wrote our contracts, and in the brutal winters the restaurant provided a convenient way to satiate ourselves at lunch and dinner. As the operation grew, I kept adding more offices and more people (and ordering more food) until we reached a sales team of over thirty men and women.

At thirty years old, four years after arriving in Canada, I felt the responsibility of leadership. People needed me and looked up to me. To improve my situation further, I went through a process called industrial psychological analysis, which helped me identify my strengths and weaknesses as a boss and as a person. I was not surprised to find that I excelled at relationships and communication; I have always loved being with people and creating connections.

One of the main weaknesses they found was that I project myself onto others. I had the erroneous belief that if something was easy for me, it should be easy for others. However, such an outlook generates a lack of empathy. If I could stop assuming we were all so alike, I could be more compassionate when others struggled and realize that others had strengths where I had weaknesses. I could stop blaming people for not living up to my standards of capability and thinking, and instead help elevate them and improve their sales. I took this opportunity to figure out where I needed people to complement my strengths and make up for my weaknesses. I hired someone to do the advertising, someone to do the books, and someone to manage the salespeople.

I had been listening to tapes and viewing slides to study the salesmanship techniques and attitudes of successful entrepreneurs like Dale Carnegie, Jack Lacy, Earl Nightingale, and Zig Ziglar, and I would play the tapes to the sales team to encourage them. Being the boss gave me a great sense of importance and responsibility, and I wanted to live up to it. I taught the men and women who were selling how to entice homeowners to list with us, how to analyze their potential buyers' needs and overcome their objections, and how to close the sale. I told them, "Sales begin when objection begins. No one who's buying will say okay to everything, and it is your job to find out what the customer needs and help them find it." I taught them everything I knew, and our sales quickly grew.

Within a couple of years, one of my brokers, Victor Cair, introduced me to Ron Bibace, a realtor who sold big office build-ings and had some connections to the Bronfmans (the owners of Seagram's and the richest Jewish family in North America at the time, with an extensive holding of real estate). Ron came to see our operations. We had three different offices on the same floor and a big room with a board where we tracked monthly sales. Every time someone sold a house, his or her name went up on the board. We were selling about thirty to forty houses a month.

Ron admired my techniques for selling and suggested that if I wrote a guide and taught my salespeople in a more organized way, I could go further. "With your staff and big offices, you're running

*By 1963, I had dozens of people on my sales team at Fulton Realty,
shown here at our Christmas party.*

your engine on three pistons. You need to be efficient," Ron said.
"Let's go into partnership. You will be in charge of selling, and I will
run the office and operations."

Ron had a degree in economics and was methodical in
his way of approaching business. He had created a structured
organization, perfected his budgeting, and developed an exacting
administrative approach to running a business. On top of that, he
had made big deals and came with connections in construction and
building. Between his procedures and my intuition, I knew we had
a winning combination.

We moved Fulton Realty to a large, 2,200-square-foot office
at 4480 Cote de Liesse, at Metropolitan Boulevard (an important
intersection in the prestigious city of Mount Royal). We had meeting rooms, classrooms, and space for our secretaries, and we created
a new department dedicated to large-scale investment properties

like apartment and office buildings.

The firm did very well. We had a very high gross income; we sold individual homes all over the city, outside of our primary development projects; and we became the largest seller of newly built homes. By 1965 we would be a major player in Montreal real estate.

After just five years of business, I was being invited to speak at conventions and taught classes to agents on how to sell. But I was no longer doing what I loved most—selling. Instead, I was constantly occupied with trying to solve the problems of other salespeople. I became a teacher, a counselor, a father, and a friend to many of the men and women who worked for me. In one sense I loved this; I knew they looked up to me, and I felt important. But I was being dragged down financially. In most sales businesses, 20 percent of the salespeople produce 80 percent of the business, while 50 percent drag and struggle. Rather than being part of the 20 percent at the top, I was busy with the 50 percent at the bottom. I had to correct their mistakes and patch things over if they said the wrong thing to the buyer or seller.

I was also throwing some of the salespeople extra cash, because they weren't making enough to live on. I never forgot that $50-a-week advance I got from Lew Kozlove when I was struggling. And I never forgot how generous and hardworking my father had been, how he always had an open hand for whoever was in need. But my generosity of time and money had limits. I looked at my books and realized that by managing a sales force of thirty-five, I was working longer hours and making less money than when I had time to sell on my own.

To fix this problem, Ron and I began to focus on another part of the business we had been developing: apartment building construction. He had a friend, Morris (Moishe) Robinson, who had experience in that area. Ron and I partnered with Morris, and in 1964 we constructed our first sixty-unit apartment building on Rue de Salaberry in Montreal. Morris put down 50 percent of the capital, and Ron and I covered the other 50 percent.

I had no personal experience with construction, but I knew how to get construction financed. With my connections in the banking and insurance industries, Ron's methodical way of planning and executing projects, and Morris's building know-how, we did well.

We finished the construction on schedule and on budget and sold the building soon after its completion. We netted about $30,000 on the project, a lot of money at that time, and immediately started planning our next project for the following year.

My next step seemed clear. In 1965 I began to phase out of the brokerage and focus on development. Not only would I make more money, but I would also have more time to spend with Ruby and our growing family.

Celebration, Mourning, and Forgiveness

While I was building Fulton Realty, I worked seven days a week and put all my energy into the business. Ruby had settled into our home in Chomedey, making friends with neighbors, taking care of the house, and tending to Sharon. I delighted in playing with Sharon when I was home, though most often I was working.

Regardless of my long hours and Ruby's new twenty-four-hour job, the next munchkin was already in the making. On March 5, 1963, our second daughter, Lisa, Aliza in Hebrew, was born. It was a joyous time, and we were grateful to bring such a beautiful girl into the world.

However, the old Iraqi notion that a family needs boys had stuck with me. Of course I loved my daughters with all my heart, but I had grown up in a family of seven boys in a society with

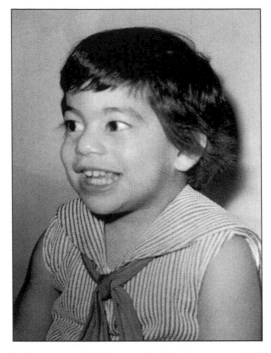

Lisa, born March 5, 1963, added to our daily happiness with her smiles and joy.

severe prejudices against girls. After Lisa was born, I was initially disappointed that we had another girl.

In April I left Ruby with three-year-old Sharon and one-month-old Lisa and went to visit my family in Israel for Passover. A year earlier, in 1962, I had received the sad news that my father had died. He had suffered from diabetes for years and his eyesight was failing, but his passing was unexpected and was very difficult for me.

I had not seen or spoken to my Baba in the six years since I left Israel, but he would write me letters in Judeo-Arabic and I would write back in Arabic, and we sent each other photographs for Rosh Hashanah. He always expressed to me that he was proud of the life I was building and that he longed to see me in person.

After I heard about Baba's death, I sat *shiva* in my home and went to the synagogue to say *Kaddish*. I remembered the sense of caring and love I had always received from Baba, especially in comparison to my abusive brother, Shumail. I always felt that Baba was warm and kind, even though he would occasionally give me a good smack. He showed his love by always making sure I had something in my pocket, even when we had little money. When he came into wealth, Baba's generosity was remarkable; it is from him that I learned the pleasure of giving both to those I love and to those in need.

I also learned from him to always be optimistic and plan for the future, even when life is difficult. Baba knew how to take responsibility—at age thirteen he supported his family. For my whole life, he always looked for solutions instead of getting worn down by problems. When I was a teenager, he inspired me to change my attitude and to love education, and to aspire to make something of myself.

The fact that Baba had entrusted Yaakub's care to me by giving me control over his percentage of the Ben Yehuda building in Tel Aviv meant so much. He had many sons to choose from, but he concluded that I would best see to my disabled brother's needs. Even though that arrangement changed when I moved across the world, it still held meaning for me.

By the time I went to Israel for Passover, I had made an important decision to forgive Shumail in my heart for his behavior toward me. For most of my life, I walked around with a heaviness and hatred toward him. He treated me so harshly during my childhood and tried to impose his will on me when I was a young adult. I admit that as a child I was rebellious and always looking for trouble, but Shumail's discipline was too extreme. And as adults, we constantly clashed.

After I moved to Montreal, I felt that my anger and resentment were weighing me down. Shumail was far away, and I had time to think about our relationship. Now that I had the perspective of a father, I could understand his past disciplinarian attitude toward me. Looking back, I realized that he hadn't hated me or wanted to hurt me. In the only way he knew how, he was trying to help me grow into a responsible adult and wanted to lead me towards a good life. Before meeting again, I decided to forgive him totally and unconditionally. It was a sobering moment and completely internal. I did not have a conversation with him; I just decided to finally let go. I felt relieved and free, and my hatred gave way to understanding and love toward him.

I celebrated the Passover Seder in Ramat Gan at Shumail's house, along with my mother and Yaakub. I had the joy of reuniting with my brother Eliyahoo and his wife and children. I visited my sister and brother-in-law, Marcelle and Sasson. Sasson and their eldest daughter, Myrna, were curious about life in Montreal, and that summer Myrna, who was in college, came to visit Ruby and me.

That Passover was a wonderful experience, and Shumail was pleasant to me. Even though we didn't have a conversation about my change of heart or our past, he could feel that I was no longer holding onto any resentment. We were able to speak freely, and we saw each other as equals. We were there to enjoy our brotherhood, and the tension of the past was off our shoulders. He gave me a beautiful *Haggadah* to take home, decorated with delicate silver trimmings. I invited Shumail and my mother to come to Montreal, and he started planning their trip.

That moment of forgiveness was an important milestone for me. It taught me the benefits of being a forgiving person and that everyone can make mistakes, even with the best of intentions. I started to believe that most people are good and don't set out to hurt others.

While I enjoyed my return to Israel and the warmth of its people, I realized how much I had changed and how much I preferred my life in Montreal. Montreal was now my home, and Canada had become my country; within it lay my new family, friends, and evolving aspirations.

Over time, the family that I dearly missed had begun leaving Israel and coming to me. My brother Elisha was first. During
his second visit to Montreal, he could see that there were more
opportunities in Canada than in Israel, and he asked me to sponsor
him for immigration. I applied for the visas, and he and his wife,
Valentine, and their eighteen-month-old son, Charlie, arrived in
October of 1959.

*Elisha with his bride Valentine in 1957 in Israel. My mother stands in the back
row on the left, and her sister, Khalla Freeha, stands third from left. Albertine
and Shumail are to the bride's left, and my father, in the hat, is to Elisha's right.*

Elisha and his family stayed at our home in Chomedey until
they found an apartment to rent in Snowdon. When I opened my
new office for Fulton Realty, Elisha came to work with me. But the
work didn't interest him, and I could only pay commission, while he
needed a salary to support his family. So he took a job with a private

company as a customs expediter and eventually built up his own successful business in that field. Nory, Elisha, and I loved to play *shesh besh* together and celebrate Shabbat with our families. Elisha's second son, David, was born in Montreal in 1961.

After my trip to Israel, and with three of her boys now in Montreal, my mother agreed it was time for her to connect with her grandchildren. In September of 1963, she arrived to stay in our home for a few months.

While my mother was elated to spend time with her children and grandchildren, she was still experiencing the insecure feelings that had plagued her in Israel. In a short time she managed to stir up trouble between Rachel, Ruby, and Valentine, the daughters-in-law she was just getting to know. She tried to pit them against each other and made wild claims, including that they were trying to starve her. I knew my mother was not well, and I scrambled to keep things in order, explaining her emotional condition to the family and urging them to ignore the crazy things she was saying.

But I never disrespected my mother. I take the fifth commandment to honor your mother and father very seriously.

A few weeks after her arrival, I received an unexpected call from Israel. After a joyful night of celebration in honor of his son Freddie's bar mitzvah, Shumail had suffered a second heart attack. That night, he had passed away. He was only fifty-three and left behind his wife, his son, and his two young daughters.

I knew I had to break the news to Nana gently, for fear of how she might react to such tragedy. She could have a heart attack or a nervous breakdown. Shumail was her oldest and favorite child, and I knew this bad news would be hard for her to accept. To ease her into understanding, I first told her that Shumail had suffered a heart attack and was recovering in the hospital. This alone sent her into shock and caused her to break down and cry incessantly. After waiting another day, Nory, Elisha, and I explained that Shumail's condition had worsened and that he had passed. Her crying ampli-fied, and she began hitting herself on her chest and face in grief. Thankfully, we had arranged for a doctor to be at the house when we broke the news, and he gave her a sedative to calm her down. It was a terrible day.

It was shocking for me, too, but I was grateful that Shumail and I had made peace just a few months before. For my mother, on the other hand, Shumail's death was life changing. She was dependent on him. My father had died less than a year before, and Shumail was the one who lived close to her and supported her, watching out for her and Yaakub. Shumail's death was a hard reality for her to accept, but she was surrounded by three of her sons and their families to help soothe her abrupt transition.

My mother stayed in Montreal for almost a year. We took her to the World's Fair in New York during the summer of 1964, where she was excited to see the Disney exhibition. She was mag-netized and thrilled by the It's a Small World ride, with its little boat and rolling sights. Her beautiful green eyes sparkled with joy, and a big smile lit up her aging face. I put my arm around her and felt her head swaying gently while the children were singing. We went on the ride three times, and she wanted to do it again. During those few moments, she was living the childhood that had been stolen from her. My mother had never known spare time. She had such a hard life—married at age twelve and a mother by fifteen, with twelve pregnancies and eight living children. The sight of her happy made me cry with joy.

By the end of the summer Nana was ready to go back to Israel, but it seems that life was simply too difficult and lonely for her there. Just a short time after her return, I received a call that my mother had died.

Truly, I felt mostly a sense of relief for her. I viewed my mother as someone oppressed and suffering, with so little happiness in her daily life. She had spent her life serving first her parents, then her husband and her children. And with my father and Shumail gone, she had returned home with only Yaakub left to care for.

Unlike when my father died, I had just seen my mother, and we had spent time together. While there were some difficulties, overall it was the happiest I had ever seen her. I kept in my heart my memory of her on the It's a Small World ride, her eyes shining and her smile bright. I was blessed to have that last time with her. I sat *shiva* and went to synagogue to say *Kaddish* for my mother, as I had for my father.

After my mother died, Marcelle, who had been living in Israel since 1951, decided she, too, wanted to come to Canada. I helped her and Sasson with the visa arrangements, and in 1966 they and their three children, Myrna, Yudit, and Yossi, moved to Montreal. Years later, Myrna and her husband, Chanoch, moved to Ottawa so that she could complete her residency in dermatology while Chanoch finished his doctorate. Yudit stayed in Montreal

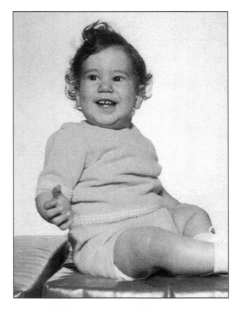

On May 5, 1965, Jeff was born, completing our family.

and became a Hebrew teacher at Jewish People's School. Yossi eventually went to medical school at McGill, then at New York University, and became an orthopedic surgeon. Not a bad legacy for a pair of refugee parents who never had a chance to go to college.

On May 5, 1965, I was absolutely elated when our son, Jeffrey (Sasson in Hebrew), was born. How happy I was to have the baby boy I had dreamed of. I invited everyone I knew to celebrate at his *brit milah*, and while the rabbi was performing the *brit*, I fainted. I still do not know if it was from my fear at the sight of blood or my joy at having a son.

"The prince has arrived," our friends joked.

The Life I Wanted to Live

Life was not easy with three little kids. The children were starting school and needed attention. Ruby, with no outside help, was feeding, dressing, and taking the children to school, to shop, or to the doctor. In the winter, every time she went out she had to bundle the kids in multiple layers with coats, boots, and mittens, then get all the snow and dirt and clothing cleaned up when they came back home. Taking care of the kids and the house was a full-time job. Meanwhile, I was still concentrating on building up Fulton Realty, leaving home early in the morning and coming back late at night seven days a week.

In a way, we were living in two different worlds. Ruby was frazzled and exhausted from taking care of the children and the house, and I was tired and tense from the nonstop drive to make Fulton succeed. She needed my comfort and I needed her appreciation, but we were too worn and too stressed to support each other.

We began to drift apart. Ruby was not happy, and neither was I. We talked less and more abruptly, and the cold and brutal winter only expanded the ice between us. Though I was working with the intention of improving the lives of our family, the business was taking over my life. I was neglecting my wife, and the children would ask, "Where is Daddy?"

I loved my wife and I loved my children, but I also loved my work. I finally realized that the answer to my problems lay only within my choices. I wanted to provide my family with the best life possible, but I saw that I was hurting them with my behavior. Although I felt and acted rich even without money, my goal was never to accumulate wealth at any cost. Losing connection with my family was much too high of a price. That was not the life I wanted to live.

I had been allowing myself to think only of the worst-case scenarios, fearing that if I took time away from work, even on the weekend, I might miss something important and face a major disaster. I now understood this was not a healthy approach. By reexamining myself, relying on the industrial psychological analysis report I had commissioned early in my work at Fulton, I began to assure myself that I'd make it in the business world and resolved to put a stop to my anxiety toward achieving immediate success. I still had to keep the business growing—I was the boss, and the people who worked for me depended on me—but I decided I could slow down a little and still maintain a stable and growing business. If I made less in the present and took longer to reach my financial goals, that was okay; my first priority had to be my family. I realized I had been delaying the real joys of a fleeting present with my family for the unpredictable achievement of the future; I needed to enjoy the journey and be flexible about the timeline.

I slowly began to change my lifestyle. I bought the book *Richard Hittleman's Yoga: 28-Day Exercise Plan* and practiced every day, sometimes with Sharon and Lisa trying out the poses by my side. Lisa still remembers how she and Jeff would climb on my back as I assumed the cobra position. After a year of yoga, I could stand

Though I was busy with work, I always made time to enjoy my family.

on my head for three minutes. I ate less and enjoyed food more by eating slowly, putting the fork back on the dish after every bite. I lost twenty pounds. I learned to take a break and breathe deeply while looking at the lovely greenery or pure snow outside my window.

Practicing yoga also introduced me to transcendental meditation. Ruby and I began to attend meditation classes, learning how to relax together. That was the first step to bringing us closer, and it helped. I would come home early, disappear into the bedroom, and meditate for twenty minutes, emerging with a clear head, refreshed and calm enough to deal with whatever was going on. I was able to offer more help and empathy to my beautiful wife and budding children.

I enjoyed this new style of life so much that I decided to explore hypnotherapy. Mostly, I used the techniques for self-hypnosis. It was a great way to get myself to relax; it helped me let go of all my

Ruby, left, had strong friendships, including with her sister Eliza, center, and our friend Miriam Grosz.

tension and even helped me fall asleep.

I also practiced hypnotizing others, mostly for fun but sometimes with a specific goal, and found that I was pretty good at it. One of my friend's daughters had been terrified of taking exams. When she sat down for a test, she would vomit or blank out, even if she had studied and knew the subject. After I did two hypnosis sessions with her, not only was she able to take tests, but she did well. Her father thanked me a million times. I helped others with weight control. I even tried to hypnotize Ruby to help her stop smoking, but she was too resistant and it didn't work for long.

For fun, I would make a show of it. I would get my kids and their friends together and play tricks. I would put down a $100 bill and say they could have it if they could lift it. But I hypnotized them to believe it was too heavy to lift, and they couldn't raise it an inch!

At the same time, Ruby found strength and balance through her family and good friends. Evelyn Azar and Miriam Grosz both lived down the street from us, and the three women supported each other in their struggles. Whether it was the kids or another family issue, they all eased each other's problems and in the process helped us become closer as a family.

Our life in Chomedey was brightened by the changes in our actions and attitude, and Ruby and I started enjoying more quality time together. Life began to shine, and the days seemed clearer. We had become close friends with Joe and Evelyn Azar, whom I had met as soon as I moved to Montreal. As couples, we had much in common and often had Shabbat dinner together. All of us were from Iraqi families—Joe had been born in India and Evelyn in England. When Ruby and I moved into our neighborhood, I urged Joe and Evelyn to buy a house there, and they ended up moving in right across the street from us. Joe was an electrical engineer who worked for the Marconi Company and repaired televisions and radios in the evenings to make extra money. When he and I were out working late, his daughters, Terri and Debbie, would play with our children while Ruby and Evelyn chatted away in the kitchen. Sometimes

Sharon (bottom row, second from the left), as well as our other children, attended Jewish day school.

Ruby and Evelyn would take a bus for an hour to go into Montreal and have lunch at Woolworth's.

As Fulton stabilized, I had more time to think about the kids. Giving our children a good education, especially a Jewish education, was a priority for Ruby and me. There were quite a large number of young Jewish families in Chomedey, and soon after we moved there the Talmud Torah School of Chomedey opened, which was connected to a larger chain of Hebrew schools in Montreal. Ruby was on the PTA and was actively involved in the school.

Most families at the school were Ashkenazi, and my kids sometimes felt they were different—their parents had different accents, and their hamburgers were more likely to come in pitas rather than on a bun. But these distinctions did not hold them back. Everyone was friendly with everyone.

I began to drive the kids to school every morning—Sharon and Lisa both remember listening to Zig Ziglar, or Norman Vincent Peale's *Power of Positive Thinking* on our cassette player as we went—and I made it a point to take at least one or two days a week to do activities with them. Almost every Sunday in the summer, we went to Messina, New York, about a ninety-minute drive from Montreal. We often went with Elisha and Valentine, Joe and Evelyn, and Imre and Miriam Grosz. We would spend the day by the lake, and the kids would play on the beach or go out on rafts while we barbequed and played *shesh besh* on the shore.

Our favorite place for fun and relaxation was the Thousand Acres Dude Ranch north of Lake George, New York, about 160 miles from Montreal. The first time we went, Ruby was pregnant with Sharon. We continued going after the kids were born, sometimes on our own, sometimes with family or friends. Either way, we ended up there a few times a year, whenever we felt the need to get away.

There was no formality at the dude ranch. Meals were

served at the long communal tables of the dining hall and families stayed in rustic log cabins. There was an indoor pool, horseback riding, archery, ping-pong, and basketball, and the kids especially loved the pinball machines. In the summer the lake was open for swimming and boating. As the kids got older, they enjoyed all the activities and were free to roam without restriction, giving all of us a sense of freedom and relaxation. These getaways were a great escape for Ruby. She was meticulous about the house and keeping everything running smoothly, but once we crossed the bridge out of Montreal she was a different person—calm, communicative, playful, and admiring of the everyday beauty that often passed her by in her busy routine.

When the kids were a little older, we rented a winter house in the eastern township of Dawson and took the kids skiing nearly every weekend, often with friends. This is where Ruby learned to cross-country ski and where all my kids became expert downhill skiers. I couldn't keep up with the kids, but I did pretty well myself.

When we were in Montreal, we worked to make our tiny house comfortable and filled with joy. We finished the basement so the kids could hang out with their friends, and I planted my first garden—some tomatoes, zucchinis, and peppers. It was hard to grow things in the short summer season of Montreal, but I found that working the soil and nurturing a seedling into a full living plant gave me great pleasure and serenity. My gardening hobby began to take deep roots in my weekly routine.

Another great source of mental health was my increasing involvement in the Jewish community. Now that my life had settled a little bit, I wasn't angry with God anymore, as I had been when I lived in Israel. As a parent, I was finding some joy and beauty in the rhythm that religion created in my week and my year. Going to synagogue filled me with serenity and inspiration. It gave deeper meaning to my life and filled in something that was missing.

Allowing myself to pause for Shabbat became particularly meaningful to me. When I was growing up, I never understood the need for rest. But now I could appreciate the peace of mind that Shabbat brought and used it to recharge my batteries.

I also realized the importance of my obligation to instruct my children in moral values. In Israel, my heart had been my only guide, but my heart gave me different answers depending on my immediate emotions, moods, needs, desires, and external circumstances. Now that I had others depending on me, I could no longer trust my heart alone. I started to connect the dots between the Torah's manual of ethical code and the long-term strength it would give my family by observing its tenets.

I started going to the Spanish & Portuguese Synagogue in Snowdon, one of the oldest synagogues in Montreal. I can remember crossing the Cartier Bridge from Chomedey to Snowdon, where I would sometimes wait patiently to get through the bottleneck of heavy traffic. It may have slowed me down, but it didn't stop me. Harone Kattan established an Iraqi community within the synagogue, and I was there to support him. The congregation included quite a few Iraqis who migrated to Montreal, either directly from Iraq or via England, Israel, or India. We prayed in the main hall on Shabbat, and we converted the social hall into our sanctuary for holy days. We held dinner parties and social events there, as well as *kiddush* on Shabbat. I helped to lead the prayers for Rosh Hashanah and Yom Kippur, and soon I was on the board of the synagogue. Harone got me involved in the Combined Jewish Appeal, a community-wide fundraising agency that supports local and international Jewish causes. And I continued to be involved in B'nai B'rith, which, like the synagogue, was a big social center for me.

In the process of it all, Ruby and I became great friends with Harone, who was the president of the synagogue, and his wife,

Suzanne. Harone was still involved in real estate, and I looked up to him as a mentor both professionally and for his spiritual leadership. Not only did he give me good advice, but he and Suzanne were always inviting us to lively dinners and parties at their home.

In addition to my time at the synagogue, one of my greatest joys was hosting my brothers and their families for the holy days, which Ruby worked hard to prepare for. We celebrated all the festivals as we had as children in Baghdad: Pesach, Rosh Hashanah, Chanukah, Purim, and a few others. Since Ruby's family also came from Iraqi origins, she made the traditional food I remembered from childhood, similar to what my own Nana had made in Baghdad— *tibeet*, *arook* (rice patties), chicken rice, and *kubbas*. Of course, my kids also wanted hamburgers and hot dogs, and Ruby made that for them as well.

As a father, I was happy to be giving my children a chance to experience some of the most joyous parts of our Jewish tradition. And I enjoyed watching them running around with their cousins, causing the same mischief I used to cause with Eliyahoo and my two cousin Aboudis. My kids were living in a completely different time

Sharon, Lisa, and Jeff looking their best for Rosh Hashanah.

and place, and it was not possible to give them the same experiences I had, but these were the celebrations that had formed some of the best memories of my childhood. I knew this was possible for my children as well, and in my heart I hoped they would carry with them the warm memories of family, food, and tradition.

Our Trip Around the World

As I built my business, I became involved in the Greater Montreal Real Estate Board and the International Real Estate Federation (IREF). I took and taught classes, and sometimes gave major addresses to audiences for both organizations. Through the Montreal Real Estate Board, I addressed nearly three hundred aspiring saleswomen on the skills and techniques of qualifying a buyer, making a presentation, emotionally involving the customer, and closing a sale. I also sat on committees for the Montreal Real Estate Board.

In 1966, the IREF announced that its annual convention would be in Japan. Japan had always been on my bucket list, and its being halfway around the world offered me an unprecedented opportunity to fulfill my dream of circling the globe. Not only would Ruby and I get to explore the wonders of the world and connect with different people (partially tax-deductible, I might add), but it was also a chance for me to take Ruby back to the city of her birth, where I could meet her mother and sister, who had never left Bombay.

But could we afford it? We had just put most of our savings into purchasing a parcel of land in the upscale neighborhood of Hampstead, where we planned to build our dream house. Fortunately, Ruby was willing to agree with my proposed scheme. We sold the land, knowing we could afford something better when we got back, and planned a five-week trip across the globe. Sharon was six, Lisa was three, and Jeff was only about a year old. Our regular babysitter, who stayed with them when we went on short weekend jaunts, agreed to watch them during this long trip.

"Look, girls, Mrs. Brazel is here!" Ruby said when the day came for us to depart.

"Hi, darlings," Mrs. Brazel said. "We are going to have such a good time together! We'll do some drawing and go on walks and learn to knit…"

"That's what you said last time," Sharon boldly interrupted, "and then we did nothing."

In the end, things went well, except that when we returned, baby Jeff would cling only to Mrs. Brazel. He would not even look at Ruby for a few days until he finally forgave her for abandoning him.

The trip was an incredible experience. We flew from Montreal to Vancouver to Hawaii, where we stayed for three nights. We got a taste of Hawaiian hospitality at a hip restaurant where topless hula dancers served the food. On the beach, I saw surfers out on the majestic waves and thought I would give it a try. I rented a surfboard, paddled out, and was so proud when I was able to stand up. Immediately, a huge wave knocked me down, and the board slammed into me. I paddled back to shore and returned the rented board. That was enough surfing for me.

From that volcanic paradise we went on to Japan, staying in the brand-new Otani Hotel in Tokyo for a week to attend the IREF convention. The mayor of Tokyo welcomed the attendees, and the Japanese imperial prince addressed the convention. Afterwards, Ruby and I traveled through the ancient city of Kyoto, the business center of Osaka, and the hot springs of Kobe. We rode the bullet train, tasted sushi for the first time, went to a kabuki theater, ate dinner at a geisha house, attended a tea ceremony, visited the Hiroshima memorial, and stayed at a traditional Japanese hotel consisting of an empty bedroom with just a futon in the cupboard to put on the floor for sleeping. The Japanese were extremely polite, and we didn't always know how to act. Taxis were clean, white-gloved drivers opened doors, and you were always welcomed and seen off with a smile and a bow.

From Japan, we hopped over to Hong Kong to take in the unique crowds of British-influenced Chinese. Even then, Hong Kong was ahead of its time and its storefronts were flooded with neon light. One evening I ordered custom-tailored shirts, and they arrived at my hotel the next morning. In the bazaar we acquired a gorgeous statue of a mother and child made of lapis lazuli, which still rests in our dining room cabinet. Ruby and I had never seen so many people walking through the streets, and although we had a good time, it felt like work to get ourselves through the crowds.

After four days, we moved on to Bangkok. The city's famous floating markets, within easy walking distance from our hotel on the water, sold food and clothing from boat to boat in the hot humid weather. If you needed to buy cheap clothing or counterfeit watches, the night market stayed open until midnight, and stalls there served pad thai and other local specialties to the hungry masses of locals and tourists. Thai temples were unlike temples anywhere else and were filled with beautiful Buddha statues. The Reclining Buddha of Wat Pho was the largest we had ever seen.

Unlike Japan, Thailand was cheap, and unlike Hong Kong, it was relatively calm. Each Asian country showed us its unique side and taught Ruby and me more about each other's likes and dislikes, our pleasures and our fears.

Ruby had not been back to Bombay since she left in 1948, eighteen years earlier, and it was finally time for a visit. Ruby's mother and sister were both still living there. On the way we spent a few days in Delhi at the Ashok Hotel, where we were lucky enough to see a performance by the famous sitar player Ravi Shankar. Despite the Ashok's distinction as a five-star hotel, the electricity would often go out, sometimes getting us or other guests stuck in the glass elevator for everyone to see.

While in Delhi we bore the three-hour taxi trip through the heat of the Indian desert to visit the ivory-white mausoleum of the Taj Mahal in Agra, where we marveled at what truly is one of the wonders of the world. There, snake charmers attracted many tourists and locals to watch cobras dancing to the music. When we made it to Bombay, we stayed in a landmark hotel facing the bay, the luxurious Taj Mahal Palace.

Our hotel was in Colaba, which was right next to the Fort area, where Ruby grew up. While Colaba was a desirable address when Ruby was growing up, now many homes were ready to collapse, with wooden beams supporting the balconies to keep them from falling over. Beggars camped in the ground floor entryway to the houses, protecting the inhabitants from other intruders. There were beggars everywhere. When I gave money to one, other beggars would swarm towards me, pushing and pulling at my arms and my clothes. In one case, I had to drop some money on the floor and run to the nearest taxi to get away.

"How did I ever live here?" Ruby asked. During British rule, the Fort area had been a wealthy enclave for Jews with servants and beautiful homes, insulated from the grittier parts of the city. However, it, too, was now run-down, and Ruby could barely recognize it.

Ruby's mother and sister, Eliza, lived in the family home of Eliza's husband, Ezekiel Moses, in the nearby neighborhood of Byculla, which was in somewhat better shape.

It was great to meet Ruby's family, and I instantly connected with her mother, who treated me like her son. Throughout our visit she cooked traditional Iraqi food and made special dishes with an Indian flare. It was during our conversations with the family that Eliza and her husband, who everyone called Eze, decided they wanted to leave India and possibly move to Canada. At the same time, Ruby's mother decided she would move to England to live with her son Victor. They started the process soon after we left.

From Bombay we continued west to Beirut, which at that time was known as the "Paris of the Middle East." As an Israeli citizen, I could never have imagined being in Lebanon. But with my Canadian passport, I was free to travel wherever I pleased. The ruins of the Roman megaliths at Baalbek were a tremendous sight, matched only in height by the cedar trees of the Lebanese countryside. The Casino du Liban offered not only extensive gambling but entertainment venues featuring cabarets, belly dancers, and topless performers. Women there wore more jewelry than we had ever seen on anyone. Beirut was a peaceful and cultured city, and we were fortunate to be there before it was destroyed by years of civil war.

We then spent a couple of days in Amsterdam, cruising the canals and visiting the Anne Frank House, which had opened a few years earlier. Amsterdam was our last stop before we returned to Montreal, completing our circle around the globe.

That trip was the first of many international adventures Ruby and I would take over the next decade with the IREF convention as impetus. We went to a convention in Madrid and tacked on a trip to the southern beaches of Marbella and Costa del Sol. The year the convention was in Paris, we started in Nice and Cannes and drove north to Paris, taking the scenic route through Grenoble and the Alps. We took a cable car up to Mont Blanc; at a mile in length, it was the longest vertically ascending cable car in the world. When we got to the top, around twelve thousand feet altitude, the air was so thin I could barely breathe, and my heart palpitated when I climbed the summit's stairs. We took another cable car that floated over the glaciers and crossed the border from France to Italy. To Ruby and me, moments like this were heaven on earth.

On many of these trips, Harone and Suzanne, who also

attended the conventions, joined us on our adventures. Together, we visited the Yugoslavian city of Dubrovnik on the Adriatic Sea and explored Italy, Sweden, Greece, and numerous other places. In every new city I toured, I always made a point to visit synagogues and Jewish sites, which Harone and Suzanne also appreciated. It was remarkable to feel a connection to Jews around the world.

Before setting out on these trips, I would get my hands on tapes or records that taught the local language. First, I would just listen—to hear the lilt and music of each language, like a baby listening to his parents. After taking in the sounds, I would set out to master around 150 words, which was usually enough for me to get by. I found that if I showed I had made an effort to learn the local language and attempted to speak it with the proper accent, I was treated warmly and my experience was often greatly enhanced—except in France, where I spoke fluently but they only accepted perfection.

I usually forgot the language soon after a trip but was able to revive it when we traveled there again. I can still pull out Spanish and Italian pretty easily if needed, but of course my most comfortable languages are English, French, Hebrew, and Arabic (reserved mostly for jokes, wisecracks, and cursing with my friends and family), and I still understand and read Judeo-Arabic. Each language revealed a certain charm about the native culture, and I was never able to get enough.

Soon after we got back to Montreal from our first trip around the world, Ruby's mother, along with Eliza and Eze, started applying for British passports, which was not easy at the time and required some bribery. Later that same year, they all made the move from Bombay to London to live with Ruby's brothers, Victor and Eze. After about eight months there, Eliza and her husband made their way to Montreal, where we helped them find an apartment in Côte-des-Neiges. Ruby's mother stayed in London, but she missed Eliza and followed her and Ezekiel across the ocean just a few months later. Having her family nearby was wonderful for Ruby. We had Shabbat dinner with them nearly every week, and our kids became good friends with their cousins, Allen and Michael.

It was a rough transition for Eliza and Ezekiel. In Bombay, Eze ran the family's retail store and made a good living by Indian standards. They had servants and a good life. But all his rupees amounted to nothing when he came to the West because of the poor exchange rate. He had a hard time finding a business to get into, so he took a job as a shipper at a clothing manufacturer for $50 a week, and Eliza took a job as a secretary at Union Electric for about $30 a week. We wanted Ruby's mother to come live with us, but she felt that Eliza and Ezekiel needed her help.

I really loved my mother-in-law, and she treated me like a king. Sometimes she would stay with us for months, and she became like a true mother to me. All I had to say was, "Nana, I really love…" and she would jump to make it for me.

Every Friday I stopped in the bakery to pick up Nana's favorite cake to bring to Shabbat dinner. I would enter the Jewish bakery and say, "Give me your best cake for my mother-in-law."

The ladies at the bakery got a real kick out of this. "Sarah, the crazy man is back," they said. "He wants the best cake for his mother-in-law!"

Chapter 11

Building Our Dreams

From the Ground Up

Back in Montreal, I had nearly completed the phaseout of the brokerage part of my business, and just a few salespeople were left on the Fulton roster. Now my attention was on my new company, Eagle Development, which focused on constructing apartment buildings. I had done very well with Morris Robinson on the first two buildings in 1964 and 1965, and in 1966 I went into business with Morris's cousin, Jerry Robinson. He was a young man and his father had some money to invest, so Eagle Development teamed up with Jerry's company to start a new project together.

I enjoyed the big-picture planning—performing a cost analysis and rent projection, obtaining a mortgage from lenders, and working with architects to plan the project. Jerry loved the day-to-day supervision of working with the contractors, dealing with labor, and ordering materials. Together, we felt we had all the skills necessary for success. We purchased our first parcel of land on the Island of Montreal, in the city of Lachine close to the St. Lawrence River.

Over the next three years we built Chatelaine Terrace

*Chatelaine Terrace in Lachine, completed in 1969, was a sprawling,
park-like complex of seven four-story buildings, each with 47 apartments.*

Lachine, a sprawling, park-like complex of seven four-story buildings, each with forty-seven apartments. We constantly consulted
with each other to keep costs within the budget and to make it a
viable project. Rent was competitive at that time, and most owners
were asking $125 a month for a typical two-bedroom. To get an
edge, we aimed to ask just $100, which meant we had to build very

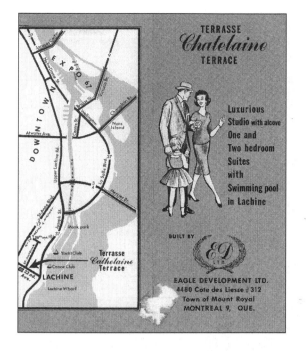

efficiently. Through hard work and diligent planning we succeeded, and the buildings quickly filled up.

While I was occupied with this major project and with my family, I continued my education. I took courses for my CPM (certified property manager) certification to help me become an effective property manager.

We sold Chatelaine Terrace Lachine by 1970 and made quite a bit of money, which prompted us to move on to our next project. In 1971 we bought a large parcel, this time on the east side of Montreal in Ville d'Anjou, where we planned to build 560 low-income units.

While I was working toward my CPM certification, I took classes alongside Jean-Guy Tanguay, who worked for the federal government agency that managed government properties and issued loans and mortgages for low-income housing. We became good friends, and I turned to him when we needed approval for our large mortgage on Anjou. We planned to build up the parcel in two

Our ambitious 560-unit development in d'Anjou was big enough to attract attention from the mayor and a member of the Quebec Parliament. I am standing in the middle, next to the mayor, and Jerry is to his right, (1971)

phases, but Jean-Guy approved our loan for both phases at once.

For phase one, we built two T-shaped wooden buildings with 140 units in each. Once those were completed, we started phase two—also two T-shaped wooden buildings—across the lawn. Between the buildings we had a large green space and a playground for the residents to enjoy. We called this 560-unit complex Chatelaine Terrace d'Anjou.

It was a huge development for a small city. The mayor and other city dignitaries came to our groundbreaking ceremony to welcome and thank us. The project brought a lot of business to the neighborhood, and the local retailers and restaurants were overjoyed.

Everything was going great. Within two years, we had built and filled every apartment on the property. Then, one night in January of 1973, I got a phone call that sent me running to the project. One of the buildings was on fire. A young child, whose mother was not home, had been playing with matches, and an entire wing had ignited as a result. Jerry and I stood with the firemen in the subzero weather, bringing them coffee and sandwiches while their breath froze in the air and ice clung to their faces.

The fire was a big deal; the newspapers, radio, and TV news covered it, with photos and everything. A wing of the building was destroyed, and several areas of the complex were damaged by smoke. Thank God no one was hurt, though many residents were temporarily displaced. Insurance covered us, and we were able to rebuild. Even with that huge setback, we were able to sell the buildings by 1974 and turned a huge profit.

Meanwhile, my dear friend Joe Azar and his wife, Evelyn, had moved to Kitchener, Ontario, in order for Joe to take a job with Raytheon, a large American aerospace company. Joe saw how well I was doing with apartment buildings in Montreal and decided he wanted to try it as well. He located some potential land zoned for apartments in a well-to-do area of Kitchener and wanted me to partner with him for their development. I encouraged him to get into it alone, but he wanted my expertise.

We joined forces and built two buildings of thirty units each. I did a lot of the budgeting and planning and worked with the architect. Joe handled the daily supervision and personal communication with tenants. When we sold the buildings, Joe decided to quit his well-paid engineering position and move back to Montreal and join me as a full-time builder.

However, our next venture was not in real estate, and we learned a good lesson. One of my neighbors, Harry Glanz, who was in the *schmatte* (textile) business, introduced me to Sam Marom, an Israeli who was a technician in a knitting factory. Sam and Harry wanted to open a new drapery and textile factory in Montreal. The government was offering bonuses for anyone to start factories that employed people. We got $30,000 from the government, and Joe

*Nory owned and ran a service station in Montreal in 1957,
before becoming an insurance agent.*

and I partnered with Harry and Sam to open Sabra Industries.

The business expanded quickly, with Sam and Harry running the day-to-day operations. Soon after we opened, Sam convinced Harry they didn't need Joe and me; they decided to buy us out and go on their own. But when it came time to sign the deal, Joe turned it around. He convinced me that it was a successful business, and we bought Sam and Harry out instead, and Joe started running it.

Neither Joe nor I knew anything about the knitting, manufacturing, and marketing of textiles, and the factory soon started going downhill. Joe wanted to put more money into the business, but I could see it was no use, and I didn't want to sink any more time or money into it. In fact, I didn't want to be in the textile industry at all; I only wanted to get out of the arrangement. Joe continued with the business, and I just walked away and gave him my share. Joe tried hard, but eventually he lost the business and our entire investment. Fortunately, we had a strong friendship, and even though we lost money together we stayed friends.

I was less fortunate with my brother Nory. He had arrived in Montreal as I had—with some money from our father but not enough to hold him for long if he didn't work. He took the money from Baba and bought a gas station in Montreal with another man. But he soon discovered that his partner was stealing from him and got out of that business. He moved from job to job until he landed in the insurance industry as an agent.

In the early 1970s, while I was developing the d'Anjou property, Nory wanted me to insure the project through him. I asked him to prepare a proposal, but his quotes were much higher than the other bids. I told him I couldn't justify paying that much, to myself or to my investment partners. I had shown my partners the other quotes, and it would not make sense, or be honest, to choose the highest one. Sadly, Nory took my actions personally, and refused to speak to me for years.

I was hurt by his choice. When we were younger, I was his protector and we were close. And in Montreal, we had seen each other often and spent holidays together. But having grown up in a big family, I knew that we each had our own distinct personality. I came to the realization that we can choose friends but not family, and while it's beautiful when we like a family member enough to be friends as well, the dynamics of our personalities might not always be compatible. If Nory did not want to talk to me, that was his prerogative. But I loved my brother, and I was saddened by his decision.

Now that I had made it in business, I could hear my Youmma's words ringing in my ears: "*Ayuni*, you are going to be rich."

As I began to acquire my wealth and saw the challenges that came with it, I clearly saw what had made her words a reality—honesty, hard work, and family.

"*Ayuni* Youmma, I am rich."

Where the Heart Is

Going into the apartment construction business tipped me into a new category of wealth. In eight years, Jerry Robinson and I built and sold over eight hundred apartments. Still, I stuck to my decision not to become enslaved by the desire to accumulate money for the sake of accumulation. I could have worked harder, built more, and spent less time with the family, but that was not my goal. I wanted my family to be comfortable and to be able to enjoy life together. I was determined to continue to maintain a balance.

In 1973, Ruby and I bought a piece of land in Hampstead—a corner lot facing a park, not far from the first parcel we had purchased and sold seven years earlier before traveling around the world together. It was time for our dream house to become a reality.

We built our dream home at 3 Applewood Road in Hampstead and moved in just before Passover 1974.

We bought the lot from a Mr. Rosenthal, a rough but congenial Holocaust survivor who owned a lot of real estate and had commissioned Fulton to sell his homes in the past. I was able to reduce the cost of the build-out by getting breaks from contractors I knew from doing the apartment buildings. It cost me the low price of $100,000 to build a luxurious 4,500-square-foot home at 3 Applewood Road in Hampstead, which was like the Beverly Hills of Montreal.

Although I was an experienced builder, designing and building a house can be tough for a couple; I had seen it enough times to know. I hired Boris Moroz, a third-party construction manager, to resolve any design disagreements between Ruby and me while maintaining the function of the house. If Ruby wanted an outlet in one place and I wanted it in another, Boris helped us figure out where it should go. Boris's fee wasn't cheap, but the money spent may very well have saved our marriage and definitely saved us a lot of unneeded tension.

We moved in just before Passover 1974. Sharon, Lisa, and Jeff each had their own rooms, painted in the color of their choice—Jeff chose blue, Sharon chose purple, and Lisa chose pink. Our house in Chomedey had been cozy but tiny. We were all excited to now have more space and more privacy.

Ruby put her soul into decorating the house in stunning fashion, while also making it comfortable to live in. She worked with a talented and well-known decorator, Andrea Myers (Nory's sister-in-law; it was at her wedding that Ruby and I met in 1957). Ruby and Andrea found elegant crystal chandeliers, sat through long hours at the auction house to buy beautiful paintings by famous artists, and designed the kitchen with the finest modern appliances. We even had an indoor barbeque. Ruby was absorbed in creating the perfect home for our family, and she took it so seriously that she developed chest pains. After learning from the hospital staff that

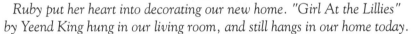

*Ruby put her heart into decorating our new home. "Girl At the Lillies"
by Yeend King hung in our living room, and still hangs in our home today.*

she was not having a heart attack but was suffering from anxiety,
she tried to take things easier.

I put much of my efforts into two areas—the den and the
garden. The den had handmade, engraved wood paneling, oak
flooring, floor-to-ceiling windows, a marble fireplace, and a state-
of-the-art entertainment system with built-in ceiling speakers and a
large television. In the winter, while Ruby sat next to me reading a
novel, I would listen to classical music and gaze out the windows to
watch the falling snow. I was mesmerized by the snowflakes dancing
in the floodlight and softly settling into a white carpet across the
concrete deck. Watching the sparkling snowfall was a meditative
act for me, a chance to be grateful for this magical moment of being
alive and to appreciate that I had more than I could ever have
imagined. It was an added relief to appreciate its beauty while not

having to worry about digging out my car, which was safely parked in my new garage.

In the summer we spent time out on the deck, where we barbequed meats and vegetables. And beyond the porch was my garden. The garden became my place of refuge. Especially in the winter, when everything green was encased in snow, I loved to be able to get close to nature. In an alcove of our two-car garage, I installed some heat lamps over a covered bed of soil and coaxed seeds to life, using specialized light bulbs that replicated the sun. In the spring, I transplanted the saplings. The warm season was too short for most plants, so I built a greenhouse to lengthen the season and help my saplings grow into a successful vegetable garden—cucumbers, peppers, zucchinis, and gourds. I attended gardening classes and even entered my gourds into a local competition, but my fifty-one-pound pumpkin was still not enough to take a prize. I also planted some hearty fruit trees—cherry, apple, pear, apricot, and a variety of plums. Only the apricots didn't work well.

I found great comfort and release in the physical work of tending to the cycle of life. Gardening became my second favorite hobby after traveling. I had many other hobbies that helped me break the hectic rhythms of existence and slow down and appreciate life. I continued to do yoga and meditate every day, and I became quite flexible. I could do the splits, put my legs behind my head, and stand on my hands. I had started jogging in Chomedey and continued doing so in Hampstead. I jogged every day with Harone, except for Shabbat, when we went to synagogue. When Lisa had a day off from school, she would join us. We jogged no matter the weather, even through blizzards. It may have been crazy, but the exercise helped me forget about the world and focus on what was most important.

Now that Ruby and I were living the easy life, I knew we would have to work to teach the kids the delicate balance of enjoying what you have without feeling entitled. A sense of entitlement—believing the world owes you something not because you've earned it but because of who you are or who you know—is, in my opinion, one of the worst character traits a person can have. This mentality stifles the desire to build yourself into something more. How can you get better if you already believe you have it down?

I taught our children that you should never spend more than you earn. I taught them that if you put money away, even a little amount grows. I taught them that spending money on experiences, like travel, skiing, classes, or hobbies, enriches your life so much more than any material possessions you accumulate.

When my kids were teenagers, I figured out a system to teach them responsible spending habits and money management, and to appreciate the value of a dollar. Rather than a weekly allowance, they received an allowance for six months or the whole year and had the responsibility of managing it. If they kept the money with me, I acted as their bank. I showed them statements, paid them interest, and never questioned their withdrawals. When they worked or got gifts of cash, they could deposit that money into Dad's bank as well.

I think my system worked well. When Sharon was around fifteen, she went to visit her uncle Victor in London and while there bought a coat for $200. That purchase drew down her balance, but she made the decision to suffer it out and not borrow money from me. All of the kids grew up to be responsible with money while understanding that money wasn't everything. They know that it is important to have enough to live the life you want to live, but it is equally important to spend the money and time you earn in a way that enriches your life and the world around you.

Sharing the World

One indulgence engraved in my psyche was travel, and I

was thrilled to include my family in that experience. Montreal had treacherous winters, with black-ice-covered roads and slick sidewalks posing hazards for cars and pedestrians. The days were short and the trees were bare, causing nature to fold into a deep sleep. Every winter vacation, we found relief by getting ourselves out of the blistering cold and into temperate climates.

We often stayed at the hotel next to the airport the day before we left Canada, just to be sure we wouldn't get iced in at home. We traveled as a family to Acapulco, Barbados, Jamaica, and Miami. We cruised on warm blue seas, which made the gray blanket that hung over Montreal seem even further away. Who could think about anything bad in the comfortable warmth and green beauty of

A fire-breather in Jamaica impressed the kids, one of many family vacations. (1969)

The kids on their second trip to Israel. (1977)

the tropics? And it gave the kids good exposure to people of other cultures. In Barbados, Jeff, exclaimed, "I saw a black Santa Claus! How could it be?"

In 1970 I took Ruby and the kids on their first trip to Israel. Sharon was ten, Lisa was seven, and Jeff was five, and this was also Ruby's first trip to Israel. My cousin Aboudi found us a furnished apartment in Tel Aviv, next to where he lived and across the street from a fire station. There was a *makolet* on the ground floor where we purchased necessities, and the kids loved buying watermelons from the horse-drawn carts in the neighborhood. Apart from the sirens from the fire station, the apartment was perfect and housed us happily for two months.

Because Ruby didn't speak Hebrew, it was hard for her when we got together with my relatives or interacted with shopkeepers and others in the country. My relatives had spent so much time in Israel that when we got together, even though we would start talking in English to make sure Ruby was included, we would unconsciously drift back to Hebrew peppered with Arabic. Ruby would put on a clear look of dissatisfaction. And she couldn't believe how pushy and rude the people could be at times. Ruby is more proper; she grew up in a very British atmosphere.

Even so, it was a delight for me to spend time with my brothers, my cousins, and some old friends. Eliyahoo knew I loved the sciences, and he took me to his lab to show off his equipment and research in the field of optics. Whenever we saw each other, we would pick up where we had left off with our joking and reminiscing. We talked about all our old times together—flying kites, terrorizing the neighborhood with our jar of bees, scaring people with our bike horn. We were both adventurous little kids, and I think that spirit remained within us as we got older. For us to see our children getting to know each other and enjoying being together was such a blessing.

During that trip I visited the Old City of Jerusalem for the first time. I had left Israel in 1956, and it wasn't until after the Six-Day War in 1967, when Israel captured the Old City from Jordan, that Jews were allowed to visit the holiest sites of Judaism. When I first saw the *Kotel* (Western Wall), I was flooded with emotion. I had the sense of being connected with my ancestors and my history. It was a stronger spiritual feeling than I had ever experienced.

I also caught up with my old friend Jacob Bar-On, my roommate from my short-lived days as a student in Tel Aviv. He had succeeded in becoming a lawyer and was also trying his hand at various businesses. I borrowed Jacob's car, and Ruby, the kids, and I drove everywhere—to Hebron, to Bethlehem, to the Dead Sea. There was a lot of freedom to move around the areas Israel had captured in the 1967 war, and the country was still safe at that time. We stayed at a beautiful hotel outside the city of Eilat, in an area that Israel eventually gave back to Egypt.

After we visited the tombs of the three patriarchs of Israel

(Abraham, Isaac, and Jacob) in Hebron, the radiator started leaking. I stopped at an Arab garage, and the mechanic gave me a story about how the repair was such a big job and would take so long and cost so much. My army training as a mechanic saved the day: I bought a pack of gum, chewed it up, and plugged the leak. That was good enough to get us the twenty miles back to our apartment in Jerusalem, where I found someone to fix the radiator at a good price.

Whenever I visited Israel, I made sure to spend time with Yaakub in Ramat Gan. He lived alone at Rechov Hasneh 5, the house my parents bought when they first moved to Israel. When my mother was alive she tried to get Yaakub married off, but nothing came of her efforts. With both of our parents gone he was lonely, and it was terribly sad. He had such a sharp mind—he read the newspapers daily and had taught himself Hebrew. He could get to the market and get groceries on his own; sometimes a neighbor helped him carry the food home. He lived off the income from Ben Yehuda 5, which was distributed by his attorney, Nissim Kadir, who also managed the building and collected the rent. But sometimes Yaakub complained the money wasn't enough, and I always gave him more. Eliyahoo visited Yaakub often and took him shopping or brought him food that Ahuva cooked for him. Yaakub managed, but I don't think he was really happy.

In 1976, the Olympics came to Montreal, and this was a great excuse for family to finally come visit us. Ruby's brother Victor came from London with his family, and we enjoyed showing them around our city. After the Games, Ruby and I took a trip to the American Southwest with our kids, and we invited Victor's daughter, Debra, who was around the same age as Sharon, to come along. We flew to Phoenix, where we rented a station wagon and drove to Sedona, the Grand Canyon, and Las Vegas. From there we drove to Los Angeles, staying at the Century Plaza Hotel right in the middle of the city, and visited Disneyland. To get to San Francisco, we took a luxury coach tour up the coast: the California Parlor Car Tour, a four-day drive up the state complete with stops at Hearst Castle, Monterey, and other scenic locations. Jeff, the jokester, wore the Mickey Mouse ears I had bought him in Disneyland the whole ride up. We visited the gorgeous 17-Mile Drive near Pebble Beach, and for the second time I stopped at Point Joe to take a picture, this time with the kids in the frame. We hiked through the tall pine trees of Yosemite to see the impressive views of Half Dome and stayed at the Ahwahnee Lodge before ending the tour in San Francisco, where we explored for four more days before making the flight home. I had been to some of those places with Ruby on our honeymoon, but it was a special feeling to be able to show them to my kids.

Adieu, Montreal

By the mid-1970s we were settled into our new home; the kids were learning English, French, and Hebrew at Herzliah High School; and I was doing well in my businesses. Jerry and I had sold all of the units at d'Anjou. I had finally found a good balance between working hard to improve our financial situation and spending time with Ruby and the kids. Between my new house, my travels, my hobbies, and my methods of relaxation, I was living a life that I could never have imagined.

But failure is an inevitable part of success. In 1974 an opportunity arose to build a twenty-one-story, 241-unit high-rise on Lincoln Avenue, a prime location on the English-speaking west side of downtown Montreal. I had never worked on high-rises before, but Joe Azar was convinced this was a great opportunity. Conditions were just right—the demand was strong, financing was favorable, the economy was booming, and on top of all this, a zoning freeze limited construction of new high-rise buildings in the area while our parcel had been grandfathered in with approval to build up to twenty-one stories.

These were heady times for Montreal. The city was preparing to host the 1976 Olympics, and prospects were everywhere. Joe and I set our sights on having the building ready to rent out for the visiting guests. We got an architect, an engineer, and construction contractors lined up and continued to pour concrete through the subzero winter to be ready in time. I tried to bring Jeff on as an aspiring architect, but at ten years old he was more interested in the great Greek *souvlaki* down the street.

Joe and I completed Chateau Lincoln right on schedule. It featured luxury furnished studios and one-bedrooms with new high-speed elevators, a heated rooftop swimming pool, and a fully equipped gym to service the corporate and business professionals of downtown.

Chateau Lincoln served as a premier hotel for the Olympics and was fully booked. We housed tourists, Olympic delegations from China and Russia, and the Canadian Broadcasting Company, which rented seventy units for their employees. We did extremely well during the Games.

Through the guests staying in Chateau Lincoln, we got privileged tickets to see some of the Olympic events. We watched Nadia Comaneci, the Romanian gymnast, win the gold medal in all-around gymnastics with a perfect score of 10. We were truly amazed by the state-of-the-art sports stadium and its retractable roof. When the rain started coming down during the basketball championships, the roof glided shut and blocked the elements from reaching the court and the crowd. As a builder, I knew this was a terrific feat. At the end of the Games, we were even invited to the Russian ship MS *Aleksandr Pushkin* to celebrate.

Nineteen seventy-six was also the year we celebrated Sharon's sweet sixteen. It was not yet customary for girls to have

Our family celebrated Sharon's sweet sixteen in 1976.

a bat mitzvah, so we gathered the family together and honored her with a sixteenth-birthday party. Seeing Sharon dance and sing with all the great friends she had made in Montreal brought tears to my eyes. I felt so proud knowing that my children were growing into such incredible adults. When I was their age, I lived in fear of the Iraqi authorities and was always afraid for my life. But here my children were, blossoming in freedom and excelling toward a bright future.

While everything was great in our personal lives, Montreal as a city was experiencing some growing turmoil. In the Quebec general election of 1976, the French-separatist Parti Québécois won on a platform of Quebec seceding from Canada and becoming an independent, French-speaking country. It wasn't just talk:

in October 1970, Québécois extremists had kidnapped Quebec's provincial deputy premier, Pierre LaPorte, and held him and British diplomat James Cross hostage in the name of the French-separatist movement. LaPorte's body was found a week after he was kidnapped; Cross was released that December.

Quebec was (and still is) the only French-speaking province in Canada; even so, Montreal was majority English-speaking except for some parts in the south and east of the city. As a result, French-speaking Canadians in Montreal were required to know English to advance their career, and they resented this fact.

The 1976 election victory of the Parti Québécois ushered in a period of great economic and social uncertainty for English speakers in Quebec. Many Montreal residents left for other provinces of Canada, and some left the country altogether. Major companies such as Sun Life Financial and the Royal Bank of Canada moved their headquarters to Toronto, leaving many Montreal offices and apartments vacant.

For Joe and me, these politics pulled the rug out from under our feet. By 1977 tourism started to taper off, and the English-speaking population of downtown Montreal, where we built Chateau Lincoln, was abandoning the area. We lowered rents, tried new incentives, and pushed our advertising, but nothing helped fill the empty apartments. Unlike merchandise, which can be sold at a later time, each day those apartments were empty equated to permanently lost income. This, on top of the property taxes and operating expenses of the building, left us facing a major deficit.

Within one year of the Olympics, our dreams were melting like the spring ice, and our investment was going down the drain. We weighed all of our options and came to the tough decision to abandon the project. We couldn't sell it, but I did not want to have a defaulted mortgage on my record. So I found someone who agreed to take the building with no down payment or investment;

*The 1976 construction of Chateau Lincoln, in the heart of Montreal,
turned out to be a valuable lesson in resilience.*

he would simply buy it for $1 and assume the remaining balance of
the mortgage.

Even with an exit in sight, Joe wasn't sure he could walk
away. "Give me your share of the building," he said to me. "I think
I can make this work. Why abandon this altogether after we put so
much money into it?"

"Joe," I said, "you are my best friend. I cannot allow you to
throw your last dollars into this black hole and go completely broke.
Please, just walk away."

He did, and we ended up losing almost all of our assets on
the whole ordeal. Years later, Joe thanked me for preventing him
from digging himself deeper into that disaster.

The experience was a huge blow, but I refused to panic. I knew that there was no success without suffering and that to improve and achieve, one must accept failure and learn from experience. I asked myself what I did wrong and how I could do it right the next time.

I stayed calm. I had built myself up from nothing—from a scared teenager on a smuggler's boat to a refugee holding out a tin plate to owning my own business and building a luxury home for my family. I had used my ingenuity and my chutzpah to create opportunity and success. I knew how to get back up. I always had a positive outlook, and that propelled me forward.

I left the high-rise business for the time being and went back to the kind of buildings I knew. All of my success so far had been with three- or four-story buildings, which could be built or renovated efficiently and rented out quickly.

I found a thirty-six-unit apartment building at 75 Glengarry in the affluent city of Mount Royal. In 1977, I borrowed money and bought the building for $750,000. My plan was to convert the units to condos and sell them, but that was not an easy thing to do at the time; these were large units and the building was rent-controlled, so people did not want to move.

To begin the transformation, I started by making improvements to the building. I divided the electricity so that each unit had its own system and spruced up all the apartments. I put a heater into the pool system and renovated the elevator. I beautified and furnished the lobby and turned one unit into a communal recreation room. To prove to the city that buyers were waiting to fill the units, I offered current tenants an excellent deal to buy their apartments: a $40,000 starting price for a fully renovated two-bedroom. A few residents jumped at the opportunity, but even then some said I was extorting them and forcing them out.

I hired Irving Adessky, a prominent lawyer who was also the

After the debacle with Chateau Lincoln, I recovered in 1977 by converting a 36-unit apartment building in Mount Royal to condos.

mayor of Hampstead. In court, we called our interested applicants to testify that they were motivated to buy the units and that they thought the conversion to condos would increase the overall value of the property. The judge ruled in our favor, and we were allowed to convert the whole building.

I started to sell the units. I gave at-cost deals to Marcelle and Sasson and to Eliza and Ezekiel, in units right down the hall from each other. By 1978 I had only a few units left to sell and had climbed out of the hole created by the failure of Chateau Lincoln. I was elated and felt back on top.

To add to my euphoria, we celebrated Jeff's bar mitzvah on May 6, 1978, and it was an unforgettable event. He had been preparing for it through all the troubles of the previous couple of years, and it was a rewarding experience to watch my boy become a man. I had been looking forward to this day for all his life and was thrilled to have the whole family there, celebrating together.

The event inspired a reconciliation with Nory, who hadn't spoken to me since our falling out over the insurance policy for d'Anjou. Before the bar mitzvah, Nory asked Elisha to help us come

Jeff's Bar Mitzvah on May 6, 1978, gave us a much needed opportunity to celebrate.

back together. He wanted to celebrate with the family and go back to our having a good relationship. By the time of Jeff's big celebration, everything was forgiven.

The event also brought some special visitors: my brother Eliyahoo and his wife, Ahuva, from Israel and Ruby's brothers Victor and Ezekiel from London. Having everyone together for something so special was a blissful moment that helped reinvigorate my spirit and make me excited for our future.

This was the first time Eliyahoo had left Israel since arriving there in 1942. It was his first time ever flying on an airplane, and I'm pretty sure it was also his first time wearing a tie. He loved our new house, and it was a pleasure to have so much room for him and Ahuva. Like he had done to me as a kid, I played tricks on him: I would make strange noises on our intercom system while he was

Eliyahoo and Ahuva left Israel for the first time to attend Jeff's Bar Mitzvah, and we showed them the beauty of Montreal.

asleep, and he would get scared and confused.

We showed our guests the beauty of Montreal. We took them to Mount Royal, a little hill with great panoramic views in the very center of Montreal Island, and enjoyed the excellent French Canadian cuisine, especially the delicious *soupe à l'oignon* (French onion soup). We visited Saint Helen's Island, which hosted the World's Fair in 1967 and still had many of the Expo pavilions and exhibitions (some had already been turned into casinos). We drove to Sainte-Agathe-des-Monts to see the mountains and have lunch by the lake, where Eliyahoo commented that he had never seen so many trees. We traveled to Quebec City to see the quaint European architecture and to Ottawa to see Canada's parliament buildings.

Jeff's bar mitzvah was a wonderful celebration, but it came amid a bigger change in our lives. Ruby and I had decided that the political atmosphere in Montreal was too turbulent and uncertain; six weeks after the bar mitzvah, we would be moving to Los Angeles.

The Quebec provincial government, headed by the Parti Québécois since its 1976 electoral victory, was planning to hold a referendum on the question of separation. The newspapers and pundits believed there was a good chance that the party would get enough votes for Quebec to secede from Canada and become an independent, French-speaking country. I was concerned. (As it turned out, the promised referendum was defeated in 1980.)

English-speaking Canadians continued to leave Montreal. Since most Jews were English speakers, we worried about what an independent Quebec would look like. We loved Montreal. We had dear friends, both French and English; we were important members of the Jewish community and especially the Iraqi community; and our kids were thriving. Sharon was eighteen and had finished high school and one year of junior college. She was brilliant and was preparing for a bright future. Lisa was fifteen and Jeff was thirteen, and both had wonderful friends and were happy in school. But Ruby and I felt that the declining economy and decreasing opportunity posed too much of a threat to our security, and we decided the time was ripe to leave Quebec.

We began to explore our options. Having traveled quite a bit, we knew we wanted to be somewhere warm. Both of us had grown up in places that did not have harsh winters, and we were done with bundling up against subzero weather, slipping on ice, and shoveling snow. That eliminated Toronto from our list. After visiting Vancouver, Miami, Houston, and Los Angeles, we chose LA.

We had visited Los Angeles a few times before and felt like it was a good match for our family. We loved the weather, which reminded us both of our childhoods, and while I had no business connections there, it was a big enough city that I wasn't worried about my ability to create a network and find opportunities.

I felt that America was one of the best places in the world to live, if not the best, and had wondered about life there since I was a boy in Iraq, thinking about college. I was drawn to what I saw as open-mindedness and freedom of expression, without the divisive politics of Quebec. It seemed to me that if you worked hard in America, there was opportunity to succeed. I was confident that there was great potential for me and my family to thrive there.

It was hard to abandon our dream home, which we had built from the ground up and lived in for only four years. Ruby was especially attached to the house; she had poured so much love and energy into it. But in the end we decided this was the right move at the right time.

Now I needed to decide whether to rent out our house or sell it. I was offered $180,000 for our castle. I asked myself, if I had that money in my pocket, would I then buy the house and rent it for profit? The answer was a clear no. Renting would require time and absentee management, and I could do more with my money and effort. I was starting anew, and if I had to choose between investing in Montreal or Los Angeles, I would choose Los Angeles. So we sold the house, knowing the money would be essential to creating our new life in the U.S.

Ruby and I applied for and received visas to the United States. Ruby had a cousin in LA who helped me get a business visa, an L-1, which would allow me to start working right away. Moving to America was a big deal for us. We were Canadian citizens who had been in Montreal for twenty-two years, with a fantastic network of friends, a strong and supportive community, and a lot of close family nearby. None of that was waiting for us in Los Angeles. We had reinvented ourselves before, but this time was going to be different: we had money in our bank account, I had vast business experience, we spoke English fluently, and even if the culture was slightly different than Montreal's, I knew I had the skills to make connections in a big city. And I wouldn't have to change my name again.

We packed all of our belongings into a moving truck that would meet us at the opposite corner of the continent, and on June 24, 1978, Jean Baptiste Day in Quebec, we set out. Seeing the bare walls of our home had a powerful effect.

Ruby looked at me through her tears, "This is going to be a big move."

"It's going to be a *great* move, honey bunch," I assured her. We were scared of the unknown but as ready as we could be. Lisa was in Israel for six months on a school program, so with Sharon and Jeff in the car, we took a final look at the house and said, "Adieu, Quebec!"

In 1978, Ruby and I bid adieu to Montreal.

PART 4

⟫⟫ LOS ANGELES ⟪⟪

1978-Today

CHAPTER 12

NEW SHORES AND HORIZONS

A Warm Welcome

We bought a new station wagon, specially outfitted with air conditioning, to cross the continent—no need for ice blocks to keep Ruby cool this time. For the second time, we began to cross North America and were excited to show Sharon and Jeff places they had never seen before. It was June of 1978, and it was the perfect time of year to travel and see the country. The trip could have only been made more complete if Lisa had been with us, though she was having a good time in Israel.

First, we stopped in Boston and stayed at my niece Myrna's house for a few days. We showed the kids Faneuil Hall and Harvard University and visited the Paul Revere House, from which the American patriot set out on his 1775 ride to warn of the approaching British troops.

We continued down to New York City to take in the panoramic view from the Empire State Building, eat a meal amid the bustling commotion of Chinatown, and stop at the headquarters of the United Nations to observe the Israeli flag flying in the sea of world flags in front of the building.

Sharon and Jeff in the Luray Caverns of Virginia, on our way to California. (1978)

We visited the Luray Caverns in Virginia and stopped in Greensboro, North Carolina, to see my old high school friend Edward Obidiah, whom I had sponsored to immigrate to Montreal. He had struggled with the French language and with finding work he liked, so he moved to Toronto and married Olivia, an Iraqi-American woman. They later moved to Greensboro. When we reunited, he and Olivia had two children, and he was planning to go into construction.

Driving southwest, we were excited to reach Louisiana. The bustling jazz scene of New Orleans was a completely new experience for the kids. The atmosphere and architecture of the French Quarter is truly unique, and it fascinated them to see such a culture. We had breakfast at Brennan's, a famous stop for Creole cuisine, and tried loads of unhealthy fried street foods. My cousin Elisha happened to be there on an organized tour from Israel, and it was wonderful for the family to meet him again. Elisha's great humor kept us laughing the entire time—often at his own expense. Elisha was only a bit taller than three feet, and when he tried on a pair of cowboy boots he joked, "They come all the way up to my balls!" We were sad to leave him and move on.

From New Orleans we hopped on Interstate 10, with Ruby behind the maps as navigator, and continued west. Houston and Phoenix were nice stops, but we were eager to get to Palm Springs. We passed through Indio, where we ate so many dates—mostly Iraqi varieties, like barhi, zahidi, and halawi—that we walked around high on sugar. We relaxed for a night to bask in the heat and beauty of the California desert before completing the last leg of our journey.

The swaying elegance of the palm trees welcomed us to Los Angeles, just as they had ushered me down the Tigris River on the summer excursions of my youth and out of Iraq on the Shatt Al Arab.

Ruby and I had flown to Los Angeles about a month before to figure out where we would live. We knew we didn't want to live in the city of Los Angeles because, at the time, children were being bused to any school in the sprawling district in an effort to make sure that the schools were integrated and diversified. We wanted to have more direct choice in our kids' schools. The only choices were either Beverly Hills or Santa Monica, as each had only one high school. Beverly Hills was excessively opulent, so we chose Santa Monica; the suburbs felt like less of a culture shock for our quiet Canadian kids.

Driving through Santa Monica, we had passed a beautiful

two-story Tudor with a "For Rent" sign on the front lawn. The house, at 321 24th Street, had a pool, which was an enticing novelty. We thought the kids would love it. The owner wanted $1,600 per month, a staggering amount compared to the Montreal market. Still, we signed a lease for one year.

Now our family had arrived. In eight days, we had covered over three thousand miles, but this third move to a new country proved to be the easiest. The house had four bedrooms and a large garden. It was older and smaller than our brand-new luxury home in Hampstead, but right away we felt at home. The Tudor style of the house beautifully fit Ruby's English antiques and fixtures, and the kids especially enjoyed the consistently good weather and the backyard pool. Ruby's cousin from Bombay, Richard Moualim, and his American wife, Marcie, lived nearby on Anita Avenue and San Vicente Boulevard in Brentwood, and we got together often.

Sharon immediately applied to the University of Southern California for the fall of 1978. With a certificate of honor from high school and a letter of recommendation from her principal, she was easily accepted. She continued to live at home and commuted in her small Pinto to the downtown campus daily.

When Lisa returned from her semester of high school in Israel, she enrolled in Santa Monica High School (which everyone referred to as Samohi), and Jeff started at Lincoln Junior High. We looked into sending Lisa and Jeff to Hebrew high schools, but the Jewish options in Los Angeles seemed limited—the schools were far away and too religious for us. While I attended synagogue on Shabbat, we were not very observant. Jeff was happy to go to a public school, and Lisa didn't mind.

But the move itself was difficult for Lisa. At age fifteen, friends meant everything to her, and it was hard for her to leave her circle in Montreal. The only way to keep in touch was through letters; long distance phone calls were still expensive and reserved for urgent or special matters. And, of course, there was no Internet and email in those days. However, after some adjustment, she joined the drama department and managed to make new friends. She had a good two years at Samohi before she graduated in 1980 and was accepted to UCLA.

Jeff had his own challenges. In Montreal he had struggled at the Hebrew school because he didn't have strong religious feelings. But in his new school he faced a different environment and a diverse population of students. Some of them were tough, and he complained about being bullied. It was a big adjustment for him, and I had to visit the principal to see how we could fix the problem. Eventually, Jeff settled down socially, though he didn't focus enough on his studies. He was more interested in his skateboard and the ramp he built in our driveway. He had a rebellious streak—similar

Our first summer in Santa Monica with my sister Marcelle, her family, and our friends Julie and Jack Iny from Montreal. (August, 1978)

to myself in my teenage years, but he was holding onto it longer than I had.

Just six months after we moved into our house, the owner wanted to sell. Newly enacted rent-control ordinances were being introduced in Santa Monica, and he wanted to avoid the problem altogether by selling the property.

He wanted $300,000, which sounded astronomical. The house in Santa Monica was nearly half the size of our house in Montreal, ten times as old, and nearly twice the price. But for me, purchasing a home is not the same as making an investment. I was not looking for a good return; I was looking for a place to raise our family and to enjoy my life. I remembered Ruby's stress and anxiety around the move and her sadness over the few pieces of furniture that had arrived damaged. I did not want to put her or the rest of the family through that experience again.

Ruby was especially keen to stay in the neighborhood. Our house was in an area north of Montana Avenue that the realtors had dubbed Gillette's Regent Square. Ruby had been told over and over how "north of Montana" was desirable. Together, we decided we loved the house and the neighborhood and did not want to move.

I put $50,000 down to purchase the house and got a mortgage from Bank of America for $250,000 at 15.25 percent interest. Our monthly payment was $3,211 for principal and interest, not counting the yearly property tax. We had owned our home in Hampstead free and clear, because mortgage interest is not deductible in Canada. In the U.S., taking out a mortgage was more enticing, because the interest was tax-deductible. Even so, it seemed insane to pay that much for our house at the time. But looking back, it turned out to be one of the best investments I ever made. We still enjoy living in that house today, and its value has appreciated tremendously.

One of the first things I did after we bought our house was to create my own garden. I ripped out the shrubs and green trees that the previous owner had planted in the backyard and put in railway ties to terrace the earth for herbs, vegetables, and fruit trees. Around the pool and upper terraces, I planted the fruit trees—navel and Valencia oranges, Eureka lemons, kumquats, Santa Rosa plums, Black Mission figs, and Blenheim apricots—and experimented with some more exotic types, including pineapple and strawberry guava, cherimoya, white sapote, loquat, and passion fruit. On the lower terrace, I planted a mixed herb garden and miniature roses. It was a dream come true: my own little Garden of Eden. The summer weather reminded me of the hot Baghdadi climate and made me think of all the apricots, peaches, and nectarines we picked in the gardens of my family's *mush tamal*, our country house outside Baghdad.

Ruby and I originally joined the Sephardic Temple

We loved the sunshine, but we also sought out California's wintery beauty. (1979)

Tifereth Israel, which had a few Iraqi members. Soon after, our new friends, Flo and Maurice Shamash, suggested we join Kahal Joseph Congregation, an Iraqi-founded synagogue on Santa Monica Boulevard. Kahal Joseph had many families from Iraq, as well as Iraqi-originated families from India, Burma, and Singapore. Upon joining, Ruby and I immediately felt that we had found our social and spiritual home.

My lawyer in Montreal urged us to meet his cousins Sybil and Seymour Pressman, native Montrealers who had also recently left because of the French-separatist movement. They lived not far from us in Los Angeles, and Ruby and I became good friends with them, sharing holiday meals and going out.

But we all missed our relatives. I missed playing *shesh besh* with my brothers, Ruby longed for those family Shabbat dinners with her sister and her mother, and our kids complained that our Shabbat dinners were too quiet and holidays felt incomplete because they had no cousins to run around with. Though we had left many friends and family members behind, in time we realized we had everything we needed: a home, a pool, a dream garden, perfect weather, and a great neighborhood close to the ocean. We were ready to explore the boundless mountains, deserts, lakes, and beaches in the sprawling expanse of the Golden State.

Golden State Indeed

As we settled in, I refocused on building my real estate business. Soon after we arrived in Los Angeles, I connected with Leon Vahn through John Costin, a common friend and lawyer in Montreal. Leon was a handsome bachelor in his mid-thirties who had also just arrived in Los Angeles with the similar ambition to start his own business. I asked him if he wanted to go into some investment properties together. He had been employed at Xerox in

Montreal and had the motivation to escape salary and employers.

Leon was born in Shanghai, China, after his parents had fled Russia in the chaos of the 1917 Bolshevik revolution. He grew up in luxury in Shanghai, where his father was a successful banker. But after Mao Zedong and his Communist Party took over China in 1947, the family lost everything. So they packed up and moved to Yokohama, Japan, and then to Calgary, Alberta, before settling in Montreal in 1955. We didn't know each other in Canada, but I was happy to meet him now. He, too, had worried about the French-separatist movement in Quebec and decided Los Angeles was the right place to be. We became good friends as we shared many values, work ethics and, specifically, goals of establishing ourselves financially.

Leon started looking in the newspaper for properties and quickly spotted a four-line ad in the *Los Angeles Times* for a six-unit apartment building for sale at 321 Palm Drive in Beverly Hills. The building already had a white slip, which meant it had been approved for individual sale as condominiums. The owner was asking $800,000 ($135,000 per unit).

"It's too much," Leon said. "I don't think it's a good deal. I'm not comfortable with this; we may lose money."

"I agree that it seems like a lot of money," I replied. "But if we do some cosmetic fixes and dress the place up, I think we'll be able to increase the value and get buyers. And even if we break even, it will be an opportunity to get our feet wet and learn the market," I assured him. Over the years, I had accumulated enough real estate experience to sense what might be a good deal and what might not. The trick is to correctly identify the difference between taking a risk and taking a gamble.

In this case, the property was in an excellent location in Beverly Hills, and the effects of the 1973 recession were finally fading. People seemed buoyant, optimistic, and ready to buy. The odds

*I partnered with Leon Vahn to convert the apartments at
321 Palm Drive in Beverly Hills into condos.*

were with us. I was confident that this building in Beverly Hills was
a calculated risk, not a gamble.

"I don't have enough money," Leon said.

"I will lend you what you need to go fifty-fifty."

He smiled and nodded in agreement. We went for it.

We spent some time and money fixing the building up. I
dealt with the market survey and sales prices, while Leon made
impeccable choices to make the place look excellent. New carpets,
new appliances, an updated elevator, and a fancy lobby; we made it
fit the Beverly Hills scene. We understood what people wanted to
see and knew how to attract the customer we were looking for. We
created a glossy, full-color brochure to entice high-end buyers.

When I started walking around in the markets of Santa
Monica, I saw how it all worked. American pricing was wide open.
The Brentwood Country Mart priced figs at $1.69, while you could

buy the same figs in a less fancy market for $0.39. There was no such thing as a set price, like I was used to in Canada. Here, vendors set the price according to the target audience. One customer was willing to pay for convenience and presentation, while another customer wanted to save. Both were viable targets. If we tailored our presentation to suit the exact audience we were looking for, they would be willing to pay the extra price.

Our timing was perfect. The Shah of Iran had recently been deposed, and tens of thousands of Iranians had come to Los Angeles, many of whom were well off. When they started buying real estate, Beverly Hills was their location of choice. Within six months we sold every unit. We asked for about double the price per unit it had cost us, leaving plenty of room to bargain down. We ended up making so much money on the property that I actually felt guilty.

"Wow," I thought to myself, "Los Angeles is really something." I had never made that kind of money in such a short period of time in my life. It was quite an encouraging introduction to the California real estate market.

Leon and I have stayed friends for 40 years. (2018)

And through the process I made one of my best friends and business partners. Leon would come over for Shabbat and holidays, bringing along various girlfriends to relax and laugh with us at dinner. He got along well with everyone and became like a member of our family.

Not long after we finished up with the Palm Drive project, I was offered a twenty-three-unit building in North Hollywood that was also approved for conversion to condos. I asked Leon to join in, but he wasn't interested. After our first success he wanted to stick with premium locations like Beverly Hills, and the Valley was considered a middle-class suburb. I decided to go for it alone.

I took out a loan and purchased the building at 12014 Kling Street. This was in the late 1970s, the Carter era, when interest and inflation were absurdly high. I went to State Savings Bank and met with Art Lucier, a vice president of consumer lending. The interest rates were ridiculous: 21 percent interest per annum, plus additional points and lending fees. And part of the deal was that I had to keep some of the money I borrowed in a savings account at his bank, with very little interest on the account.

I invested a lot of money fixing the building up to make it modern. I installed air conditioning in every unit and updated all the old appliances and decor before I started selling off the units. Within eight short months, I sold enough units to pay back the loan. When I tallied up all the interest and fees I had to pay, the actual interest rate came out to 43 percent per annum. "I don't know about you," I told Lucier, "but I'm pretty happy. I know you made your 43 percent, but without you I would not have made much more than that." Another calculated risk had paid off.

After I finished with the Kling Street project, the same owner was selling another twenty-three-unit apartment building on Coldwater Canyon Avenue near the 101 Freeway. I borrowed money at a better rate from Toronto-Dominion Bank and invited

*I partnered with friends from Montreal to buy the building
at 4660 Coldwater Canyon Avenue in Studio City.*

my friends from Montreal, Harone Kattan and Andrew and Steve
Gaty, to join me. All were real estate experts and could see the
potential.

Unlike previous properties, this building was not yet approved for conversion to condos. To be able to sell the individual
units, I had to hire an experienced surveyor to request a white slip,
the permit from the city to allow the change from an apartment
building to condominiums. It took over a year to get the permit, so
I started fixing up the building in the meantime.

This was a precarious time for real estate in America. Due to
the still-soaring interest rates, the banks' prime rate was around 15
percent. The interest rate was so high that individuals weren't buying, and because of rent control policies that limited their return,
investors could not justify buying, either. Many people who had
expanded their holdings too quickly were having difficulty paying
back their loans and were losing their properties. Some building
owners went broke. I knew that once I got the white paper, I would
have to be creative to sell the condos quickly.

Luckily I had faced reluctant buyers before and had

succeeded in changing their minds. I had learned what motivated buyers in America: People wanted to feel like they were getting a deal—a discount or something free thrown in. They wanted to feel like their purchase gained them entry into an exclusive group (like Ruby's "north of Montana"), and they wanted to feel like the seller really felt connected to them and cared about them.

I set up an office in the building and sat down with each of the current tenants.

"I have a permit to sell your apartment as a condominium for $110,000," I started, "but I want to offer you an attractive deal as a current tenant to stay here that will eventually cost you less than you are currently paying for rent." That got their attention. "Right now, a two-bedroom goes for $900 a month," I said. "Instead of $900, I will ask you to pay me $1,000. For the additional $100 a month, I will give you the option to buy your condo within a year. If you decide to buy, I will give back one year's worth of paid rent ($12,000) to serve as part of your down payment."

At first, the tenants looked at me like I was crazy. How was raising the price by $100 an opportunity for them? I explained how it was actually a good deal. If they opted not to buy, they would be out $1,200 in additional rent and might be forced to move if a potential buyer came along. If they opted to buy, they would have already put in $12,000 as part of the down payment. Plus, they were already living in the unit, so they knew what they were getting.

I also explained that if they exercised the option to buy, they could deduct the mortgage interest and property taxes from their income tax, effectively reducing the price per month to less than they were currently paying for rent. In the 1980s, income tax rates were as high as 70 percent, making tax deductions critical.

"When you put all this together," I told them, "it ends up being cheaper to buy than to rent. Plus, there is the potential in-crease in the value of the condo going into the future."

My approach ticked off all the boxes: a discount, an exclusive offer, and my personal attention to their well-being.

I worked day and night, thinking about nothing but fixing up the building and filling it up. I rented every condo and chose people who looked like good prospects who would qualify for a mortgage. While others in the real estate market were losing their shirt and pants, I found a way to make it happen. I put all my eggs into one basket, and I watched that basket until all those chicks hatched. In time, all the tenants except one exercised his right to buy. Again I was able to quickly pay off my high-interest loan and make a great return on my investment.

I bought one more building in the Valley in 1983, also with Harone and the Gaty brothers. This time, it was an office building at the intersection of Coldwater Canyon Avenue and Victory Boulevard, only about ten blocks from the last endeavor. It was a terribly mismanaged property that needed a lot of maintenance, and I knew I would have to work extra hard to fix this one up. But after my calculations, I felt it was still economically viable. The value of real estate is not the brick and mortar but the income it generates.

I ran my business from 6442 Coldwater Canyon Ave.,
an office building my partners and I purchased in 1983.

I knew that owning property out of town was risky, but AP Parts in Toledo, Ohio, turned out to be a good investment.

Luck was with me again when, two years later, construction started on the new, state-of-the-art Century Theatre next door. The owners were obliged to add an additional two floors to the parking garage, which provided ample free parking for the surrounding offices and brought more traffic to the area, increasing the value of the property I had just purchased. I moved my office into a first-floor unit and started to run my business from there.

I was always on the lookout for the next lucrative investment, once I felt my current investment was stable enough for me to put my attention into a new prospect. In 1984 I was unexpectedly given the chance to diversify with an out-of-town proposition. When Ron Bekker, the nephew of my old law school friend Jacob Bar-On, moved to Montreal in the mid-seventies, Joe Azar and I had accommodated him in an apartment at Chateau Lincoln. Ron ended up working with a schoolmate of his, Ezra Harel, and Ron introduced us. Ezra now lived in New York, and he really knew how to finagle a deal; he did not have any money, but somehow he could buy property by getting other investors to take him on as a partner. I had sold Ezra one of my condos on Kling Street as an investment, and we got along well.

Ezra owned AP Parts—the exclusive supplier of GM truck mufflers—and wanted to raise cash by selling the corporate headquarters, a six-story building in Toledo, Ohio. I decided to purchase the building with Harone and the Gatys.

From my experience as a certified property manager, I knew well that owning out-of-town-property could be risky, and since the owner was not on site, building mismanagement could become an issue. To avoid this problem, I organized a triple-net lease agreement with Ezra. In this plan he would continue using the building for his company headquarters and paying the net rent going forward and would also be responsible for paying the taxes, insurance, and building maintenance. It was a win for everyone: Ezra got his money, and we didn't have to worry about the renting and management because, with AP Parts the only active tenant, Ezra was likely to manage the building well.

But a few months after our purchase, the labor union, United Automobile Workers, at AP Parts went on strike. Under these conditions, I felt nervous about the company's ability to continue paying the rent. Only nine months after my purchase, I decided to sell. I put a small ad in the *Wall Street Journal* and sold the building within a month. Again, my partners and I split a huge profit.

Success came with a new problem—this time, one that I was happy to have. I was earning quite a bit, but that amount of money was taxable at a rate of about 70 percent. By the time the government was finished with me, I would have had only 30 percent of the earnings left. I began to look for ways to delay paying taxes and I found that the best legal option was a deferred-tax pension fund. I could put 100 percent of my pretax profits into the pension fund and let it grow till retirement. I could also invest this money without paying taxes to generate more income. I would only pay taxes when I started to withdraw from the fund at retirement.

But one can only put a limited amount into the fund per year, and my profits exceeded that limit. I found a way around that as well. Since my corporation's fiscal year ended in October, I would put in the maximum amount then and the maximum amount a month later, in November, which was during the next fiscal year but within the same calendar year. In this way, I contributed double the usual limit in a single tax year. Instead of keeping 30 percent of the profit, I got to keep nearly 100 percent by tucking it away for the future. As the saying goes, the fruit becomes sweeter for those willing to wait until it ripens.

Everything I did was according to the law. I paid my fair share of personal taxes every year so I could sleep at night, and the one time in my career the IRS audited me, it was because of a clerical error and was totally cleared.

While everything was great at home, my extended family was dealing with a terrible mess. Back in Israel, Yaakub had slowly lost all his teeth and couldn't chew anymore. In 1987 I got a call from Nissim Kadir, Yaakub's lawyer, in a panic; he was at Yaakub's house, and something was wrong. By the time he got Yaakub to the hospital, Yaakub had died. He was about sixty years old.

I went to Israel to try to settle the estate, but I could see things were complicated. First, there was the house at Rechov Hasneh 5, where my parents and Yaakub had lived since 1952. We all agreed we needed to sell this house, but it was attached to another house, and we had to sell the property as one unit. After I met with the neighbor a few times, he finally agreed to put it on the market. Soon after we sold, a developer came in and demolished the house to put up an apartment building. The proceeds from the house were divided among the remaining five siblings and Shumail's son, Freddie. When I was cleaning out the house I found some bearer bonds among the piles of paper and added those to the estate to be divided among us.

The situation with the building at Ben Yehuda 5 was different. Shumail had owned 49 percent of the building, which Freddie took over after he passed. Yaakub had inherited my father's 51 percent, which was to be divided six ways: among Elisha, Marcelle, Eliyahoo, me, Nory, and Freddie (who took over his mother's portion). But to protect himself from losing the property, Freddie, with the help of the lawyer, Kadir, carefully orchestrated it so that the five siblings could not sell their portions to anyone but Freddie.

After ten years of Freddie managing the building, we all wanted to sell, but he refused to buy our shares at market value and refused to sell the building to a third party. My niece Myrna finally suggested we get a lawyer, since most of us were far away in Canada. I eventually went to court in Israel to testify to the facts of the story, and the judge ruled in our favor: Freddie either had to sell the building on the open market or buy our shares at market value. But Freddie refused to accept the judgment and threatened to appeal.

The experience was excruciating. It was costing us a fortune to fight and, even worse, it was ripping the family apart. After it dragged on for a few years, we couldn't take it anymore, and around the year 2000 we all agreed to sell our shares to Freddie at an absurdly below-market price.

The whole ordeal was miserable and gave me more bitterness than any other business experience in my life. Now I was just happy it was over. I had tried to stay calm throughout the affair through yoga, meditation, gardening, and jogging. We all were relieved to be done with it, but scars from the episode lingered, and my personal relationships with Marcelle, Myrna, and Nory suffered as a result of that ridiculous battle.

The Fruits of My Labor

Through all the ups and downs in Los Angeles, Ruby and I had become involved in the community. I joined the board at Kahal Joseph Congregation. Ruby became the treasurer for the sisterhood, volunteered for the United Jewish Fund's Sephardic Division, was active socially at our local YWCA, and worked out almost every day. She also decided that, since the kids were now older, she wanted to go back to work and took a job at a jewelry store in Santa Monica. I was hesitant about having my wife work, but it turned out to be a positive and enjoyable activity for her, and she was quite good at it. It even provided Lisa with a high school summer job of stringing pearls for customers.

Ruby and I also joined a *chavurah* (Jewish fellowship) focused on marriage enrichment. Members would meet at each other's homes, and the host couple would present a topic for discussion—it might be about house duties, kids, communication, sickness, or even minor annoyances The discussion would be followed by expressions of appreciation for one another's caring and understanding. For every issue, some people had questions and others had answers. The *chavurah* was an exercise in listening and thinking, prioritizing the real issue at hand, and accepting that there are many routes to address the same problem. Participating helped Ruby and me become closer and understand how to better deal with personal conflict and to compromise; by improving our relationship, it became easier and more pleasurable to spend time together. And we made good friends in the process (especially Sam and Doris Engleman).

As always, travel remained one of our favorite ways to spend time together. In addition to our continued international travels with the IREF, we also traveled with the family. In 1984 I took the family, with the exception of Lisa (who couldn't get away from her studies at the University of Pennsylvania), on another trip to Israel for the wedding of my brother Nory's son, Michael. He was devout, so men and women were separated during the ceremony, the meal, and the dancing. I had never been to such an Orthodox event, and it was a unique experience for all of us. I took advantage of the occasion to show Jeff and Sharon Israel from north to south: We went to the Sea of Galilee and Safed, the center of Jewish mysticism, and we traveled through the Negev Desert all the way to Eilat.

The next year I made it back to Israel and Egypt with Lisa, who was then twenty-two. It was the first time I had taken a trip alone with Lisa, and it was a special bonding experience in our relationship. Besides viewing Egypt's historic pyramids and mummies, she could see how people were jumping through the windows of buses for seats, just like I had experienced as a boy in Baghdad. For lunch, we ate pigeon while looking down on the Nile River from the Cairo Tower.

Nineteen eighty-six brought Ruby, the kids, and me back to London to attend the double wedding of Ruby's nephews, Colin and David, followed by a well-organized trip to Scotland with her sister, Eliza, and Eliza's family. We even went to Loch Lomond and to Loch Ness, where we did some hunting for the mythical Loch Ness Monster.

In 1988, Ruby and I went on an African safari with Meir and Odette Saltoun, friends we had met on a trip to Australia. The two of us started in Johannesburg, South Africa, where we took the Blue Train, an overnight luxury liner like the Orient Express, savoring a seven-course meal accompanied by champagne and what seemed like dozens of forks and knives as we made our way to Cape Town. After a week in Cape Town, we flew to Zimbabwe to see the largest waterfall in the world, Victoria Falls, before meeting the Saltouns in the capital of Harare.

From Harare the four of us flew to Nairobi, Kenya, and drove to the Ngorongoro Crater in Tanzania, an extraordinary caldera full

We offered Sharon, Lisa, and Jeff guidance, but not pressure, as they moved into adulthood in the early 1980s.

of wildlife. We lodged on the rim of the crater and took jeeps down into the valley where elephants, rhinos, hippos, giraffes, and zebras roamed freely. We took pictures of birds in the sky, crocodiles in the river, and monkeys all over our car! In an intense moment, we videotaped three lionesses circle a wildebeest near a watering hole. Somehow, the lucky wildebeest was able to outrun them, and the poor lions remained hungry.

Back on the home front, our kids were growing into young adults. Ruby and I decided that once they turned twenty-one, we would let them make their own choices and learn from their own mistakes. We had done our fair share of forceful suggestions when they were growing up, and now that they were of age, we didn't want to pressure them to take one path or another. We wanted to let them discover what worked in their own lives.

In 1979 Sharon had transferred from USC to UCLA to study psychology. She graduated with a bachelor's degree in 1981 and moved to Cape Cod to work in a residential facility the following year. After gaining work experience there, Sharon went to Utah to ski while supporting herself with a job as a waitress at the Goldminer's Daughter ski resort, which we had visited as a family in 1979. When the snow melted, she came back to Los Angeles and found a job with Bentley Industries, a marketing company for corporate branding of knickknacks and gifts.

While working there, Sharon met and fell in love with Keith, and they married in 1987. This, of course, was a perfect excuse for us to have another family adventure. After the wedding, we hired a tour company and took a bus trip from Los Angeles to San Francisco. It became a real family reunion with Marcelle and Sasson, Nory, Elisha and Valentine, and their children from Montreal; and Ruby's brothers, Alex, Victor, and Eze, along with their spouses, from Ottawa and London. It was a wonderful trip and a great opportunity for us all to be together.

We took the kids to one of our favorite spots from our honeymoon: Point Joe!
(1987)

Before we knew it, Sharon was starting graduate school at the California School of Professional Psychology, where she became a teaching assistant for classes in statistics. Five years later, in 1989, she received her PhD in psychology. She was our first child to earn a doctorate, and my heart was filled with pride and elation. I couldn't help but think back to my own dream of higher education and was happy that I was able to give that opportunity to my kids. Immediately after graduating, Sharon secured her first job as a psychologist, working at the Veterans Administration in downtown LA.

Lisa graduated from UCLA in 1984 and first pursued becoming a commercial photographer. Eventually, she decided to be a medical doctor. She moved to Philadelphia to take her premed requirements at the University of Pennsylvania and, after some traveling in Europe and Southeast Asia, returned to Los Angeles

EGBOK (Everything is Going to Be OK) Bus Tour (August 25, 1991)
Standing left to right: Victor & Thelma Isaac, Eze Moses,
Morris & Flo Shamash, Rachel Gher, Charles Samuel, Rachel Jacob,
Joyce Isaac, Doris Shukur, Eze Isaac, Sasson & Marcelle Ovadia,
Sass Khazzam, Julius Baran, Grace Khazzam, Alex Stenson, Ruby Samuels,
Rachel Shamash, Eliza Moses, Lulu Jason (partially hidden), Nory Samuel,
Ahuva Sasson, Eliyahoo Sasson, Sharon & Keith Jablon, and baby
Elana Jablon (Halawa Baklawa) Sitting left to right: Jeff Samuels,
Charlie Khazzam, Eli Samuel, David Samuel, Dorit Shmueli, Joe Faraj,
Margaret Baran, Aviva Shmueli, Myrna Junowicz, Val Samuel,
Ann Stenson, Kora & Lenor Junowicz, Benedicte Bossut,
Nadine Faraj, and Joe Samuels

*I, with my siblings Elisha, Eliyahoo, Nory, and Marcelle,
had come a long way from Taht Al Takia. (1991)*

to start medical school at UC Irvine in 1988. I was proud to see her learning and happy to know I had bequeathed her with the travel bug as well.

While Lisa was working toward her medical degree, she married Glenn Benest, whom she met through Jeff. Glenn came from a Lebanese Jewish family, and he and I got along great. For their wedding adventure in 1991, I took the trip planning into my own hands and organized the Samuels Family "Everything Is Going To Be OK" Bus Tour, or EGBOK Tour for short.

There were forty-three of us—thirty-eight family members and five friends. My cousin and friend, Aboudi Meir, was too sick to come, but his wife, Aviva, and daughter, Dorit, came from Israel. Eliyahoo and Ahuva also made the long trip from Israel. The last time Eliyahoo had visited was for Jeff's bar mitzvah in 1978 in Montreal, and it meant so much to me that he made the effort to join us in Los Angeles. Elisha and Valentine and their two children came. Nory was there, of course, and Marcelle and Sasson, along with their daughters, Myrna and Yudit. We had Ruby's entire family: Alex and Ann from Ottawa; Victor, Thelma, Eze, and Joyce from London; and Eliza and Eze from Montreal. Ruby and I each had three brothers and a sister in attendance.

I hired a private tour bus, and we set out on an eight-day adventure. I had planned our itinerary meticulously and designated a committee to prepare all the food so that we were ready for picnics along the way. We started every morning by reciting the "Daily Inspiration" and holding a Dumb Joke of the Day competition, complete with gag prizes like farting pillows and pills to cure bald heads. Above all, we enjoyed being together and seeing the unbelievable scenery God had created on the western coast of the United States.

Daily Inspiration

This is the day the Lord has created
To rejoice and be happy at it.
Day by day and in every way,
I feel better and better and better.
I feel fine, I feel wonderful and I feel terrific.
Oh what a beautiful morning,
Oh what a beautiful day,
I have this wonderful feeling
Something is going my way, my way.
And the start of a beautiful day.

From LA we drove to Las Vegas to see the unique shows and gamble for a couple of nights before driving through the mountains of Zion National Park and spending a day at Bryce Canyon to enjoy

*Our EGBOK Tour, commemorated in this scrapbook page,
brought together 38 family members and five friends.*

the striking red hoodoo rock formations. We then headed south to hike for two days in the awe-inspiring vastness of the Grand Canyon and continued to work our way down to the pristine nature of Scottsdale, Arizona, before heading back to Palm Springs for a bathing suit competition and a night of dancing to a great trip's end.

What a time we all had! I really wanted everyone to be together and had worked hard to make it happen. Family always meant a lot to me, and I was grateful to have this opportunity to see everyone at once, especially my remaining brothers and sister.

Soon after the wedding and EGBOK Tour, Lisa began her internship at the UCLA internal medicine department. Just one year later, she was offered an unexpected opportunity at New York Medical College for a residency in dermatology. When she accepted the position, she had only four days to move to New York; fortunately, Glenn agreed to rent out his condo in Santa Monica and forego his screenwriting instructor job in LA to join her. I contacted Ezra

Harel in Israel, who offered his condo in Manhattan. Lisa stayed in his fancy place on Broadway and 73rd Street for a few weeks until she was able to find a suitable place for herself and Glenn in Yonkers.

While Lisa and Glenn were in New York, I tried to rent out their condo in Santa Monica, which Glenn had purchased before they were married. But their unit was in a converted apartment building, and because of rent control I could only get about a third of what they were paying in monthly mortgage payments. Selling it made no sense. We were in a recession, and market prices were so low they wouldn't be able to ask enough to allow them to pay off the mortgage. So rather than continuing to pay mortgage on the vacant condo, or dipping into their own funds to supplement the pathetic current market value, I advised them to walk away. They would lose the equity, but they wouldn't have to come up with the money to pay off the mortgage. It was a tough decision for Glenn, who had left both his job and his home to move to New York, but in the end he took my advice.

Jeff graduated high school in 1983—much to our delight, because he had struggled through school. We didn't pressure him to go to college, and he decided to move to Colorado to become a ski instructor. He did well at it; I went to visit him once and could see the students really loved him. But after a year, he decided to come back to Los Angeles and asked to work with me in the real estate business. I was overjoyed with the idea and couldn't wait to start his training.

The Hardest Decision in My Life

I grew up in a culture that rarely allowed women to be part of business and never looked at women as equals. Some of those prejudices against women stayed ingrained in me for too long. For that reason, I never even thought about bringing Sharon or Lisa into my business. I supported them both throughout graduate school, and when they started their careers I was immensely proud of their achievements and happy to be proved wrong in my assumptions about women. But for most of my professional life, I had dreamed about bringing my son into my business. I imagined the scenario many times, thinking up names for our future partnership—Samuels and Son Real Estate, or maybe Samuels and Samuels Real Estate. So I was thrilled when Jeff asked if he could come work with me in 1984, when he was nineteen years old.

Initially, he spent some time in the office building on Victory Boulevard to learn about property management. In 1985 I gave him his first assignment—to find properties to buy. I instructed him to comb through the classified ads in the newspapers every day to look for office buildings, commercial spaces, or industrial properties for sale and bring me anything he thought might be a potential prospect.

Every week he came to me with five to ten leads. And every week I said, "No. No. No. No," and explained why. I wanted to show him how to find something with real potential and pointed out what was wrong with the properties he brought me so he would learn how to find investments with upgrade potential. I sat down with him to identify various problems with properties—mismanagement, vacancy, neglect—that might signify that a prospect has potential for enhancement and, thus, an increase in value. Each time something seemed reasonable, I recommended he go visit and report back about the location, the condition, comparable properties, and the accuracy of the advertisement. I paid him a salary, but I told him there was a nice bonus if he brought something that was a good investment.

After a few months of trial and error, Jeff brought me information on a property on 6th and Harvard streets, in the

Mid-Wilshire-Koreatown area just west of downtown. It was a six-story, sixty-five-thousand-square-foot office building right across the street from the Wilshire Boulevard Temple. The property was in bad shape, and the management team was located in San Francisco. Only 15 percent of the building was rented out. On top of that, the owners had a high mortgage rate at 12 percent. Under these conditions, the owners were in serious trouble if they didn't get out soon.

I called my usual partners, Harone Kattan and the Gaty brothers. They approved of the purchase over the phone at my recommendation. Joe Azar was living in Houston at the time, but he wasn't happy there and was not doing well in his real estate ventures. He had come to Los Angeles for a few months to help me with the purchase of the Toledo property and management of the Victory building, where my office used to be. He was in LA when Jeff found the 6th Street property, and I invited him to get involved. That ended up giving him and Evelyn a good excuse to move to Los Angeles.

Together, we prepared a bid far below the projected value. In terms of the cash equity required, Harone invested one-third, the Gatys invested one-third, and Joe and I split one-third. In addition, Joe and I would be the general partners, which meant we would manage the building for 33 percent of the final profit. The remaining 67 percent would be divided among the five of us.

But before I entered into another partnership with Joe, I had to have a talk with him. In our last venture in Montreal, Chateau Lincoln, we had nearly lost everything, and I still remembered our bad experience with the textile company. Joe was an engineer—he was trustworthy, smart, and analytical; he worked hard; and he was my best friend. But he didn't always have the best business sense. I needed to set up some parameters.

"Joe," I told him, "I respect you, and I value your friendship and your talent. I will always listen to you and hear your opinion. But if we can't agree on something about the building, I will have the final word."

I knew it sounded harsh, but I needed to be clear so that we could continue in both our friendship and our partnership. Joe readily agreed.

"I know you have a better business head, and I will go along with these terms," he said. In our long-continuing partnership, I only had to exercise that veto power once.

To clean up the legal matters, I made a new contact that would stay with me for a long time: David Miller, a lawyer at Greenberg Glusker, joined the team. From the beginning, I had a good feeling about him. Not only was he a knowledgeable real estate lawyer, but he was a good listener and had a practical business sense that would help to protect our interests.

We acquired the funds and purchased the building at 3727 6th Street in December 1985. We set up an office there and worked like crazy. Rather than pay a premium and hire a general contractor, Joe organized subcontractors—specialized workers and professionals to do sheetrock, electrical, carpentry, and plumbing—which drastically cut down our costs and time. He was a master supervisor in this regard and kept everything moving ahead of schedule. While he worked on the daily progress of designing our renovations, I focused on the areas that I was stronger in—administration, rentals, and marketing.

We reformatted the existing units in ways that made more sense for the modern office and upgraded the decor of the entire building. We modernized the elevators to increase speed and access and remodeled the front and lobby to create an impressive entrance, with vibrant bougainvillea climbing up the outer walls. We put a sign out front, with the magic words:

$AVE! $AVE! $AVE!

Office space built to suit.

Management on Site.

Beat the Market!

If a potential tenant came in, I wouldn't let him leave until we had a deal. Let's say we were asking $1,000 a month for an office suite, but the potential tenant only wanted to pay $700; I would offer him three months of free rent—two up front and one at the end—and we would close the deal. The place probably would have stayed empty for two months anyway, and now I had a tenant who would soon pay $1,000 a month. Once they were established, it was doubtful they would move out. When we acquired the property, we were losing about $1,200 a day. Within eight months of our purchase, we had rented enough space that we were breaking even. Within another six months, we almost had the space fully rented and were turning a substantial profit. The property turned out to provide a great income.

Jeff was delighted that we had bought the building and was

Jeff found the office building at 3727 6th Street — a stellar investment.

281

rewarded handsomely for his find. But while he was learning a lot, I could see he was developing an attitude of privilege; he was the boss's son, he had earned some money, and now he thought he had made it. He was buying stocks and spending money as if he were a professional, and I did not like the know-it-all way I heard him using to talk to coworkers and employees. They knew he lacked experience.

I realized that Jeff's personality was being overshadowed by my presence. With me there, he didn't have to struggle to find solutions; when he had a problem, he looked to me. I began to think that he needed to face life independently and learn to build his skills on his own if he was to grow into the astute businessman that I knew he could be. Not only would he learn different things than I could teach, but he would also gain the sense of pride that comes with succeeding and failing on his own terms. At the age of twenty-one, he needed to start owning his actions.

I was certain that was right for him, but my biggest struggle was with myself. Although I loved having my son around and had dreamed of working side by side with him for years, I knew the time had come to put that dream aside.

I first phrased it as a suggestion.

"Jeff, I think you really need to get yourself out there. I suggest that you go work for someone else for a year and see what it's like working in the real world, without the protection of the family. After that, we can apply all your learning here."

But Jeff was too comfortable and dismissed the idea. With his welfare in mind, I decided that I had to be firm.

"I love you," I said, "but I have to let you go. I am hurting you by sheltering you from the real world. You have much to learn and need to face the reality of life and struggle with it on your own."

This was the hardest decision in my life. It felt like I was a mother bird pushing her chick out of the nest to teach it to fly.

It was an uncomfortable situation, but I was confident in him and would be there if he fell. But Jeff did not take it well.

In July 1986, when we all went to London for the double wedding of Ruby's nephews, Jeff made a friend and decided they were going to go to the Far East together. He left from London and traveled for a full year, barely calling us at all. Sometimes we didn't know if he was alive.

We did unexpectedly get word of him that long year. While traveling in Thailand and Indonesia, Lisa was having dinner at a restaurant in Yogyakarta, on the Indonesian island of Java. Suddenly, she heard a familiar voice and turned around to find her brother! Neither had known the other was in the same country, let alone the same restaurant. We were delighted and thrilled to get word that Jeff was okay.

It was only at Sharon's wedding in the summer of 1987 that Jeff reappeared. He looked gaunt; while on a camel caravan in India, he had suffered from dysentery. But we were all happy to have him back.

Jeff had changed in Asia. He was no longer interested in just making money and having fun. He had become more spiritual, and you could see him thinking. He had seen poverty and had experienced responsibility. He had matured and learned some of the lessons he needed to appreciate life in his own way. He told us he was ready to go to college; Ruby and I were happy to hear it and to support him.

In January 1988, Jeff moved to San Francisco and started his studies at City College of San Francisco. He was riding the bus to his first day of school when he met a beautiful blonde from France and started speaking French with her. She was on her way to the college as well. It was love at first bus ride, and Jeff started saving her a seat every day. During the summers, in an attempt to be self-sufficient—another sign of his growing personal responsibility—he drove a cab to make money.

In 1990 Jeff transferred to UC Berkeley to complete his bachelor's degree in religious studies. We were thrilled that he was going to a top-tier college and was on a good path, and we saw that his girlfriend, Benedicte Bossut, was a good partner for him. She was hard-working, kind, caring, thoughtful, and uniquely able to keep Jeff focused.

After Jeff graduated from Berkeley in June 1992, he and Benedicte moved to Boulder, Colorado. Jeff started working on his master's degree, studying Buddhism and Asian cultures. One month later, he called to say that he and Benedicte were going to Boulder city hall to get married. I would have loved it if the two lovebirds had let us throw them a party, but they refused my offer and eloped.

CHAPTER 13

WHAT COMES NEXT

A New Generation

When my children were newborns, I was afraid to hold them so I never did. They seemed so fragile, so tiny, and I felt so inept. It was only when Elana was born in December 1990 and Sharon placed her four-day-old baby girl in my arms that I first felt what it meant to hold such a beautiful, delicate life in my own hands. It's a moment I will never forget. Ruby and I immediately loved being grandparents.

Rebecca was born four years later, while Lisa was in the middle of her dermatology residency at New York Medical College. We went to visit her in Yonkers quite often and couldn't get enough of our second grandchild. We took Lisa and Glenn to nice restaurants and babysat at their apartment so they could spend some alone time together. Ruby came equipped with ingredients for matzah ball soup, and I brought oranges and tangerines from our garden for Rebecca to enjoy.

Only twelve days after Rebecca was born, Sharon blessed us with Eden, her second daughter. Sharon had been working full-time as a psychologist at the Veterans Administration. But after Eden was born, she cut back on her hours there so she could have more time to be with her growing children. Her choice to reduce her hours at the VA, coupled with her desire to be more flexible with her work, led her to start taking tutoring more seriously. Sharon had enjoyed tutoring since she was a student at UCLA and found that there was a large market in preparing graduate students for their psychology-license exam.

She not only loved the work but also found that it was lucrative. She scaled back at the VA more and more, eventually reducing her time to one day a week, and began to build her group sessions into a business. Under the corporate name PsychPrep, she developed courses, guides, online packages, and audio programs to prepare graduates for the mandated psychology-license exam. She hired others to help and quickly built up her enterprise. I was proud of her entrepreneurial spirit and her willingness to take risks. She still runs the entire operation from her home on San Vicente Boulevard in West Hollywood. So much for my inherited doubts about women in business! My brilliant daughter had once again upended my deeply held prejudices.

Unfortunately, Sharon's relationship with Keith began to deteriorate. After having continuous arguments, Sharon and Keith decided to divorce in 2000, and it ultimately became her responsibility to raise her young ten- and six-year-old daughters. I convinced them to come to a mutual agreement without the stress and cost of divorce lawyers, and I believe this helped them avoid years of heartache and pain. We were sad about the situation, mostly for the grandchildren, but we knew it was for the best.

It was important to Sharon to give her girls a Jewish upbringing. She sent them to Gindi Maimonides Academy, a Jewish day school, and they continued to join us for a traditional Shabbat dinner every Friday night. Ruby always prepared scrumptious dinners of Iraqi specialties like chicken with rice and lentils and *kubba*, or Indian dishes like curries, *bhaji* (a fritter), and *kichri* (a rice and lentil dish). But for all the Iraqi and Indian fare she cooked up, the girls' greatest demand was for Grandma's matzah ball soup and her beef brisket.

Lisa and Glenn had moved back to Los Angeles in 1996, where Lisa worked in a dermatologist's office. After a few years of experience, she opened her own practice in Burbank in 1998.

However, Lisa and Glenn were going through some difficulties in their relationship as well. To smooth things out, a friend suggested they try Scientology. They did, but it could not help them avoid their mutually agreed-upon divorce in 2002. As with Sharon and Keith, we were sad to see the separation, but we were mostly worried about Rebecca. Luckily, Lisa and Glenn had a friendly breakup and agreed to share custody of Rebecca, who was eight at the time. Glenn and I kept up a good relationship as well, talking often and continuing to go out for dinner, which Lisa didn't mind. Glenn had lost his father when he was young, and he looked up to me as a father figure. Glenn was also the father of my granddaughter, and I wanted to maintain healthy relationships in their family and stimulate love in any way I could.

For me, it was a huge joy to have the three granddaughters together for Shabbat. After lighting the candles, the girls and I sang "Shalom Aleichem," welcoming the angels of peace, and "Eshet Chayil," a song for the women of valor from the book of Proverbs. Then we made kiddush and *hamotzi*. After dinner, I'd sit one on each knee and hold the other in my arms while singing *"Yom Hashabbat Ein Kamohu,"* tickling them all the way through. Having the family gather around to laugh and sing was a scene that was comfortable and familiar to me. I knew from my own experience that these were the moments that could bond a family for a lifetime and, I am happy to say, my granddaughters did indeed become close with each other.

From Boulder, Jeff and Benedicte moved on to the University of Virginia, where Jeff started on his PhD and Benedicte began her

287

master's in teaching. I encouraged them to buy a house instead of renting in the center of Charlottesville. In 1995 they bought a bungalow in Lake Monticello, a nearby suburb. Not only was it a wise investment, but they could also enjoy the privacy and intimacy of their own home. It was in Lake Monticello that Claire was born in early 1997.

Claire was the fourth member of a magical coincidence that had developed: each of my four granddaughters' birthdays was within just two weeks of the others, and they surrounded my own birthday on both sides. Elana was born December 26, 1990; Rebecca arrived on December 20, 1994; Eden joined us on January 1, 1995; and Claire was delivered on January 7, 1997. I was right in the middle of it all, December 31. When I chose December 31, I wanted to make up for lost birthdays—but I only expected one party, not five!

Following Claire's birth, Jeff spent a couple of years in Sri Lanka working on his PhD thesis, focused on the reasons children joined the Buddhist monastery to become monks. When I practiced transcendental meditation in Montreal, Jeff had often practiced with me, and this had possibly influenced his area of study. Ruby and I visited him and his family in Sri Lanka in 1999. We went hiking, toured many ancient temples, saw the tropical orchid gardens, and had a wonderful time. After completing his PhD in 2001, Jeff got multiple job offers and ended up taking an assistant professor position at Western Kentucky University in Bowling Green to teach Buddhism and ancient religions.

After he had worked for a few months, I encouraged him to buy a house. Benedicte also worked, and thanks to the affordable cost of housing in Bowling Green, they were able to buy a lovely and spacious four-bedroom home for only $120,000, which they still live in today. In 2006 Benedicte gave birth to Zach. Zach is not only the sole grandson, but he is also the only grandchild who is an

*We visited Jeff, Benedicte, and Claire in Sri Lanka, where Jeff
was researching Buddhist monastaries.(1999)*

Jeff and Benedict purchased a beautiful home in Bowling Green, Kentucky, when he got a job there as an assistant professor of religion and ethnography.

outlier to the December/January birthday tradition—he was born on March 9—but I love him just as much.

When Jeff's next-door neighbors moved and the house went up for sale, I advised him to buy it and rent it out. Since then, he has bought several other investment properties in Bowling Green, which provide him with a nice supplement to his university salary. Over the years, Jeff has become good at spotting a profitable investment.

A few years ago, Jeff and Benedicte bought a property for Benedicte to fulfill her dream of creating her own Montessori school. She had opened a school a few years earlier but was renting space for classrooms. With a secure location, her passion, and her leadership as principal, the school has grown from just a few students to a full-scale elementary school. Zach attended, and if the other students are as smart as him, Benedicte is definitely doing something right.

My dream of education, one that I never had the opportunity to realize myself, has been fulfilled by each of my three children. I am now the proud father of three doctors—two PhDs and one

Benedicte opened a Montessori School in this building they purchased in Kentucky.

MD—and nothing has provided me more satisfaction. Between Sharon's psychology, Lisa's dermatology, and Jeff's spiritualty, they continue to fulfill our balance of mind, body, and soul.

And having four incredible granddaughters in addition to my two brilliant and successful daughters has finally allowed me to consciously combat my cultural prejudice against girls. This unfortunate bias had been ingrained in me since I was a child and affected me when we had two girls as our firstborns. In Baghdad, having a baby girl was not a reason to celebrate; only a boy was. Boys were supposed to support the family and carry on the name. But my own experience with Lisa and Sharon proved to me that girls are just as good as, and often better than, boys. They are smart, accomplished, caring, thoughtful, and passionate. I would not trade my daughters or granddaughters for any boys in the world. I not only love them, but I respect and admire them. I know my family doesn't always agree with my opinions on women and other subjects—we have some heated arguments—but I have come a long way from my Iraqi upbringing.

All Sales Final

Becoming a grandfather convinced me it was time to take it easy and continue to travel while I had my health and my love of exploration. I still had many places on my bucket list. But first, there were a few last deals to put into place.

In 1993, Leon Vahn came to me with an investment proposal. He had an acquaintance, John Webb, who could go in with us as an on-site partner and manager of a sixty-thousand-square-foot office building in the Denver area.

In the past, I had been in charge of every aspect of development—acquisition, building, renovation, rentals, and management. This time, I would invest as a limited partner and be available for consultations or to offer my experience if asked, but I would keep my hands out of the day-to-day operations. I was ready to leave the reins to Leon and John. My investment came entirely from my pension fund, so any future gains would not be immediately taxable but would be available for more investing.

At the time of purchase, the building was almost completely empty. The price we paid—$1.1 million—was a real bargain: less than $20 per square foot and less than 20 percent of the cost of building a similar structure from the ground up. This was during the recession of the 1990s, and prices were down. The property had been repossessed by an insurance company for nonpayment of mortgage, but insurance companies aren't in the business of building management, and they wanted to get rid of it. With hands-on management, we knew that we could turn it around and that there was a serious profit waiting if we did. Jeff was living nearby in Boulder, and I invited him to use his savings to invest.

We went into action, just as we did with the property on 6th Street. Our team immediately began major improvements inside and out and, one office at a time, they filled the building. John proved to be a smart, honest businessman and was an exceptionally good property manager. He oversaw daily needs and was responsible for negotiating deals with tenants and working on the renovations.

Within a year, our investment was already providing a handsome income, which paid for the mortgage and operations. Seeing the obvious success unfold, we bought the property next door, which had been built by the same builders in the same style. The following year, after refinancing the loan on our first building, we bought a third.

While the recession worked in our favor for the Denver investments, we didn't have the same luck with our 6th Street building. The market in LA was tough, and we were having trouble with vacancies and high rates of interest. We tried to make a deal with our lender to reduce the interest rate of the loan, but with no luck.

We had acquired the building on a deal known as a land lease, where we purchased the right to generate income from the building on the land but didn't actually own the land itself. We paid a percentage of the rental income plus an annual fee to the landowner, Northwestern Mutual, and at the end of the lease term the building would revert back to the landowner. We purchased the lease with thirty years remaining on it and from 1986 to 1994 earned a nice income from the property. But in 1994, it was no longer worth it. We negotiated with the bank and came to the agreement that they would take ownership of the lease as payment for the remainder of the loan. In a sense, we would sell the building to the bank. As with Chateau Lincoln, I made sure that I would not have a default on my record.

I refused to let this market mishap dampen my spirit. Reaching this level of optimism was not necessarily natural for me; when I was growing up in Iraq, I never got positive feedback from my parents or Shumail. No one ever told me I did a good job, or that I had talent, or that I was good at anything. Instead of praise, I received criticism; as a result, my natural reaction was to be hard on myself. If I gave a talk or sealed a deal, I always picked on myself afterward about what I could have done better, even if everyone congratulated me on doing such a good job. When I missed a good deal or got myself into a bad one, I had to fight the instinct to second-guess myself.

It actually took work with a psychologist to learn to give myself enough credit. I had to be taught the healthy way to do a postmortem and how to accept what was in my control and what was out of my control—to accept that the actions of the past cannot be undone, to understand where I had excelled, and to determine what I could do better the next time. By this point, I had been through enough of these tough situations to successfully put these theories into practice. While I was disappointed about the 6th Street building, I did not let its failure get me down.

With my mind clear, I spotted the next opportunity immediately. Northwestern Mutual, the insurance company that owned the land for the 6th Street building, wanted to sell. So before we gave up the lease on the building, I purchased the land for $600,000. This was mostly a deal for family and friends, including my brother Elisha, Joe Azar, Ezra Harel, and our attorney, David Miller (who by this point was a great friend). I owned the majority share of the land, and I gave each of my kids the chance to purchase 5 percent of that.

The bank sold the building lease at auction, and the new tenants would now pay the rent and annual fees to us. I could have won the auction and purchased the building lease again, but I had no interest in running the property anymore; I was ready to slow down, and the passive income we could collect from owning the land was enough for me.

In 1994, at sixty-four years old, I was done with showing

up every day at 9 a.m., done with responding to complaints from tenants, done with making decisions about the building, and done being involved in the operations and rentals. Now I owned the land instead.

Over the years, I kept an eye on our investment properties in Denver, and in 2007 we sold the land on 6th Street for nearly six times what we had bought it for.

The good life was about to get even better.

Celebrating Life

With a lifetime of work behind me, I began to focus on the many opportunities that lay ahead. One of the biggest blessings in my life has been my diverse interests and my insatiable desire to learn new things, meet new people, and improve myself. In a way, I was made for this time of life. I could hardly consider it retirement, because I loved doing what I did. I see many who work until retirement, then stop doing everything altogether. Unlike this traditional picture, I was ready to take classes, continue with my hobbies, seek out new adventures, share my knowledge with others, and enjoy the blessings of my family.

And, of course, travel. Every time I travel, I'm grateful to my dear mother for taking me on that trip to Mosul at the age of eight. I can still remember the vast scenery zooming by as I leaned my face out of the open train window, hearing the sounds of vendors shouting, "Hot chai! Baklava! Laffa! Namlet [soda pop]!" I snuck away from my seat to stand by the door, which had a larger window. For much of that 250-mile train ride between Baghdad and Mosul, I stood there watching the rivers, the mountains, the flatlands, and the people. I knew then that I wanted to see everything this vast world had to offer.

I have had some memorable trips over the years. By this

In our world travels, we visited The Grand Canyon (1991), the Himalayas (1999), and the Western Wall in Jerusalem, with Eliyahoo (1991).

writing in 2019, I have been in every state across the U.S. I have traveled to 104 countries, including Uzbekistan, New Zealand, South Africa, Dubai, Myanmar, China, Australia, Nepal, Argentina, Lebanon, and nearly all of Europe, stepping foot on each of the seven continents along the way.

In 1994, following the collapse of the Soviet Union and the opening up of the Communist countries, Ruby and I went to Russia. This was during *perestroika*—a period of post-Cold War revivalism when everything was just starting to open up to the outside world. There, we were given the chance to observe the remaining vestiges of Communism: the government agents on every floor of our Moscow hotel, the fixed menus of food, and the unbearable queues everywhere. We saw *Swan Lake* at the Bolshoi Theatre and walked around Red Square. After trying out my few Russian words, I made friends with a woman I met on the street in Saint Petersburg. She got us excellent tickets to the *Nutcracker* at the Kirov Ballet and invited us to her house for dinner the next day.

In 2005 I fulfilled a lifelong dream: Ruby and I went to Antarctica. Our ship, the *Crystal Symphony*, went right through Iceberg Alley, a region surprisingly full of life. We saw whales, seals, penguins, and scores of fish and birds. It was a breathtaking trip, and apparently rare: we were among the lucky two hundred thousand people who had made this trip south.

In between all my travels, I went back to Israel every few years to visit my brother Eliyahoo, my nieces and nephews, and my cousins. I always stayed in touch with my two childhood friends, Katsab and Ambar, who had both made their homes in Israel. To me, staying in touch with friends is natural and always worth the effort. When they are friends who share childhood memories, it is even more meaningful. In 2000, I took a four-day bus trip to Jordan with Katsab and Ambar. I was the only non-Israeli on the bus, and I was the only one who had to pay a visa fee to cross the border. We

*In 2004, I took my friend and CPA, Vernon Baptist, to visit Israel.
We toured the Golan Heights with Eliyahoo and his daughter, Yalta.*

were in Amman for two nights and Petra for two more. As an added bonus, we got to see Pope John Paul II in his popemobile pass by our hotel in Amman.

In 2004 I took a trip with Vernon Baptist, my good friend and CPA for more than thirty years. As an evangelist born in Trinidad, he had always dreamed of visiting the Holy Land to walk in Jesus's footsteps, and I was happy to be his guide. We stayed in a hotel together, and I escorted him to all the holy sites. I took him to meet Eliyahoo and my nephew Yigal in the heart of Jerusalem. Vernon gathered water from the original baptism site on the Jordan River, visited the Church of the Nativity in Bethlehem, and explored Nazareth, the city where Jesus lived. He had an experience of a lifetime, and it was a special thing to watch. I was glad to give him a rich spiritual experience. A few years later Vernon's sister also visited Israel, and my family was happy to show her around.

My favorite way to travel is with as much of my family as possible. At least once a year, and usually more, we take the whole tribe on a vacation. In 1999 we acquired a real bargain on a time-share in Cabo San Lucas, Mexico, from one of my tenants on Coldwater Canyon Avenue who could no longer afford the annual fees on the four-bedroom penthouse (complete with a pool and Jacuzzi). Until 2017, every Thanksgiving break, the whole family— all of our children and grandchildren—would fly to this stunning retreat at the tip of Baja, California. Clear blue skies, sandy beaches, warm ocean water, and lots of activities for both the kids and the grown-ups made these holidays as heavenly as could be imagined. During the nineteen years we went, the only negativity we faced was being robbed twice—both times by police who shook us down after claiming we were speeding. Even this we laughed about and considered it part of the adventure.

In December 2018 we continued the family vacation tradition in Puerto Vallarta, where thirteen of us enjoyed a week together in a modern penthouse facing the ocean.

We have taken the family to Israel, Italy, Greece, the Czech Republic, Hungary, and Poland, as well as on cruises to Alaska, the Panama Canal, the Caribbean, and the Mediterranean. Sometimes

Traveling with family is one of our greatest joys. Our granddaughters Elana, Rebecca, Eden, and Claire in Cabo San Lucas in 2000 and in 2017.

I take a trip with just one child or grandchild, but more often we are all together. Ruby and I love these times of family togetherness, especially when we can see how much everyone enjoys being with each other. I know that the vacations we take together create memories that will bind us to each other for a lifetime, which is so much more valuable than any material gift. Even as the grandkids get older and it becomes harder to get everyone together in one place, most of them make the effort to join in on our family excursions.

Between trips, we all stay in close contact. Wherever I am, I always FaceTime with my grandkids on Friday evenings. I recite to them the traditional and priestly blessing *Yevarechecha*, which parents give their children to grace them with God's protection, peace, and light.

Yevarechecha
May the Lord bless you and keep you.
May the Lord shine his face upon you and be gracious unto you.
May the Lord lift up his countenance upon you and grant you peace.

I give the blessing in Hebrew and English, and I always add to the translation that they should be blessed with passion, patience, and compassion.

I know that I am the strongest Jewish connection in my family, and I have been blessed to be able to teach my grandchildren Hebrew, Jewish history, and our family's traditional prayers.

Elana and Eden went to Hebrew schools, and Sharon organized beautiful ceremonies at Temple Beth Am, where they were called to read the Torah. It was a *simcha* (joy) to celebrate the bat mitzvah of Elana in 2003, and it was equally wonderful watching Eden step into womanhood in 2007. It continues to give me great pleasure to see Elana and Eden stay so connected to the traditions.

When Rebecca was around ten, Glenn would drop her off at our house every Monday and I would have a few hours with her before Lisa picked her up. I used that time to teach her Hebrew and prepare her for her *bat mitzvah*. We would also talk about Judaism, Jewish history, and Israel. In 2008 Ruby and I made Rebecca a lovely bat mitzvah at Kahal Joseph. Girls aren't allowed to read from the Torah in our Orthodox synagogue, but Rebecca had the opportunity to study with the rabbi. At the ceremony, she recited the *Shema*—the prayer that is so central to Jewish services—and addressed the congregation with the topic "The Women of the Torah." It was a great experience for me to teach and study with her, and I continued the practice with the rest of my grandchildren.

I prepared Claire for her bat mitzvah using the Internet to reach her in Kentucky. I taught her to read Hebrew, and we studied some of the Torah together. We also made her a celebration at Kahal Joseph in 2010, where she spoke on a sensitive topic: "Is Lying Ever Justified?"

I started teaching Zach for his bar mitzvah when he was twelve. Once or twice a week, we met on video chat and I taught him Hebrew and Jewish history and culture and shared my life experiences with him. He is a great joy to be around, and I was overcome with emotion and pride when he read from the Torah at Temple Emanuel in Beverly Hills in the summer of 2019.

One of my greatest pleasures is when we can share Shabbat dinner and festivals in person. Nowadays, Ruby and I celebrate Shabbat, Rosh Hashanah, and Passover at Sharon's house. She always cooks a delicious meal, but some nights we make *kiddush* at home and go to a restaurant together so nobody has to cook and clean. Our pleasure is only enhanced when Lisa can join us.

Elana graduated from Northwestern University in 2013 and became a teacher with Teach for America for a few years. When one of her best friends from Northwestern, Taylor, was converting

Elana's bat mitzvah at Temple Beth Am in Los Angeles in 2003.

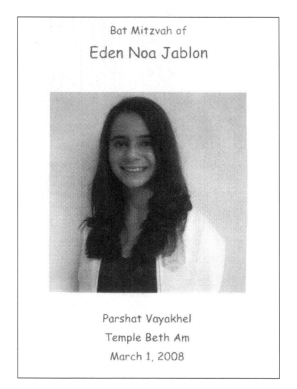

We felt immense pride at all of our grandchildren's bnai mitzvah.

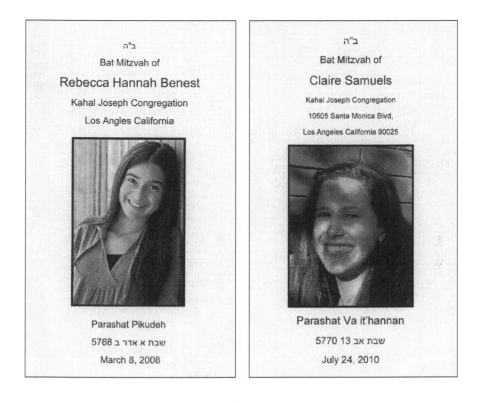

ב"ה

Bat Mitzvah of

Rebecca Hannah Benest

Kahal Joseph Congregation

Los Angles California

Parashat Pikudeh

שבת א אדר ב 5768

March 8, 2008

ב"ה

Bat Mitzvah of

Claire Samuels

Kahal Joseph Congregation

10505 Santa Monica Blvd,

Los Angeles California 90025

Parashat Va it'hannan

שבת אב 13 5770

July 24, 2010

I taught Zach for his bar mitzvah at Temple Emanuel in Beverly Hills in 2019.

*Every Friday night, we call each of our grandchildren
to bless them for Shabbat. (December 2016)*

to Judaism and wanted to learn Hebrew, I was happy to help. Taylor converted and had a wonderful Jewish wedding in June 2018.

In December 2017 Sharon organized a ski trip in Vermont with her daughters; Elana's longtime boyfriend, David Meritt; and David's parents. Unfortunately, the weather was so cold that they couldn't ski. Nevertheless, with both their families present, it was a warm occasion for Elana and David to get engaged. We all gathered together again for Elana and David's wedding on Dec. 28, 2019, at the Culinary Institute of America in Napa Valley. The wedding was emotional and beautiful, made even more joyous by the fact that we could all celebrate our birthdays together! Elana is now at the University of Virginia in Charlottesville working on her PhD in psychology, and David works as a consultant.

We watched Eden graduate from Wesleyan University in

May 2018. She's interested in traveling and took a year to explore Nepal, India, Japan, and other parts of Asia. I can't wait to see what she does next.

Sharon continues with her business, PsychPrep. Her program has become one of the leaders in the industry, and people come from around the country to attend her courses.

Lisa lives about an hour away from us, and although we don't see her as often as we'd like, we still manage to get together. She is a wonderful cook. She comes for holidays like Passover and Rosh Hashanah, but she is mostly disconnected from Judaism. She bought a beautiful home in Shadow Hills (located in northeastern San Fernando Valley), where she has an expansive herb and vegetable garden and forty-five fruit trees. She recently sold her successful dermatology practice and is now pursuing a degree in homeopathy to equip her with even more tools to help patients who prefer a more natural approach.

Rebecca finished high school at age sixteen and graduated from UC San Diego at twenty. She was proud to share with me how she stood up to a professor who had unfairly condemned Israel. She moved to Guatemala and Tanzania to help underprivileged kids through the nonprofit Save the Children and has since traveled through Australia. She has an adventurous spirit and even climbed Mount Kilimanjaro when she was volunteering in Kenya. She now lives in Puerto Rico and calls me often. She and her boyfriend, Alexis, look forward to my weekly Friday night blessings.

Claire is a student at Centre College in Danville, Kentucky, and Zach is in middle school. I talk with them every week. We visit them in Bowling Green regularly, and they visit us too. Jeff and his family have little connection to the religious side of Judaism, partly due to the lack of Jewish community in Bowling Green, but they still feel connected to our history and heritage, and Zach and Claire enjoy our Friday night FaceTime of *kiddush* and blessings.

I was privileged to attend the swearing-in ceremony when Benedicte became a U.S. citizen in March 2011. It was a unique ceremony for the thirty-nine new citizens from nineteen countries. Families gathered at Mammoth Cave National Park—the largest cave system in the world, with 390 miles explored—to be sworn in and celebrate their status as United States citizens.

Surrounded by guests and family members, the candidates were each called to the opening of Mammoth Cave, and we all walked into a large chamber of the cave decorated with star-spangled flags and floodlights. The judge welcomed the new citizens and encouraged them to take an active role in American society. After some speeches, they recited the Pledge of Allegiance, and we all put our hands to our hearts to sing the national anthem with them.

On the way out of the cave, I met a ranger. He asked me what I thought of the ceremony, and I told him how elated I was to witness it. I remembered when I was awarded the privilege to be a U.S. citizen in 1994. I stood with some 1,500 new citizens at the Los Angeles Convention Center and we, too, said the Pledge of Allegiance and sang "The Star-Spangled Banner."

I told the ranger I was proud to be a citizen of the greatest country on God's green earth, where I and my children and grandchildren can enjoy freedom, equality, and countless opportunities that I could never have known in my country of birth, Iraq.

He looked at me, his eyes shining, and with a broad smile on his face said, "Amen."

*In March 2011, Benedicte was sworn in as a U.S. citizen
at Mammoth Cave National Park in Kentucky.*

Chapter 14

Creating Meaning

Every Day a Blessing

I am thankful every day for the good life Ruby and I continue to enjoy after sixty years together. Marriage is hard work. But through hard work, we have learned to accept each other's weaknesses and support each other's strengths. We are Mr. Right and Mrs. Always Right.

I managed to keep myself healthy and out of the hospital (aside from my eye surgery and appendectomy in Baghdad and my tonsillectomy in Israel) until I needed back surgery at age eighty-two. Two years later, in 2015, I developed an aggressive prostate cancer. But the miracle of modern medicine and some brilliant doctors saved me, using a procedure called the DaVinci robotic prostatectomy.

I have been cancer-free since then. It did not get me down, as I have long seen life as a gift and have celebrated every day as best I could. The whole experience enforced my perspective: live today as if it is your last day on Earth and plan for tomorrow as if you are going to live forever. I react as if every moment is a part of my destiny, the continuation of a story that has to end someday, somehow.

*Sharon had pillowcases made for me and Ruby
for our 60th anniversary. (2019)*

I am ready to face whatever God gives me, and I am happy I have made it this far.

In 2000 Ruby developed colon cancer. It was a shock to all of us. She had always taken excellent care of herself by eating well and exercising often, even when the kids were little. It was caught completely by luck during a routine colonoscopy exam, and we have Dr. Ron Chitayat, a longtime and faithful friend, to thank for this early discovery. The chemotherapy was a terrible process, but her healthy attitude and habits helped her stay strong throughout the treatment. She responded to the disease by becoming even more active, tackling her illness head-on with exercise classes and volunteering at the YWCA and at the Cancer Support Community Los Angeles, a nonprofit that provides a variety of programs to cancer patients and survivors at no charge. Thank God, she has been cancer-free since and still goes to CSCLA to take classes and help others battle their condition.

The religion I distanced myself from as a young adult in Israel now holds deep meaning for me. I have learned that Judaism teaches us what is right and wrong in a world of moral relativism, as well as how to have hope in our darkest moments—as a people and as individuals. It provides forgiveness in light of human fallibility and demands human responsibility to repair all that is unjust or in disarray in our world.

I continue to live by the words of the prophet Micah:

"He has shown you, O mortal, what is good.
  And what does the Lord require of you?
To act justly and to love mercy
  and to walk humbly with your God."
                    - Micah 6:8

Every morning, before I put on *tefillin*, I take a deep breath and meditate in my daily prayer. I start and end each paragraph by saying three times, "Thank you, Ribono Shel Olam"—Master of the Universe. Then I add:

...for the capacity to be able to think with my mind and be able to concentrate and remember, and be grateful for the capacity to think.

...for the capacity to see with my eyes and gaze at the beauty of your creation, and be grateful for the capacity to see.

...for the capacity to hear with my ears the multitude of sounds of your creation, and be grateful for the capacity to hear.

...for the capacity to smell with my nose the various aromas of your creation, and be grateful for the capacity to smell. Thank you, Ribono Shel Olam.

...for the capacity to taste with my tongue the many flavors of your creation, and be grateful for the capacity to taste.

...for the capacity to feel with my hand the different temperatures

and textures of your creation, and be grateful for the capacity to feel.

…for helping me communicate with my body to have it function as you created it to be, from the top of my head to the tip of my toes. Thank you, Ribono Shel Olam.

Thank you, Ribono Shel Olam. I am grateful.

This meditation is my spiritual breakfast, a part of my morning ritual of mindfulness and gratitude that centers me for the rest of my day. The next part is my "Daily Inspiration," which I sing out loud with Ruby and with my walking partners; this recitation helps me look at even more positives in my life. I used to attend classes at the synagogue, and I still read our synagogue's weekly *dvar Torah* from Rabbi Melhado and another *dvar Torah* online from Rabbi Jonathan Sacks. I read the weekly Torah portion in both Hebrew and English.

I go to my synagogue, Kahal Joseph, every Shabbat. I drive, but I don't listen to the radio on the way in order to feel the distinctness of the day. I take this day of the week for reflection and spirituality. I use it as a special time to spend with family and friends without the distraction of radio, television, or computers. After lunch, I take a pleasant walk with Ruby, and I make sure to rest, relax, and recharge.

When I am on my travels, I make sure to attend a Shabbat service wherever I am in the world. I have prayed in synagogues from Cairo to Cape Town, from Bucharest to Bombay, from Singapore to Sydney, and from Paris to Prague. It makes me feel like an MOT (Member of the Tribe) to connect to my religion with different people around the world and see different ways of respecting the same faith. I am often invited by strangers into their homes and get to see their culture firsthand.

One of my favorite ways to express gratitude is through charity, and I strive to be as generous as my father was. I follow

Judaism's rule and give 10 percent of my annual income to the poor, the needy, and the unfortunate. The main focus is my synagogue, but I also sit on the board of JIMENA (Jews Indigenous to the Middle East and North Africa) and give to other Jewish organizations that feed children in Israel. We support the Cancer Support Community, the Salvation Army, Christians United for Israel (CUFI), and many other causes.

For a few years I volunteered through a Jewish eldercare program, driving a woman from West Hollywood to visit her husband at the senior care center in Santa Monica. I usually sat down to talk with them and kept them company. Helping people makes me so grateful for what I have.

Through Monona Wali, my Santa Monica College memoir-writing instructor, I was asked to coach an at-risk youth for the Intergenerational Arts and Literature Program, an SMC outreach initiative. I was paired up with a teenager, Eric McKandes. We met for two hours a week for ten weeks. Prompts from the instructor helped us open up and candidly talk about our lives. He grew up in tough circumstances that I had never faced or even encountered in all my relationships: he never knew his father, his mother's boyfriends were abusive, and he was overweight. His stories were horrible and heartbreaking to hear.

We came up with a joint project idea—we wrote poems about each other's lives and how we connected over the belief that we are not in control of the past events in our lives, but that we have the power to control how we react to them. We emphasized that we must be the advocates of our lives, struggle to improve ourselves, remember our past but avoid living in it, and avoid seeing ourselves as helpless victims in order to define our own destiny. We must see a bright future and work towards it. We are the ones responsible for holding ourselves accountable, rising up, and making ourselves heard regardless of color, class, or creed. Our project ended up winning first place for the 2011 Santa Monica Human Relations Council presentation.

<u>Eric</u>
July 29, 2011

Life is not a bowl of cherries,
but there are lots of cherries to enjoy.
Life is not a bed of roses,
but there are plenty of roses to smell.

At six months Eric's father left
his mother accountable for his debt.
She struggled and labored alone,
to care for Eric, after his father was gone.

From job to job she was always hired,
Working hard, she was never tired.
Under pressure and worry, at times
Lost her cool but not her love for Eric.

At seventeen Eric has learnt
To face life, sit, stand, or bend.
To taste cherries and smell roses,
Opportunities come in small doses.

Hard work, courage, and determination
Are essential to life's compensation.
Faith, love, and caring through life
Bring hope and meaning to the strife.

In today's world education is a must,

Persistence, self-reliance, and trust.
Financial management with integrity
Can take life's struggle to prosperity.

Giving makes me realize that I have enough, and more. I have faced many difficulties in my life. When I wasn't clear about how to face a problem or which direction to proceed, there was always someone with a good word, a hot meal, a smile, or a hug who unlocked my mind and delighted my heart. An open door or sincere advice gave me hope and clarity. In return, I have learned to give back the same to others—both with resources and with compassion. It brings me joy and pleasure when I share my experience, advice, laughter, or a positive comment.

Eric McKandes and I worked together in the Intergenerational
Arts and Literature Program at Santa Monica College in 2011,
where our poetry project won first place.

It is through Judaism that I have learned that my temporary life on earth is for a purpose. Judaism allows me to appreciate my achievements and earthly possessions but requires me to share my blessings. By doing so, I feel I can truly enjoy them. I must be accountable for my actions and leave the world a better place than when I came into it.

I need to fulfill my obligations and duties before demanding privileges. When I do something wrong, as I often do, I must admit it, correct myself, and promise not to repeat it. When difficulties interrupt my unpredictable journey through life, I recognize that this, too, will pass. God's infinite mercy guides me to live in a righteous way, and the values of family, friends, and community that Judaism instills provide me with a sense of security that "I am not alone."

No Time for Boredom

In addition to my daily prayers, I keep myself motivated and relaxed with a combination of meditation, yoga, exercise, and recitations of inspirational quotes. When my children were young and I worked like mad, these practices helped me stay focused. The physical activity continues to offer me an opportunity to center myself now that the pace of life has slowed down, though I have given up doing the splits and standing on my head. I do water exercise, cardio, and some weight training at the YMCA whenever I have the chance. I have a physical trainer, and a masseuse comes to my house once a week to work out the bumps and bruises of time.

Ruby took exercise classes at the YWCA for over thirty years, but it closed in 2016 after ninety years in existence. She has found other classes through the amazing programs at the Cancer Support Community. Whether it's osteoball or tai chi, Pilates or deep breathing, Ruby spends about eleven hours a week working out and walks with me three to four times a week for an hour after dinner. In between it all, she is an avid reader and finishes about one book a week.

When we moved to Los Angeles, I jogged daily with a group at Palisades Park or on a local route with Lisa. When the doctor suggested jogging was too much pressure on my joints, I started walking every day instead. It became a regular habit, and while I began to pass the same people every morning, I am always meeting new friends on the way. Five or six of us start our walk with my daily inspirational message, then walk through Palisades Park to watch the waves and absorb the gorgeous stretch of golden, sandy beaches of the Santa Monica Bay at sunrise, ending with the song "Oh, What a Beautiful Mornin'."

More than twenty years ago, I met some friendly men on the path and was invited to join their group for lunch on Thursdays. They called themselves the Lunch Bunch, and we continue to meet regularly. Each week, about twelve of us get together. Although members have come and gone (only three—Harry Sussman, Harvey

I celebrate the beatiful morning along the beach as often as I can.

Sisskind, and Miles Klein—are left from the original group), the traditions have sustained and evolved. We choose a restaurant, and each week a designated "birthday boy" gets a dessert and pays the bill but must also bring a topic for discussion. We have no agenda and no center of attention; it is a forum for us to express ourselves and learn about each other. At the end, no matter how intense the discussion sometimes becomes and how much we begin to rip at each other, we walk out as friends.

Ruby has her own walking partner—Eva Salzer, a ninety-three-year-old neighbor with whom she has been walking for over thirty years. They take trips around the neighborhood a few times a week, and all the neighbors know the two ladies well. Even the school bus drivers pull over to say hello!

Santa Monica has the perfect weather for a gardener. I spend hours in the garden, and I have continued to create the sanctuary I always dreamed of. I diligently attend to its needs. I

Working in my own Garden of Eden connects me
to the fragility and beauty of life.

I enjoy sharing my bounty with friends and neighbors.

have a weekly gardener to mow the lawn and blow the leaves, and someone comes every few weeks to help me with the heavy lifting—planting, digging, cutting trees, removing shrubs. Other than that, I cultivate it on my own. I lose track of time out there. I tell Ruby, "I'll be inside in ten minutes." An hour later, she comes out, asking, "What happened, Joe? Where are you?" Being in the garden, with the physical exertion and mental focus on life, is a meditative and energizing activity for me. I connect with nature and tend to the life that grows. Weeding and feeding, trimming and pruning, growing and harvesting, disease and death; every part of gardening deals with the realities of life.

I care for over thirty fruit trees, my collection of orchids, about twenty potted succulents, and dozens of miniature rose bushes. I have a vegetable garden and numerous herbs. I make my own herbal tea using fresh lemon verbena, peppermint, spearmint, oregano, lemongrass, lemon balm, sage, and ginger, which I call my "elixir of life." I love to share my bounty with friends. Every

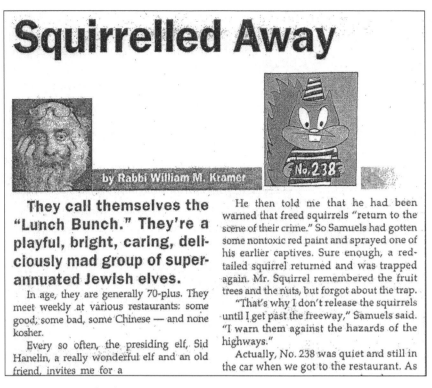

Squirrelled Away

by Rabbi William M. Kramer

They call themselves the "Lunch Bunch." They're a playful, bright, caring, deliciously mad group of superannuated Jewish elves.

In age, they are generally 70-plus. They meet weekly at various restaurants: some good, some bad, some Chinese — and none kosher.

Every so often, the presiding elf, Sid Hanelin, a really wonderful elf and an old friend, invites me for a

He then told me that he had been warned that freed squirrels "return to the scene of their crime." So Samuels had gotten some nontoxic red paint and sprayed one of his earlier captives. Sure enough, a red-tailed squirrel returned and was trapped again. Mr. Squirrel remembered the fruit trees and the nuts, but forgot about the trap.

"That's why I don't release the squirrels until I get past the freeway," Samuels said. "I warn them against the hazards of the highways."

Actually, No. 238 was quiet and still in the car when we got to the restaurant. As

*An article about me in the Jewish Journal in 2001 focused on
The Lunch Bunch and my squirrel-catching antics.*

Shabbat, I bring roses to the ladies at the synagogue.

My biggest problem in the garden is unwanted guests—squirrels. I wait for the fruit to ripen on the trees, but those greedy rascals sometimes come and grab it before I do, leaving a huge mess behind them. I've tried many schemes to keep them away—netting the trees, propping up scarecrows, hanging shiny CDs—but none of that totally solves the problem. The only answer I've found that actually works is trapping the squirrels. I set up an animal-friendly cage, plant some walnuts at the back, then wait for the rodents to take the bait. Once I've got them, I put them in the trunk of the car, take a drive, and let them go at a local park or in the woods.

When my niece Myrna asked how far I took them, she told me I needed to go farther. I told her not to worry, "I don't give them my address!" But she was sure they were coming back. To prove her wrong, I bought nontoxic red paint and marked their tails before releasing them. Within a week, I called to Ruby, "The *momzer* (bastard) is back!" I felt like he was laughing at me. Since then, I take the squirrels at least four miles away. Any closer than that, and they still come back. I have been trapping squirrels for more than twenty years. I keep track of my conquests on a "*momzer* list," and as of March 2019 I've captured and released 1,039 squirrels.

Unlike the *momzers*, wild birds are welcome in my yard. I buy fifty-pound bags of seed to scatter on my balcony so that I can watch the variety of birds that come to eat: striped and black-headed finches, mountain doves, blue jays, and even domestic pigeons. I especially love seeing the hummingbirds that come right outside my office window to drink nectar. They float for four or five seconds, drinking from the feeder, then flit away before I can even snap a quick photo.

Lisa was infected with my passion for gardening. She has an enormous, lush garden at her home in Shadow Hills and fills it with vegetables, fruits, herbs, and desert plants. When she saw my success with the squirrel cages, she bought four. When she installed a drip irrigation system to save water, I did the same a year later. We are always sharing the fruits and vegetables of our labors.

Another hobby of mine is to dry fruit in a dehydrator. Sometimes I use fruit from my garden, but I usually go to the Grand Central Market and buy wholesale cases of bananas, mangoes, nectarines, peaches, pineapples, apricots, or apples—whatever is in season. The market itself is a sight to see. When I took my late friend Abe Abraham, he was like a kid in a candy store; it reminded him of his youth in the open markets of Shanghai, where he was born. I don't add sulfur or any other preservatives in the drying process—just pure, healthy fruit. Once I have my stockpile dried, I freeze it. I take them out to eat as a snack, to take on travels, and to share with friends and family. I even give some to my doctors' receptionists, which seems to give me easy access at the office. When Elana was a toddler, she used to come over and help me cut the bananas. Only about half would end up on the tray, while the other half ended up in her mouth.

Although I lack the skill to play any instruments, I love listening to music. I have satellite radio in my car, and I love Sinatra, classical music, and all kinds of genres. Music lifts my spirit. I always have music playing in the background as I work in my upstairs office, sitting at my desk in front of a window that overlooks my pool and garden.

I also discovered that I can watch recordings of live performances of New York's Metropolitan Opera or the Bolshoi Ballet at my local movie theaters, and we go often. The sound and projection are first-rate, and they add subtitles to the performance where needed. Besides an opera or ballet, Ruby and I go to see a movie almost every Saturday night—a great opportunity to reach into the freezer for some dried fruits!

To this day, I try to keep up with technological advances. I bought my first computer in the early 1990s and have updated my equipment and skills over the years. I learned to type, and I hire young people to help me learn and understand how it all works. My best instructor is Luca Chitayat, the nephew of my good friend Ron Chitayat. I met him when he was about sixteen, and now he is in his late twenties. He not only has kept me up to date with technology and how to use it but has worked beside me to write and edit this book!

The key is to never let myself be intimidated by the continuous changes of technology. If something isn't working right, I don't start screaming at the computer. Instead, I ask myself what I've done wrong. I enjoy the challenge. I continue to look at failure as a stepping-stone to success and as an opportunity to learn how to do things better the next time. Once I succeed in the pursuit of something unknown, the glowing feeling of accomplishment is worth it. I email, discover new things on the Internet, upload YouTube videos, and have my own blog—www.joesamuels.net—where I post my writings, thoughts, and speeches. I am no expert, but I do well for my age. I had a Windows PC, but at Jeff's suggestion I switched to Apple and have found computing much easier. Now I have an iPod, iPad, iPhone, and a twenty-seven-inch iMac desktop computer—a far cry from typing with two fingers on a manual typewriter or IBM Selectric as I did in Montreal, and certainly from the quill and inkwell I had to work with in Baghdad.

Forever a People Person

Relationships have always defined me and been at the center of my existence. I love people and especially love having a shared history with people. Relationships are an essential spice to life and have innumerable benefits towards health, wealth, and happiness. My network of friends, whom I can turn to anytime and who can turn to me for anything, has immeasurably enriched my life. I appreciate the friends who know me and those who care about me. A great friend not only praises and appreciates but can sincerely criticize and comment without fear of losing my friendship. When I think about it, I recall a quote that I learned in high school in Baghdad:

"Friendship is above reason, for, though you find virtues in a friend, he was your friend before you found them." – *A. Clutton-Brock*

It is not just deep relationships that I find meaningful. I talk with everyone: the car attendant, the supermarket cashier, the teller at the bank, the Uber driver, fellow travelers, even people in the elevator or strolling by in the park. Sometimes we never meet again, and sometimes we keep in touch forever. I treat everyone as

Between yoga and jogging, I was still partying at the age of 70!

my fellow human. To any waitress who stops at my table, I love to ask, "What is your beautiful name?" My children joke that I can make friends with anyone, anywhere.

An example of this is the several interesting and strange encounters I've had at Subway. I am a healthy eater, so I never eat fast food, but I do enjoy Subway. Whether I eat it in my garden, in the park, or at the Hollywood Bowl, my order is always the same: whole-wheat bread stuffed with pepper-jack cheese, lettuce, double tomatoes, spinach, cucumbers, green peppers, olives, avocado, and cilantro, with a sprinkle of black pepper, oil, and vinegar, and topped off with jalapenos.

If I am eating my sandwich at the shop, I don't mind making friends. Once, as I entered the Subway at Pico and Lincoln boulevards, a man with a shopping cart full of bags approached me, "Can you spare a dollar?" I offered to buy him a sandwich instead. He went ahead of me in line and gave his order: "Footlong with double roast beef, bacon, chips, cookies, a bowl of soup, and a large drink."

I have bought sandwiches for others before, but this guy knew how to take advantage. He filled up his cup with a drink and started to leave. I looked at him. "Don't worry, I'll eat it later," he said, and left.

On another occasion, I went to pick up my usual veggie sandwich at the Subway on Wilshire Boulevard and 14th Street after a morning of hard work in my garden. I was wearing my full gardening outfit, down to my laceless New Balance sneakers. Standing in line in front of me was a lovely young girl.

"Are you a nurse?" I asked her.

She looked at me, "No, I'm a secretary."

I continued with my small talk, commenting on her beautiful hair and her youthful look. My turn to order came. I placed my order, the usual sandwich, and took $10 from my wallet to pay the cashier.

"You don't have to pay," said the cashier. "The girl ahead paid for you." I turned around to thank her, but she was gone before I could say a word. When I told the story to my children they said, without hesitation, "Dad, she must have thought you were homeless."

One bright and sunny California day, I picked up my veggie sandwich at the location on Santa Monica and Sawtelle boulevards. The only available table was one with a handicap sign. I didn't feel guilty taking it; I have what I call a "senior privilege" sign in my car. I sat down, unwrapped my sandwich, and took a bite. I like to chew slowly while looking around and watching the people inside and the cars outside. I took a sip of water.

A man two tables away stood up, pulled up a chair, and sat down.

"Is it okay if I share your table?"

He sat before I could answer, though it wasn't unusual to share tables at Subway. He was dirty looking: unshaven, with crooked teeth, blue eyes, and bushy long hair, covered by a camouflage shirt and khaki pants. I felt uneasy but kept my cool.

"Would you like to share my veggie sandwich?" I asked. "Nope," he shook his head from side to side. He looked a bit spaced out. I sank my teeth in and took another bite, pretending everything was fine.

He looked at me and stared solidly into my eyes. He was trying to say something. I looked at him calmly and curiously.

"Can I buy you a sandwich?" I asked him. I thought perhaps he didn't care for veggie sandwiches. He looked at me, put his hand in his pocket, and pulled his wallet out to show me his credit cards. I understood what he was trying to tell me.

"You are a good man. Where are you from?" he asked.

"Thank you. I live in Santa Monica. How about you?" I asked.

"I'm from Houston, Texas."

"Oh," I responded, "I have been to Houston many times. How do you like it?"

"I hate it."

"How about Los Angeles?"

"Don't like it either."

"Do you have any family in Los Angeles?" I asked.

"Nope," he replied. I began to wonder what to do next.

"Can I have a sip of your water?" He continued staring at me. I felt awkward and uncomfortable.

"No, I'm sorry," I replied, apologetically.

He looked irritated. He paused for a moment, turned around to face the cashier, and with a boisterous voice shouted, "Can you give me a f---in' cup of water? Yes or no?"

A sudden, deadly silence emerged in the restaurant, and all heads turned toward me, eyes wide in puzzlement. I jerked my head backward. I was disgusted. Who was this guy, and why was he sitting at my table? The cashier ignored him. The lady in front of me got up, gave me a sympathetic look, and left.

"I think it's a good idea if you go to the cashier to ask for a cup and get water from the fountain," I suggested.

He got up and slowly walked toward the cashier. I turned around. He was limping. My heart sank in my chest. He was wearing an artificial leg. I stopped eating. He quietly turned back, sat down, and drank his water. I began to feel for him.

"Did you ever serve in the military?" I asked gently.

"Seven years in the infantry. After two f---in' assignments in Iraq, I was discharged." He sounded incensed and remorseful. I looked at him again. My anxiety turned into sympathy.

"What about your leg?"

"F---in' IED, three of my friends were killed," he retorted.

I was glued to my seat, unsure of what to say. Should I tell him I was born and grew up in Iraq? Or just shut up?

He pressed on, "We've lost 4,491 Americans. We are f---in' stupid, thinking once we remove f---in' Saddam the f---in' Iraqis will be thankful. They are all the same shit. They are killing each other and especially killing the Christians. They are worse than animals. F--- them."

I took a deep breath, drank a bit of water, and waited. I couldn't eat any more. I had butterflies in my stomach. Should I tell him that most Iraqis are decent, voiceless victims and that I had once lived among them? I decided to wait. I knew I couldn't reason with someone who was so angry.

"Our country owes you a big debt of gratitude," I replied, looking at him with a sense of admiration and appreciation.

"I don't think anybody gives a shit," he continued ranting.

I decided to speak up. Maybe my story would give him some comfort. I realized that the only way to communicate with him was to speak in his dialect.

"Allow me to tell you my story in f---in' Iraq," I said. He jerked his head backward as if someone had hit him. He looked curious and puzzled.

"I was born and grew up in Baghdad. I had to run for my life from the sons of bitches." He gazed at me, his eyes wide open, eager to hear the rest of my story.

"My family lost our home and business and fled Iraq, too, only because we were Jewish," I said. "I became a homeless, penniless refugee at nineteen." He was startled to hear my revelation. I felt that we were connected.

"Were there lots of Jews in Baghdad?" he asked.

"Nearly a quarter of Baghdad's population was Jewish in 1948; we were lucky to get out alive from that shithole."

"Are you okay now, is your family okay?" he asked.

"We are all okay, thank God. We are grateful to be living in America. We are truly indebted to people like you for keeping us safe." He stayed quiet.

"Is there anything I can do for you?" I asked him. He was grappling for words.

"Love you, man. You remind me of my father. He passed away many years ago." His voice was cracking.

I couldn't eat anymore. I wrapped my sandwich and was ready to leave. I got up. As I did, he stood and limped slowly towards me.

"Can I hug you?"

"Of course, son," I replied. I saw tears in his eyes.

Before I drove home, I sat in my car. His image filled my mind. I visualized him as a child—how his mother must have run with open arms to hug him when he returned from school; how his father must have been looking forward to his bright future.

I went back the next day. I didn't want to buy a sandwich. But he wasn't there. We never saw each other again.

Saying Goodbyes

Out of all my circles of people, it is always my family and my oldest friends who remain closest to my heart. But, as is the natural course of life, I have grown older and have had to learn to say my goodbyes.

My brother Elisha died in December 1999 from Parkinson's disease. I was able to fly to Montreal for his funeral. We connected as boys in Baghdad, and I always looked up to him. And as adults, we spent much time together in Montreal—celebrating holidays with our families, playing *shesh besh* by the lake, and reminiscing about our youth. I always remembered that he gave me my only bar mitzvah gift—the gold cuff links with my initials, "JS," which I have since passed down to my son, Jeff (also JS!). Ten years after Elisha passed away, his wife, Valentine, died from Alzheimer's. Their two sons, Charlie and David, still live in Montreal. David is single, and Charlie has two boys.

Later that year, Joe Azar passed away. He was taking Coumadin, which perhaps made him dizzy because he was on a ladder when he fell back and hit his head. I left with the family for Thanksgiving in Cabo when Joe was in a coma, and he died while we were there. I felt a deep loss that I still have trouble thinking about. For four decades, he was not only a business partner but also one of my most sincere and best friends.

While we were on a cruise on the Danube around 2006, we got word that Eliyahoo's wife, Ahuva, died after having a stroke. We were not able to get there for the funeral but went to visit later to offer comfort to Eliyahoo and their children, Yigal, Yalta, and Yifat.

I continued to visit Eliyahoo often. I took him to a hotel in Eilat, where we spent a wonderful three days and nights together. We visited the Underwater Observatory aquarium in the waters of the Gulf of Eilat and went to a theater to experience a virtual reality retelling of the stories of the Israelites and the Torah. In between visits, I called him all the time. I was scheduled to visit him again in May 2011, but that February I got a call from his son, Yigal. He informed me that his father's health was deteriorating quickly. I asked Yigal to hold the phone up to Eliyahoo's ear, and I screamed out to him, "I love you!" Yigal said he saw a smile spread across his father's face.

I was on the phone with Yigal when Eliyahoo took his last breath on February 23, 2011. We cried together. I always looked up to Eliyahoo, both when he was the leader of our adventures in youth and as adults when I saw his quiet happiness with his wife, his children, and his job. All he needed to be happy were the basic necessities. He taught me about taking chances, trusting, loving, and enjoying life's adventure.

I sat *shiva* in Los Angeles and said *Kaddish* at Kahal Joseph, where I added his name to my other family members' names on the memorial wall. I went to Israel as planned in May and visited Eliyahoo's grave for a final goodbye. I spent much of my time with Yigal, and we are still close.

Marcelle died on August 15, 2012. Yossi phoned me from Miami a day before she went in for a heart operation, and I had a chance to wish her a speedy recovery. Unfortunately, she passed the next day. Marcelle's husband, Sasson, had died two years earlier. I had always admired Sasson and considered him a mentor. We became close when they moved to Montreal, and I can still remember helping them get their first condo in Mount Royal.

Ruby's sister Eliza died on May 21, 2008. We were grateful to have lived in the same city as Eliza and Eze in Montreal and to have built such a good relationship with them, including having our children grow up together. That September, Ruby and I took a trip to view the fall foliage near Montreal, and we drove to Toronto to visit Eliza's grave.

My *Khalla* Salima lived in Haifa for most of her life, and I visited her often. When I moved to Israel, she was like a mother to me. She lived a long life full of stories but left us in 2008. I am still close with her children, Hadassah, Simhah, Bella, Madeline, and Kadouri. Kadouri came to visit us in Los Angeles not long ago.

Katsab, my childhood buddy from Baghdad, died from pancreatic cancer in 2009. We went to school together at Rahel Shahmoon when we were ten and stayed friends for sixty-five more years. The other one of our trio, Ambar, died on Purim in 2017 in Israel. I was not able to go to the funeral, but Sandra, his daughter, told me that many people came to remember my dear friend, whom I never lost touch with over eighty years.

I also stayed in touch with Edward Obidiah, my high school friend who was the best man at my wedding. Ed was always on the move. I helped him get a visa and move to Montreal before he eventually got married in Toronto and went to live in Greensboro, North Carolina. Years later, he ended up in Portland, Oregon, to be near his son, Joe, who was a dermatologist. I visited him there in the summer of 2016, and his daughter-in-law videotaped us talking about our life in Baghdad and the struggles that followed. Unfortunately, Eddie passed a few months later.

When I go to Kahal Joseph on Shabbat, I always say the *Kaddish* memorial prayer at the end of the service to remember those who have passed on: my parents, my siblings, and even more distant family and friends. This spiritual way of remembering important people in my life makes me appreciate my past and my present. Saying this prayer helps me feel grateful that I have lived a long and happy life and that I am in good health and able to remember and honor my family.

It is sad for me to see so many people go, but I accept it as part of life. I have been blessed to have close relationships with so many people and to have deeply enjoyed each and every occasion with them. But everything in life is temporary, including life itself. Spiritually, I believe there is an infinite life waiting for us after. And in the physical realm, we live on through the influence of the deeds we have done. We leave our marks on this earth, and our actions will echo long after we've passed.

CHAPTER 15

A CHAIN OF MIRACLES

Baghdad Revisited

Of all the places where I've lived or have traveled to, the one place I haven't wanted to go back to is Iraq. I left there angry and disappointed, rejected and betrayed by the land of my birth.

After Saddam Hussein was deposed in the Iraq War in 2003, I thought maybe I should go. An acquaintance, Aaron Basha, a prominent jeweler in Manhattan, went with the help of one of his customers, an Arab delegate to the United Nations. They flew him to Dubai and took him on a private jet to Baghdad. He went to see the Old Jewish Quarter, where I was born, and spoke about how much had changed: wide, paved streets; old houses torn down and replaced by new ones; and no signs that Jews ever lived there—he could not even find the synagogue I used to go to, nor the school. He had security guards with him at all times, provided by his VIP hosts.

But I don't have those kinds of connections or security. More importantly, I also feel that I still don't want to visit. While I have a longing nostalgia for the beautiful times that Iraq gave me, I'm aware that there are consequences to opening an age-old wound. In seeing the past, while there is much happiness to recall, there is the knowledge that I must accept the inevitable disappointment of what the past has become. I am not sure that the curiosity of nostalgia is worth the cost.

However, after the war on Saddam Hussein, I did get a unique opportunity to peek into my past. On May 6, 2003, U.S. special forces were searching for weapons of mass destruction in the headquarters of Baghdad's feared secret police, the Mukhabarat. Instead, to their surprise, in the heavily damaged and flooded basement they discovered a trove of long-forgotten Iraqi-Jewish artifacts.

Saddam Hussein's Ba'ath Party had stolen, looted, and confiscated public and personal items from dozens of synagogues, schools, and community properties and for some unknown reason had stored them, albeit poorly, for decades. The U.S. government, with the approval of the provisional government of Iraq, rescued these nearly destroyed remains of the once-thriving, two-millennia-old Jewish community of Iraq and shipped them to the United States. At a cost of $3 million, the U.S. government restored and preserved these priceless artifacts and exhibited them in Washington, D.C., New York, Miami, Kansas City, and Yorba Linda (about an hour from Los Angeles).

In 2015, I went to visit the artifacts at the Richard Nixon Presidential Library and Museum in Yorba Linda. The moment I stepped into the two-thousand-square-foot exhibition, the history of my people came to life. On display were some of the trove's 2,700 books and thousands of documents, some dating back to the 1500s.

There was a high school diploma in Arabic that reminded me of the diploma I received in June 1948, which I couldn't take with me when I fled. There were Torah casings, stripped of the silver or gold and missing the Torah parchment that was meant to be inside. I remember carrying a *Sefer Torah* in a similar casing on my bar mitzvah; the ornate casing, with the parchment scroll inside, was so heavy that I was terrified I would drop it, which is a great sin. There were numerous prayer books, including a *Haggadah* from 1902, which took me back to our festive Seders at home.

It was a bittersweet encounter. Seeing the exhibit brought tears to my eyes and filled my heart with joy. It brought sweet memories of the wonderful life we had and of our close-knit community. Yet it also brought bitter memories of the terrible fear and horror I felt when I saw Jews arrested, tortured, and hanged for nothing more than their faith. The rampant hatred and anti-Semitism we all experienced left me, and every Iraqi Jew, with tremendous anxiety and a sense of hopelessness that I will never forget.

Regretfully, these treasured artifacts were scheduled for return to Iraq in September 2018, but that has fortunately been extended as of this writing (March 2019). I wrote an article for the

This handwritten 1902 Haggadah, saved by the Iraqi-Jewish Archive, is in danger of being shipped back to Iraq.

Washington Post on October 19, 2017—"The History of Iraqi Jews Is in Jeopardy"—with more information about the story of these artifacts and the potential loss of their legacy, and it has become my passion to actively work towards saving these relics. I have written more articles, met with members of Congress, and have made great progress with the help of JIMENA, CUFI, Kahal Joseph Congregation president and fellow Iraq-escapee Yvette Dabby, and other dedicated people and organizations. At the moment it looks as if the documents will be here to stay, at least for a few more years, but I will continue to work diligently to prevent them from ever returning to Iraq.

I believe there is only a handful of Jews left in Baghdad, if that. Our history, our artifacts, our 2,500-year presence, has all but been erased from the rivers of Babylon.

However, the city's influence on me persists. Not least of it, my early experiences made me realize just how blessed and lucky I am to be alive.

Telling My Story

I only started talking about my past in 2007, when I enrolled in a memoir-writing class through the Emeritus program at Santa Monica College, led by Monona Wali. For many years, I did not discuss my childhood in Baghdad and certainly not my harrowing escape or my difficult years in Israel. I didn't even talk to Ruby much about it, nor my children. The first time I wrote and read about my escape from Iraq to the class, I cried the whole way through. Bittersweet tears streamed down my face as the words flowed from my heart. I hadn't realized how much I had repressed—the fear, the loss, and the feeling of being thwarted and rejected from my home. It was such a release to let those tears go, to take off the shackles of my past and realize that my experience was worth remembering. I now know how important it is to get this information out there, to help make sure history remembers and understands what Iraqi Jews had to go through.

I have Monona to thank for opening my floodgates. Since this class, I have written many articles about my life. Some have been published in the Los Angeles *Jewish Journal*, the *Washington Post*, the *Times of Israel*, and the *Jerusalem Post*. I speak whenever I am asked—to large audiences of schoolchildren, college students, synagogue groups, and others—and I talk to my grandchildren about it all the time. They're always asking me for more stories about my escape and more about the happy times of my childhood in Baghdad.

In December 2016, with the help of JIMENA, I was given the opportunity to tell my story at Los Angeles City Hall. I addressed the Los Angeles City Council to help them understand the rarely told history of Jews from Arab lands. I now feel it is my duty to help the wider world understand the diversity of backgrounds in the Jewish community and to expose the hardship that Jews in the Middle East and North Africa had to go through.

My personal story is mirrored thousands of times by Jewish communities both from Iraq and from other Arab lands. We all suffered anti-Semitism, persecution, confiscation of property, displacement, false accusations, jail, torture, and murder. We were all expelled from our homelands, displaced after thousands of years of coexistence because of our religion. Of course, this has happened to Jews in many places across the globe and across the centuries; my story is only a sentence in the Jewish book of survival. But my story also shows how after every ill treatment and disaster, Jews have exemplified the power of resilience to start over. We face and accept the present and look ahead to rebuild the future. We remain loyal and respectful of the laws of society and live as faithful citizens of the countries that adopt us. We refuse to drown in tears of self-pity

Sixty-five years after my boat ride to freedom, I discovered that Haskel Abrahami, who attends my synagogue, had been on the boat with me.

and sorrow, and we reject living in a state of victimhood or demanding entitlement. We talk about our past, but we refuse to live in it.

A few years ago, I was speaking at Kahal Joseph about the horrible night I got stuck on the Shatt Al Arab as I smuggled out of Iraq with a boatful of young teens. After my talk, a member of the synagogue, Haskel Abrahami, approached me. We had known each other for many years and sat near each other at services, but neither of us had spoken much of our past. Now he was looking at me in wonder.

"Yousuf," Haskel said, calling me by my Arabic name. "I was on that boat with you! I was on that river when we got stuck overnight. I was the thirteen-year-old boy on that fateful trip when we crossed the Shatt Al Arab in December 1949!"

I was stunned; I could not believe he was that little boy. I remembered being so concerned for my youngest passenger and wondering what had happened to him. Now here he was, like me, a member of my synagogue sitting seats away, happy and living in Los Angeles with a loving family and a good life.

I thought back to the fear and hope I had felt as we sailed down the Shatt Al Arab, hidden beneath a layer of hay and a cloud of doom and hope, wondering what would become of my life as I left everything I knew behind. I could never have imagined I would have all that I have now. I could never have imagined I would feel the joy and the gratitude I feel every day.

Gratitude

A few years ago, Ruby and I were driving to Scottsdale, and I was listening to my favorite radio show, *The Happiness Hour*, hosted by Dennis Prager. No politics, no economic meltdowns, no world problems are discussed—only issues about happiness.

His topic for that day was: Can you think of the happiest person you personally know well? Why do you think that this person is the happiest you know?

During the commercial break, I asked Ruby, "Who is the happiest person you know well?"

She turned around and pointed at me.

"Why?" I asked her.

"Because you always find something to be grateful about."

While I am not sure I am the happiest, she was right about being grateful. I walk around feeling blessed and lucky. I am in good health and financially well off. I enjoy a profound sense of love from my friends and from my caring family. I am grateful for the things I have and grateful for the things that I don't have. Almost everything in life that happened to me is beyond anyone's control. While growing up, I faced numerous difficulties, disappointments, and even life-threatening situations. I had two choices to handle them: I could either blame my luck, blame everybody, succumb to the situation, wallow in self-pity, and lead a miserable life; *or* I could face my problems head on, work around and rise above them, learn from every situation, and look at each of my experiences as a step toward a better and happier future. I chose the latter.

At many junctures in my life, I have asked, "Why me?" Why did we have to suffer in the Farhud? Why did I have to run away from my homeland? Why did I end up a penniless refugee? Why did I never get to go to college? Why did this or that venture fail? By victimizing myself, I made myself miserable and, in turn, people did not want to be around me.

Eventually, a strong voice shook me awake, as if from a trance, saying, "Why are you grumbling? You did not end up tortured or hanged in the public square of Baghdad, as so many others did. Your boat made it to Iran, when the one behind you did not. You and your whole family got out, and the rest of your life has been lived in freedom, in good health, in fortunate circumstances, and with good people."

As I matured, I slowly learned that I should be asking a different "Why me?" Why have I been so fortunate? Why have I been blessed to have good health, a supportive wife, and accomplished children and grandchildren? Why have I been blessed with wealth, freedom, respect, a rich culture, and a constant shower of love? Why me?

I don't know the answers, but I know that asking the questions gives me the appreciation to enjoy every day. Not everything will go right, but we must reframe our mindset to understand that these experiences, both positive and negative, make us who we are. And going forward, we can use our knowledge and influence to decide who we will become.

It seems that I have been successful in passing along this attitude of gratitude to my children and grandchildren. In 2009, we enjoyed our tenth annual Thanksgiving vacation in Cabo

San Lucas. Late in the afternoon, I sat with my granddaughters in the Jacuzzi, watching the setting sun slowly disappear behind the mountains into the Pacific Ocean, gazing at the scattered clouds engaged in a leisurely and graceful game of transforming the blue sky into a kaleidoscope of gray, yellow, orange, bronze, and red. We were spectators in a large, open-air theater, watching a whole show performed just for us.

"Make a list of what you are grateful for," I challenged the children.

At dinnertime, after we recited the Friday night *kiddush*, we offered our thoughts:

"I am grateful to my parents for bringing me here from Kentucky," said Claire, age eleven.

"I am grateful to my mom and dad for taking me on so many trips," said Rebecca, thirteen.

"I am grateful to Mom and Dad for doing their best to give me a good life," said Eden, thirteen.

"I am grateful to my mom for sending me to the best schools," said Elana, seventeen.

"I want my Mommy!" said Zachary, two-and-a-half.

Then it was my turn.

What am I grateful for?

I am grateful to God for the gift of life, for being born healthy and surviving childhood in an age when wellness was not a given. I am grateful that I grew up with a loving and large family and caring parents. I am grateful for my Youmma, my grandmother who was always there to soothe any humiliation or pain. I am grateful for being blessed with good luck that helped me survive some dangerous situations.

I am grateful to have visited dozens of countries, and I am grateful to live in America, the greatest nation on Earth. I am grateful for the great American society that allows me to fulfill my dreams and enjoy the fruits of my labor freely. I am grateful for the freedom I enjoy and the sense of security that I longed for when I was growing up.

I am grateful to breathe fresh air, to see clearly, to hear beautiful sounds, to taste healthy food, and to exercise daily. I am grateful for being blessed with a good attitude and good friends.

And I am grateful to have found my life partner, Ruby. For over sixty years, she has been my chief supporter, my travel partner, my home manager, and my love. Despite our differences, difficulties, and discord, we have enjoyed a wonderful life together, and I am grateful we have managed to raise three kindhearted, confident, and self-reliant children who went beyond our dreams in gaining the education we never had. And I am grateful for the five grandchildren they have blessed us with, who all bring us constant joy.

Albert Einstein is credited with saying, "There are only two ways to live your life. One is as though nothing is a miracle. The other is as though everything is a miracle." If I had to describe my life in four words, it would be "a chain of miracles."

In sharing my story, I hope that others will realize the same about their own lives. We are owed nothing, and change is inevitable. In most circumstances, we can influence both our positive and negative experiences to fit our hopes and aspirations. Every day that we are alive is a gift and is a chance to improve ourselves and the lives of those around us. Don't be overwhelmed by problems; some you will solve, and some you will have to live with. Never be a victim to the uncontrollable conditions and events of life; rise above them to make your life what you believe it can be. Make every moment count.

Make your life your own chain of miracles.

APPENDIX

EYEWITNESSES TO THE FARHUD

Several of my friends have written of their personal experience of the Farhud, or have had stories written about them.

Shaoul Moshi: From Roof to Roof We Ran

I was 16 on the first day of Shavuot, June 1, 1941, when my family heard bullets begin to rain during the late afternoon. We were worried. Around 6 a.m. the next day, we heard loud screaming from the street. I peeked through the window. A man with a rifle on a horse had shot open our front door.

While the mob started looting the first floor, we all ran to the roof. My brother Haskel was helping my sister Latifa and my parents. I took off my pajamas to change, but didn't have time. I ran to the roof barefoot, in my underwear.

A young man who worked at the blacksmith shop down the street caught up with us on the roof and held a long knife at my brother's throat. Haskel started pleading.

"Please look at her, she is like your mother. She is a sick woman. Allah will reward you in this world and thereafter for sparing us. I am begging you. Please, please, take whatever you want from our house. It is all yours."

He looked at my mother, looked at Haskel, and screamed, "Go! Go, *ibn al kalb* [son of a dog]!" My mother jumped over the wall to safety, but twisted her leg. From roof to roof we ran, to a friendly Muslim neighbor, who offered us his house as shelter. We

345

all gathered there, nearly 70 Jews, till the British forces entered the next day and stopped the looting and killing.

When we went to the police station we saw many injured Jews, and one dead outside. And when we got back to the house everything was gone, including the garbage can. We stayed at my *Khalla*'s until we rented a new house in Bataween, and bought all the new furniture we needed.

I remember this like it happened yesterday. It is a trauma I cannot erase from my memory.

(I wrote this after I interviewed Shaoul Moshi in 2018.)

Charles Dabby: "Don't Worry, We Have a Guard."

On June 1, 1941, a Sunday, Charles Dabby, then 6, looked out the small recessed window of a second-story bedroom in his family's house in Baghdad. He could see men breaking into nearby homes on the narrow street below, then hoisting stolen items over their heads or hauling them away in donkey-driven carts. "People were taking sheets, pillows, everything and anything," he recalled. He also heard the shouts and crying of both adults and children.

Charles' parents pulled him and his two younger sisters, Bertha and Tikvah, away from the window, saying, "Don't worry. We have a guard."

The family felt reassured by the presence of Azawi ibn Tabra, the large, Muslim owner of the warehouse where Charles' father, Heskel, a spice importer and distributor, stored his merchandize. The keffiyah-clad Azawi was standing guard outside the family's front door, a sword in one hand and a gun on his left side, patrolling back and forth. A few men accompanied him. He had also stationed several men on the Dabbys' roof in case attackers jumped over the short wall separating the flat, attached roofs of the adjoining houses. Another guard remained inside the house, making funny faces to entertain Charles.

Later, Heskel led the family downstairs to the basement, where they slept for several nights. It was too dangerous to sleep on the rooftop, as was the custom in warm weather.

After the Farhud, when Charles walked with his father along Main Street to school, they often saw men hanging from scaffolding. When Charles asked why they had been hanged, Heskel answered, "Because they're thieves." He never explained that they were Jews.

On Nov. 29, 1947, Charles remembers listening to the United Nations vote on Israeli statehood on the family radio. "I could hear my heart. I was crying," he said. He had secretly begun learning conversational Hebrew, leaving school for an hour at a time for classes taught by young Iraqi Jews. At home, he buried his Hebrew papers in a box in the backyard, hidden from his parents. "They would panic," he said. Like most Iraqi Jews, Charles' parents were not Zionists.

Then, one afternoon in 1949, as Charles rode his bicycle home from school, two boys attacked him—hitting him and trying to steal his bicycle. Charles removed his belt and began thrashing the boys and destroying their bicycles. He returned home with torn clothes, his own bicycle on his shoulder. That night, after learning that the boys' parents had important government jobs, Heskel put Charles on a train to Basra, to stay with his uncle. In the summer, against his uncle's and father's wishes, Charles crossed into Iran with a smuggler and, after some time in Istanbul, he traveled to Israel. His two sisters followed a year later, when Iraq allowed Jews to emigrate, while forbidding them to keep their Iraqi citizenship.

Charles' parents, however, remained in Baghdad. Charles saw them again only once, in London in 1971. That same year, Charles helped his younger brother, Joseph, who was only 2 when Charles fled, escape Iraq. The following year, Joseph moved to Los Angeles, where Charles had been living since 1966, and where he currently lives with his wife, Teresa Stauring Dabby.

(From "Witness to Iraq's Farhud," Jane Ulman, *Jewish Journal*, May 20, 2015)

Steve Acre "Screams Began to Emanate..."

In a mixed Jewish and Muslim quarter, Steve Acre (born Sabah Akerib) lived with his widowed mother and eight siblings in a house owned by a Muslim.

Acre, then 9 years old, climbed a palm tree in the courtyard when the violence of the Farhud began. He still remembers the cries of "*Ithbah al yehud*" from the street, which translates to, "slaughter the Jews."

From the tree Acre could see his Muslim neighbor, the Hajji, sitting in front of their house with a green turban (a sign of a prominent Muslim cleric). He stood up in front of the door with his dagger, and when the crowd arrived at their steps he said, "There is a widow and nine children in this home, and they have asked for my protection. If you want to go in, you will have to kill me first."

The men then crossed the street and screams began to emanate from the house of his mother's best friend, Sabiha. "Later lots of men came outside and set Sabiha's house on fire. The men were shouting with joy, holding up something that looked like a slab of meat. I found out it was Sabiha's breast they were carrying - they cut her breast off and tortured her before they killed her."

(Adapted from "Farhud Memories: Baghdad's 1941 Slaughter of the Jews," Sarah Ehrlich, https://www.bbc.com/news/world-middle-east-13610702, June 1, 2011)

MODERN-DAY HEALING

Hannah and Rachel: A True Story of Love and Hope

This is adapted from an article I wrote for the Kahal Jospeh newsletter in December of 2008, inspired by the account published in Yediot Ahronot in June 2008, sent to me by my friend Shaoul Gory. The story of Hannah and Rachel brought back the hope, the despair, and the memories buried in the seams of my past.

In 1951, Hannah and Rachel's family was among the mass expulsion of Jews from Iraq who were allowed to leave the country with only one suitcase. It was the same window during which my mother, Yaakub, and other family members escaped.

"In one week we are out of this hell," their father said to the family including Hannah, 18, and Rachel, 19. Hugging and kissing with both joy and trepidation, the family said their farewells to friends and family.

Then, just two days before their departure, the family's ecstasy melted to grief and their hope spun to calamity. Hannah didn't return home that evening. The family checked everywhere and with everybody. No one could solve the mystery of her disappearance. Their obedient, mild-mannered daughter had vanished into thin air. The authorities were of no help.

The family left for Israel as planned, but Hannah's father stayed in Baghdad for two months, searching for his daughter. Finally, he arrived in Israel, a broken man. Hannah's mother died from depression a few months later. But the family had to move on. Rachel and her brothers got married and had children. Hannah's picture adorned the living room wall and her story was told and retold, to the next generation.

Flash forward 58 years.

In March 2008, Rachel Menashe of Ramat Gan received a phone call from the Israel Ministry of the Interior. Hannah was alive and she was making her way back to Israel.

The night of her disappearance had been the start of a nightmare for Hannah. A Muslim man from the neighborhood had kidnapped her. She became a sex slave, a servant to his other wives and a nanny to his kids. She had to conduct herself as a Muslim woman. Even when she heard of Jews being tortured or saw their hung bodies swaying in the public square, she could not react.

At night, she cried over a photograph taken with Rachel, which was in her purse at the time she was kidnapped. Over the years, even after the tears dried up, she kissed the photo, an icon that kept the flame of hope glowing.

Hannah's kidnapper died in 2007. She was alone and had had no children during her captivity. On her weekly shopping route, Hannah ventured on a different path, and it was there she found an American soldier.

The U.S. military had entered Iraq in 1991 for the first time, and in 2003, Iraqis finally celebrated their liberation from Saddam Hussein's tyranny when he was captured by the U.S. The U.S. still had a military presence in 2008, the day Hannah approached the soldier.

She told him her story of kidnapping and slavery. He took her to his superior, who contacted Israeli officials.

On June 13, 2008, newspaper, radio, and TV reporters were waiting at a special lounge at Ben Gurion airport in Israel. Rachel, her brothers, their children, grandchildren, cousins, and other family members were there to greet Hannah, ending 58 years of hoping and waiting. Accompanied by an airline hostess, Hannah, now 76, approached her family. "Hannah is here," one of the children screamed. There was not a dry eye in the crowd.

"I am only sorry that my mom and dad are not here to witness this moment. I knew we would meet again one day," Rachel told reporters. "The circle is complete. Hannah is here."

Hannah's legend is but a grain of sand in a vast Sahara of untold stories. Reading her tale was a seismic shock to me, an earthquake to my psyche and a whirlwind to my memory.

I remembered the two teenage Jewish girls I knew who were kidnapped. One was Miriam, a maid at our next door neighbor's home, and the other was a girl from Sandor, a small Jewish village in Kurdistan, whom I met on a school camping trip in the summer of 1947, before she was sold into prostitution. At the age of 14, I nearly lost my life when two Muslims youths chased me with a knife for stopping them from molesting my neighbor's daughter. Perhaps I saved that one girl from decades of torture. But so many others ended up like Hannah.

At least in Hannah's case, she was eventually able to celebrate the miracle of reuniting with her family in Israel. For all of us who escaped that hell, our lives are a miracle to be celebrated.

Artifacts of Iraq

My op-ed on the travesty and tragedy of Jewish artifacts being shipped back to Iraq was published in The Washington Post *on October 19, 2017.*

The History of Iraqi Jews Is in Jeopardy

For more than 10 years, the United States has served as a gracious host to thousands of Iraqi-Jewish artifacts discovered by the U.S. military in Saddam Hussein's intelligence headquarters during the Iraq War. The trove, which includes 2,700 books, Torah scrolls and prayer books, and thousands of documents dating to the 1500s, represents the lost history of a once-thriving, two-millennia-old Jewish community in Iraq.

Despite the U.S. government's valiant effort to preserve and restore this treasure, the State Department is preparing to return the artifacts to Iraq in September 2018 in accordance with an agreement made with the Iraqi government under the Obama administration.

But these artifacts belong to the Iraqi-Jewish community and their descendants. Returning the trove to Iraq is tantamount to returning stolen treasure to a thief. President Trump and the State Department should do all that they can to prevent such an injustice.

I was born in 1930 in Taht Al Takia, the Old Jewish Quarter of the old city of Baghdad. Baghdad was my home, and Iraq was my country. But my sense of national identity was shattered when Muslim mobs looted and burned Jewish homes and businesses, murdering hundreds of Jewish men, women, and children in the 1941 pogrom known as the Farhud.

I was 10 years old. There was nowhere to run, and no country to take us in.

After the failed Arab war against Israel in 1948, the

Jews of Iraq and other Arab countries faced anti-Semitism and open hostility. We suffered arrest, torture, public execution, and confiscation of property.

The Iraqi-Jewish artifacts are a rare example of what was stolen from more than 850,000 Arab Jews and the historical Jewish presence that Arab regimes are attempting to erase. At present, there are only about 3,000 Jews living in Arab countries who are continuing our story.

Decades later, the Baath Party, led by Hussein, looted and confiscated public and personal items from synagogues, Jewish schools and community properties. On May 6, 2003, the U.S. Army uncovered these artifacts hidden in a flooded basement of the Mukhabarat (Iraqi secret service) headquarters.

With the approval of Iraq's provisional government, the U.S. military rescued the damaged items and brought them to this country. The U.S. government has since spent more than $3 million to restore the archive, exhibiting it across the country. The artifacts brought tears to my eyes when I first visited the collection at the Nixon Library. It's almost as if my lost history in Iraq came back to life.

The hearts of the Iraqi Jewish community are filled with gratitude toward the heroic teams who rescued and restored this collection. Thanks to the United States, we have preserved these pieces of history for present and future generations.

But Iraq has proven itself an unreliable custodian, and we fear these historical treasures could be lost forever. Trump has the chance to be remembered as the preserver of our history, just like Moses who brought the Hebrews from Egypt and kept their message alive for future generations. I implore the administration, on behalf of all Jews from Arab lands and our descendants, to keep our icons of history from being sent back to those who stole them from us.

THE LATEST ON THE IRAQI JEWISH ARCHIVES

I have continued to follow this story closely. As of this writing (Sept. 2019), the Iraqi Jewish archives remain in the United States. The following is a July 19, 2018, story by Josefin Dolsten for JTA.

State Department Says Working to Keep Iraqi Jewish Archive in US

The State Department said on Thursday it is working with Iraq to extend the stay of a trove of Jewish artifacts from the country, after a bipartisan group of senators introduced a resolution recommending that the items not be returned as planned in September.

"We continue to work with the Government of Iraq and relevant stakeholder[s] to extend the exhibition in the US," a State Department official told JTA in an email.

Last year, the State Department said that it would return the Iraqi Jewish Archive in September 2018, to the dismay of activists who argue that the collection of thousands of Jewish religious and personal items should be accessible to the Iraqi Jewish community, which fled the country amid anti-Semitic persecution.

On Wednesday, following discussions in the Senate, a group of lawmakers introduced a resolution recommending that the US renegotiate the archive's return and keep them in the United States.

The measure was introduced by Sens. Pat Toomey, R-Penn., Charles Schumer, D-NY, and Richard Blumenthal, D-Conn., with Sen. Marco Rubio, R-Fla., as a co-sponsor.

"These invaluable cultural treasures like a prayer book and Torah scrolls belong to the people and their descendants who were forced to leave them behind as they were exiled from Iraq. The State Department should make clear to the Iraqi government that the artifacts should continue to stay in the United States," said Senate Minority Leader Schumer, who has been active in arguing for the archive not to be sent back.

Toomey noted that he had introduced a similar resolution along with Schumer and Blumenthal in 2014 that was unanimously passed by the Senate.

"It makes no sense for this material to return to Iraq when the vast majority of Iraqi Jews and their descendants live in the Diaspora," he said in a statement.

In 2003, US troops discovered the archive in the flooded basement of the Iraqi secret service in Baghdad and brought it back to the United States.

The items include books, religious texts, photographs, and personal documents left behind by Jews who fled the country amid intense persecution by late dictator Saddam Hussein. Under an agreement with the government of Iraq, the archive was to eventually be sent back there.

The US government spent over $3 million to restore and digitize the archive, which has been exhibited across the country. The trove includes a Hebrew Bible with commentaries from 1568, a Babylonian Talmud from 1793, and an 1815 version of the Jewish mystical text Zohar.

In addition to saying the artifacts should be kept accessible to Iraqi Jews, activists also question whether Iraq would properly take care of the items were they to be sent back.

Iraq and proponents of returning the archive say it can serve as an educational tool for Iraqis about the history of Jews there and that it is part of the country's patrimony.

APPRECIATIONS

I have been married to Joe for sixty delightful years. He is a dependable husband, always there when I need him, generous, kind and giving of himself.

He is a wonderful father, continuously there supporting and encouraging our children to be kind, trustworthy, and self-reliant.

Education was very important to him. Although he was unable to go to college, he saw to it that our children would value the importance of higher education. He also taught them how to manage money and be financially independent.

He is a terrific grandfather. He showered our grandchildren with unconditional love and made sure to get all the family together for Shabbat and holidays, especially for our annual family retreat in Cabo San Lucas.

Sharon, Lisa, and Jeff did not fail him, nor did his grandchildren. We are both extremely proud and immensely gratified with our family.

Love,
Ruby

Dear Dad,

Congratulations on this monumental accomplishment. Because of your dedication and hard work, our family's history, as Iraqi Jews, will be preserved.

I feel blessed to be a part of this wonderful family you and Mum have created, and continue to create each day.

We shared many special moments together. Shabbat dinners; trips to 1,000 Acres Dude Ranch; trips to Messina Beach with family and friends. I remember sitting on your back while you did yoga poses, and getting Motek, our myna bird (it was very convenient that he came to us already saying "bonjour, Joseph," from the priest who had him before we did). And all of the food: family barbeques, *hamim* eggs, the most delicious laffas that only you could make, watching you eat fish heads (which I still love doing), and Sunday dinners with you and Mum. We all benefited from your travel bug: family trips to Cabo's Club Cascadas every November, cruises to Alaska, Panama Canal and beyond!

My passion for gardening was born out of yours. I learned to love eating delicious homegrown vegetables and fruits from the greenhouse you built in Montreal, and then the bounty from your garden in sunny Santa Monica, California. I admire your efforts at depopulating your neighborhood of fruit-stealing squirrels.

I love your incessant desire to learn something new every day, and that you know how to have fun! I admire your ability to make lemonade out of lemons! Most of all, I appreciate your unwavering persistence in keeping our family together, in a time when so many people go their own ways.

With all my love to both you and Mum,
Lisa
PS: Sorry for killing all your tropical fish. I didn't realize Play-Doh wasn't food.

Dear Dad/Saba,

Mission accomplished! Congratulations on completing your story, chronicling an important piece of our family history – one of countless missions you have undertaken in a rich and full 89 years. Your ability to focus on, persist at, and realize your dreams is a source of inspiration.

But perhaps even more important than your accomplishments is that you have always been full of zest, always planning, always up for our next family adventure: from teaching me (Sharon) to ski at age 5 in subzero temperatures in the mountains outside of Montreal, to taking your kids skating on Beaver Lake, to horseback riding. As the family grew, so did the trips, with children and grandchildren: to Mexico, Barbados, Belize, Israel, Greece, and Italy, and family cruises. You brought in the extended family, even orchestrating bus trips, and always including everyone in joyfully celebrating family occasions – bar- and bat-mitzvahs, weddings, birthdays.

We love you!
Sharon, Elana, and Eden

Dear Dad/Joe/Saba,

Congratulations on finishing your biography. This is certainly an important milestone in your life and we are so proud of you! As we reflect on your life and all that you have accomplished over the past 90 years, we wanted to share with you the many ways in which you have impacted our lives.

The first thing that stands out to us is your positive attitude toward life. Throughout the years, you have always been steady with your "Everything is going to be OK" attitude. However, you didn't just stop there. Indeed, you really seemed to expand that attitude into one that says "Everything is going to be great." Frankly, your positive attitude – your daily mantra of "Day by day and in every way, I feel better and better and better," is not just inspiring, but infectious.

While you have experienced many obstacles and hindrances in your life, you seem to have always risen above them, looking at each problem that presents itself as an opportunity to learn and grow. In doing so, you challenge us to not get mired in the muck but, instead, to rise above it and be grateful for our lives and the short time we have here together.

Another way in which you have affected us is by your kindness. While you have been successful in so many ways throughout your life, you have never lost sight of those less fortunate than you. You are truly warm-hearted and generous. We just hope that we will be able to follow your footsteps in making the world a better place. From donating to charities to supporting the homeless, you seem to truly care about the world around you. What is even more inspiring is that you are not just content with giving money to the homeless; you want to learn their stories and, in taking an interest in them, touch them deeply.

Your adventurous spirit is also exceptional. From our family vacations to Mexico, the Caribbean islands, Europe, Eastern Europe

and so on, you have motivated us to travel the world and learn as much as we can from other people and cultures. Your practice of learning other languages so you could communicate better while traveling is impressive and something that we too strive to do when we travel the world.

Not unrelated to how you approached traveling and the world around you is your unending desire to learn something new each day. Whether be it be languages, yoga, writing classes, or even singing, you never seem to stop expanding your mind and spirit. You have opened your heart to learning from those around you and that interest in others and their cultures is, again, inspiring.

Finally, we have learned much from how highly you value friends and, in particular, family. From the Friday Shabbat dinners to taking all of us on family vacations, you have instilled in us seeing our families as so very important and valuing the time spent together. We are truly touched by the way you have accepted Benedicte, despite her not being Jewish, into the family and have truly treated her as your own daughter and as an *eshet chayil*. We look forward to your Friday evening calls and Shabbat blessings which not only remind us that we are an important part of your life, but also keep us connected to the others you call to bless!

We could, of course, go on as there are so many ways that you inspire us. But, perhaps, in the pursuit of brevity, it is simply better to say that we love you and are so very proud of this major accomplishment.

Love,
Jeff, Benedicte, and Zachary

Dear Saba,

Thank you for always being a great pillar of our family, a family that appreciates and makes time for one another, and values the importance of stories and laughter.

You and grandma have always been a source of love and learning. Growing up, I spent Monday nights with you, where you not only taught me how to read Hebrew, but also about interest rates, finance tips (more helpful than I thought they would be while hearing them at 9 years old), and how to do all of the Richard Simmons "Abs in 7 Days" exercises. Even when you weren't teaching, I was always happy to sit on the couch with you and watch old Carol Burnett reruns. Grandma taught me to appreciate good food, to love endlessly, to care for those around me, and to take time for myself. You and the whole family have always been a place of laughter and sharing together, in the good times and the harder.

When I think of you, I always think of one afternoon we stopped in a small town in Poland for lunch. Nobody could read the signs, so we parked in front of the restaurant, and when we got back to the car, there were two angry Polish policemen in front of the car, scolding us about something related to our parking job. We had no way of communicating with them, but you, ever the linguist, remembered a Polish nursery rhyme. You started to sing it to them, not just once but repeatedly, until the policemen were laughing loudly, shook your hand, and walked away still smiling and waving at us. You taught me that kindness and a sense of humor can never make things worse.

Love and hugs to you and grandma,
Rebecca

"It's fun to have fun but you have to know how"
- Dr. Seuss, and also Joseph Samuels. We'll never know who said it first.

The most salient thing growing up with Saba Joe has taught me is the power of perseverance. Of course his will and determination are littered everywhere in his life: from his journey to North America, his hard work in real estate, his passion for bringing people together. But his perseverance is most noticeable in everyday interactions with him. Whether it is a simple conversation, or the planning of something magnificent, he does it all the way, every single time.

He has brought our family together on countless occasions. Though I always felt miles away physically, he made sure that we would be in contact no matter what. It takes a very special kind of person to be able to do this. Because of his hard work, he has been able to do what he is passionate about – travel. From this I have learned more than from anything else in my life. He passed his passion for travel onto his children, and thus onto me. I am indebted to him with gratitude for my opportunity to experience so many cultures in the world. And while he has always been eager to learn about other cultures, he has constantly held steadfastly onto his own.

Saba Joe is incredibly proud of the culture he comes from and upholds it in everything he does. His religion and culture are littered into every conversation he has, explained to the many people he comes in contact with, and preserved in his own mind and now his memoir.

I am incredibly grateful to have grown up with his love, passion, and hard work. I hope that I can put the same passion he has toward life into my career and in the relationships with friends and family that he has exemplified throughout my entire life.

I think this memoir is going to be an inspirational story for many to read. I hope that it inspires them to live their lives with the richness and constant desire for education that he has.

Love,
Claire

My brother Joe and I smuggled our way out of Baghdad when I was 16, and he was 19. We travelled in disguise to Basra, and then by a dingy hay boat, crossing the Shatt Al Arab in the middle of the night to reach Khorramshahr, in Iran. We were lucky, as we would have been killed had we been discovered. Days later, with only the clothes on our back, we reached Ahwaz, where Joe became a supervisor looking after our needs until we were able to go to Teheran to fly to Israel by a refitted Alaska Airlines airplane. Joe continued to stay on in Ahwaz to help many other kids like me, for two months, until he finally arrived to Israel himself. We had an extremely difficult time, but luckily we arrived safely. I served in the Air Force and Joe served in the Navy.

Nory Samuels

To our family, Joe Samuels is Uncle Joe Smiles, a nickname our granddaughter Sophie conferred on him as he presented her with his signature homemade banana chips. The name has stuck all these years because it so aptly describes Joe Samuels. He has faced life's challenges and many painful situations with his ever-present smile and optimistic attitude.

One occasion which stands out is when we visited the Nixon Library to see the Iraqi heritage artifacts on display there. I could see that Joe was moved close to tears as we viewed the defaced holy writings. It was an electrifying experience and demonstrated how much pain and suffering the refugees from the Iraqi Jewish diaspora suffered. Yet they persevered and even, with G-d's help, prospered.

Ever the optimist, Joe cultivates a bountiful garden. Every Saturday he presents the congregants at his shul, Kahal Joseph, with lapel miniature roses that he grows year-round. He guards the numerous fruit trees diligently and has become an expert at trapping the marauding squirrels, which he lures into a cage with nuts. Each squirrel gets a number sprayed onto its tail before being released. Number 1001 to date. What remains of the fruits he open-handedly shares.

This generosity has carried into Joe's interaction with a wide and varied circle of friends, young and old, rich and poor, educated or not. He has a way of putting people at ease and inspiring hope and joy and laughter in them. Only last week we visited with a seriously ill person. By the end of the visit we were singing and swapping jokes. Ruby and Joe have become part of our extended family and no occasion, whether joyful or sad, is complete without them. Joe enjoys Iraqi cooking, especially spicy and hot foods and we all love to have him eat with us. We look with wonder as he downs hot chili peppers with gusto.

We are grateful to be included in his circle of friends and have benefitted immensely on numerous occasions from his sage and calm advice and guidance.

    We wish you health and long life, our Uncle Joe Smiles.

Evelyn and Fuad Salem

I met Joe initially as a patient, and slowly he became a very important and valuable mentor and friend to me. Now, it is a great honor to express my deepest admiration for this one-of-a-kind person.

In a very special manner, Joe is able to discuss and dissect a problem, and help you solve it. He is a loving husband and a dedicated family man. He is a great leader, who always works hard and successfully to get his family together for holidays and special events.

Joe is like a magnet. I love his intelligence and his analyzing power. He is a world traveler, having visited over 100 countries and always curious to see and learn more. Joe never stops learning and mastering new things – singing, writing, lecturing.

I am so thankful to have Joe in my life, and to be considered his friend. Thank you, Joe!

Dr. Ron Chitayat

Within seconds of meeting Joe, you can tell he is made of something different – Joe radiates an energy more powerful than the sun itself.

I met Joe when I was 14, through my Uncle Ronny. It started out simple: as a way for Joe to be taught his way around a computer. But, as has been proved by the last 15 years of working together, I am the actual student in our relationship.

From economics, to real estate, to gardening, to photography, to poetry and music, Joe's interests and expertise are almost unlimited. And he is determined to do it all online - YouTube, a blog, photo albums, articles for newspapers and magazines, and even getting licensed as a travel agent to finagle the best deals!

The first time Joe told me he wanted to get an article published, and had set out from the get-go with that intention, I thought he was mad. I thought, "That's not how it's done!" But thoughts like that don't stop Joe. Joe is willing to try anything. When Joe sets a goal, he goes after it, and I mean in a way that you rarely see people do, even when they say they love that particular thing. And it's every single time. I have watched in awe time and time again as a man 60 years my senior makes me feel old. With his combination of intelligence and tenacity, of course, he got that article published. And then three or four more. And then a book.

It's a philosophy that he has ingrained in me: to take whatever is in front of you, look at all its angles, and push it to the fullest potential you can. Examine how it went. Then do it again, with the exact same effort. Make every moment count.

Seeing how much Joe has expanded and evolved at his age proves to me that our capacity for knowledge and love is infinite and our experience of this life is dependent on how well we manage our limited time on Earth. Each time we are together I attempt to hold on to what he tells me, knowing that if the words have come out of his mouth, they come from wisdom and experience.

Like so many others, I could go on forever about all the facets Joe has impressed on me – financially, spiritually, and practically – and how to be happy in the face of managing them all.

Thank you for everything, Joe, especially for letting me help you in writing this book. I will carry the lessons I have learned for a lifetime. I can only hope to become the man you are, and support the people around me as you do. You are not only a mentor to me; I consider you family, and I love you. Thank you for everything that you give to not only me, but to anyone who gets within feet of you.

Luca Chitayat

Photo Credits